A Longman Topics Reader

Legends, Lore, and Lies

A Skeptic's Stance

JOSEPH CALABRESE
University of Nevada, Reno

PEARSON
Longman

New York   San Francisco   Boston
London   Toronto   Sydney   Tokyo   Singapore   Madrid
Mexico City   Munich   Paris   Cape Town   Hong Kong   Montreal

Additional Titles in the Longman Topics Reader Series

Translating Tradition
Karen E. Beardslee

Reading City Life
Patrick Bruch and Richard Marback

Diversity: Strength and Struggle
Joseph Calabrese and Susan Tchudi

Citizenship Now
Jon Ford and Marjorie Ford

The Changing World of Work
Marjorie Ford

Youth Subcultures: Exploring Underground America
Arielle Greenberg

International Views: America and the Rest of the World
Keith Gumery

Listening to Earth: A Reader
Christopher Hallowell and Walter Levy

Body and Culture
Greg T. Lyons

Issues of Gender
Ellen G. Friedman and Jennifer D. Marshall

Writing Places
Paula Mathieu, George Grattan, Tim Lindgren, and Staci Shultz

Peace, War, and Terrorism
Denis Okerstrom

The World of the Image
Trudy Smoke and Alan Robbins

Hip Hop Reader
Tim Strode and Tim Wood

The Counterculture Reader
E. A. Swingrover

Discovering Popular Culture
Anna Tomasino

Music and Culture
Anna Tomasino

Ethics in the 21st Century
Mary Alice Trent

Considering Cultural Difference
Pauline Uchmanowicz

Language and Prejudice
Tamara M. Valentine

CyberReader (Abridged Edition)
Victor J. Vitanza

Dedicated to the memory of Carl Sagan, a balanced skeptic, and to all those like him who serve the freedom of the human spirit. I also dedicate this little work to Joseph and Jacqueline Calabrese, my parents, for putting me on good terms with books and curiosity.

Senior Vice President and Publisher: Joseph Opiela
Marketing Manager: Sandra McGuire
Production Manager: Savoula Amanatidis
Project Coordination and Text Design: Elm Street Publishing
    Services, Inc.
Electronic Page Makeup: Integra Software Services, Pvt. Ltd.
Senior Cover Design Manager/Cover Designer: Nancy Danahy
Cover Image: Copyright © Digital Vision/Getty Images, Inc.
Manufacturing Manager: Mary Fischer
Printer and Binder: R. R. Donnelley and Sons Company—
    Harrisonburg
Cover Printer: Phoenix Color Corporation

For permission to use copyrighted material, grateful acknowledg-
ment is made to the copyright holders on page 244, which are
hereby made part of this copyright page.

Library of Congress Cataloging-in-Publication Data

Calabrese, Joseph T.
    Legends, lore, and lies : a skeptic's stance / Joseph Calabrese.
        p. cm.—(A Longman topics reader)
    Includes bibliographical references.
    Contents: Urban legends—Media gullibility—Alternative
    medicine—Psychics and the paranormal—Pseudo science.
    ISBN 0-321-43924-4 (alk. paper)
        1. Critical thinking—Problems, exercises, etc.
    2. Parapsychology. 3. Pseudoscience. I. Title.

LB2395.35.C25 2005
808'.0427—dc22

                                                    2006050718

Please visit us at www.ablongman.com

ISBN 0-321-43924-4

    4 5 6 7 8 9 10—DOH—09 08

CONTENTS

*L*egends, Lore, and Lies: The Skeptic's Stance offers readers the opportunity to explore and evaluate tales of extraordinary events, reports of paranormal experiences and abilities, and the claims of pseudoscience. It does so from a predominantly skeptical position, although readers will find its tone far from pedantically dismissive. Perhaps you share a belief that such a book has a place in education these days. Our culture, technologically sophisticated and grounded in a robust tradition of scientific inquiry and advancement, also accommodates the most fantastic beliefs and claims. This paradox has been frequently remarked, yet it bears repeating. Our labor, ingenuity, wealth, and focus have, for example, created communication empires. We have built libraries, research institutions, and universities that house and transmit the knowledge of millennia. That virtual servant, the Internet, grows in power every year so that many millions of people can easily access a world of data from their homes and offices. Consider that the student who might explore physics, baroque art, or American literature can also find thousands of pages devoted to ghosts, demons, psychics, healing crystals, racialized pseudoscience, and so on. The same student can watch TV programs showing a medium who contacts various dead folks at the request of his audience; she can see a televangelist healing invisible viewers far away from the studio, or hear claims that Hurricane Katrina, an earthquake, or a terror attack is the work of an angry god. C-SPAN viewers might tune in to hear a congressman claim that since evolution is "only a theory," we need to present "creationism" or "intelligent design" in our public schools. In this context, belief and knowledge become indistinguishable.

This book does not attempt to finally wean students away from paranormal or supernatural beliefs, and it does not attack faith. Instead, it presents and delineates a skeptical stance. Balance is the characteristic virtue of this stance, and not mere nay saying and reflexive doubt. However, balance is not presented here as pseudo-objectivity, or as a rigidly non-judgmental position. One must judge, finally. The point is to learn how to use basic tools, ask reasonable questions, propose useful tests, set standards of proof, and do the very human and often very difficult work of judging. Although this work is a pillar of liberal education, it can be admitted here that one book in one course isn't going to complete the task. It is an approach, and for many students a beginning.

The authors in this collection write predominantly from a skeptical viewpoint, although several readings come from a believer's point of view. The presence of the latter is not meant to suggest broadly that belief and doubt are equivalent options. Rather, readers are asked to compare standards of evidence and to distinguish between critical and uncritical approaches to claims. Hence, an essay promoting homeopathy shares a chapter with another that critiques the bases and claims of Cranial-Sacral therapy, and another on the healing powers of magnets. The story of a pet psychic's alleged communication with a pet turtle appears alongside essays that scrutinize belief in crop circles and Bible codes. More darkly, the same chapter presents an essay that examines the beliefs of the doomed Heaven's Gate cult. In another chapter, the therapeutic attempt to "recover memories" is described, and the presentation of these in the guise of sound psychology is mordantly critiqued. Still, none of the essays displays a mocking, dismissive hostility to all things unusual. The critical views are generally tempered with mild humor and a sense of the limits of human certainty. A reader will thus find among the skeptics presented in this book a steering between cynicism and the despair of achieving certainty, both of which paralyze thinking. Between these, or better, amid many extraordinary claims and much uncertainty, the skeptic seeks critical balance.

ORGANIZATION OF THIS TEXT

The text is divided into five chapters. Chapter 1 presents some urban legends, and it underscores popular gullibility and fascination with the bizarre. One essay departs from the innocuous in suggesting the role of racial stereotypes in a popular legend, and by implication, the service to a just social order that skepticism can provide. Chapter 2, "The Media and Public Gullibility," considers the role that various programs and publications play in fostering uncritical acceptance of unusual claims. Chapter 3 zeroes in on "Alternative Medicine." What is the logic of homeopathic medicine?

Who is marketing oxygen as a panacea? What dangers do quack remedies present to the public? Chapter 4, "Psychics and the Paranormal," considers such popular interests as hidden messages in the Bible code, crop circles, and mediums who claim to speak with spirits. In the essay focused on Heaven's Gate, a potentially fatal link can be seen between cults and adherence to claims of a supernatural realm. Finally, Chapter 5 looks at the distinction between science and pseudoscience. Here readers can see that governments themselves can contribute to fallacies if officials fall under the spell of pseudoscience. Other essays in this chapter explain certain typical and crucial standards by which inquiry should proceed, showing that these standards separate inquiry from mere speculation.

FEATURES OF THIS TEXT

The following features work to engage students in reading, research, and critical discussion of the phenomena and claims in the text.

- Each chapter's readings present a topic suitable for skeptical inquiry. They vary in the demands they place on readers, but all of them are accessible to readers even if they are not trained in one of the sciences.
- Brief author biographies precede each essay, giving the reader some background information that will be helpful in understanding the reading's point of view.
- Each reading concludes with "Questions for Discussion and Writing," which in the course of a semester will help students build up their own critical toolkit.
- Each chapter ends with more elaborate writing suggestions for longer papers based on different kinds of research and inquiry. These may readily be adapted for the writing skills of a wide range of students.

ACKNOWLEDGMENTS

I would like to acknowledge the invaluable help of Rebecca Gilpin and Virginia Blanford, who directed this project along the intricate path from its proposal to its publication. Kim Nichols kept the work moving as it neared completion, and provided an astute copyeditor, Betsy Webster, who has an eye for detail and an ear for phrasing. Finally, my thanks to Longman Publishing for its openness to this and many other subjects in its wonderful Longman Topics Reader series.

JOSEPH CALABRESE
English Department
The University of Nevada, Reno

The Skeptic's Stance

This Humanist whom no belief constrained,
Grew so broad-minded he was scatter-brained.

—J. V. CUNNINGHAM

Nothing has such power to broaden the mind as the ability to inves-
tigate systematically and truly all that comes under thy observation
in life.

—MARCUS AURELIUS

People often equate the skeptic and the cynic, but that is a mistake. Cynicism is not really a reasoned position; it's more a conditioned outlook, one characterized by a priori judgments that tend to be dismissive. A skeptic remains guardedly open to possibilities. Evidence matters to the latter. Her stance requires balance because she acknowledges assertions, considers evidence, and recalls her own fallibility, even while examining claims and weighing evidence. The skeptic's opinions are open to question. The cynic's are rigidly set. He "knows" that people are fools and liars, that research is pointless, that things in general end badly. H. L. Mencken said that a cynic "is a man who, when he smells flowers, looks around for a coffin." Skeptics in general are far less gloomy and nothing in their outlook needs to end in morbid doubts. Asking for evidence, for grounds of belief, for repeatable results and so on makes sense in a world full of people as fallible as ourselves.

Given our culture's fascination with extraordinary claims, with people who say they "channel" spirit counselors, with videos of Bigfoot, and with crop circles made by aliens, there is a place— if not a pressing need—for a questioning habit of mind. There is probably no city, and hardly a small town in America, that doesn't have a resident psychic ready to counsel people about their romances, career choices, or past lives. A "Center for Psychic Improvements" will offer classes that help students cultivate their powers. A 30-second Internet search will turn up claims for products that will "cause you to unleash your psychic powers— instantly!" All for under $30.00 plus shipping. So many people match alien kidnapping symptoms that it's only a matter of time until you are related to one. You could be such a victim, particularly if you experience "buzzing in the ears, interpersonal relationship problems, back problems, insomnia, craving for salts, or promiscuity as a teen."

Such beliefs are trivial and amusing. If our friends read up on the exciting messages encrypted in wheat or barley crop circles or visit a medium to hear the channeled advice of Cleopatra's chambermaid, we laugh with maybe a faint sense of superiority. Occasionally, idle beliefs take on a shade of menace. In the early 1990s, UFO chatter got mixed strangely with government conspiracy theories. Strange conventions took place in which survivalists and gun enthusiasts mingled with booksellers featuring texts about government plans to institute a new world order. Suddenly, black helicopters were spotted everywhere, ferrying FEMA agents and UN executives across the country as they scouted locations for massive detention centers. A book entitled *Black Helicopters II: The Endgame Strategy* by Jim Keith offered a tangle of black choppers, cattle mutilations, UFOs, and alien abductions all somehow connected to a plot to end America. It included a fascinating chapter on a "quadrant sign code," complete with photos showing the decal-plastered backs of road signs. One has to learn to read the decal placement in order to decipher these directions to foreign troops who will be driving across America. These days, post–Hurricane Katrina, no one fears the organizational prowess of FEMA, but for a time this sort of claim drove people into militias already staffed with armed conspiracy buffs. Confrontations between militia members and federal agents during the nineties in Texas and Montana owed some of their vigor to irrational beliefs.

It isn't only paranoid civilians who subscribe to odd notions. Our own government has invested resources into ways to weaponize psychic powers. According to a report by Michael Mumford et al., "An Evaluation of Remote Viewing Research and Applications," in the 1970s our government began to investigate remote viewing powers as an espionage tool. Eventually it was found that remote viewers, aka psychics, fared unsatisfactorily. They failed "to produce the concrete, specific information valued in intelligence gathering." But that was after someone decided to fund such a study in the first place. One wonders what led to that decision. Every year Americans spend huge sums of money on untested herbal remedies, diet pills that turn out to be ineffectual and sometimes very dangerous, healing therapies based on magical claims, and so on. We seem, collectively, to be a gullible nation.

This book offers readings that will present you with some useful tools. You can begin to build up your own skeptic's toolkit, stocked with the means to weigh and sort claims for various products, powers, entities, theories, and so on. As a start, here are some fundamental tools for your kit; you can add to or rework these as you progress through the book.

QUESTIONS

- **Who is making the claims?** If someone says that a rare planetary alignment will occur with calamitous results for life on earth, it seems reasonable to ask if the source is an astronomer or someone who only reads his horoscope.
- **Who might benefit from belief in this claim?** Like the question above, this looks into interest. If someone claims to be able to locate oil fields with a dowsing rod, are they also selling their services? Is the person who tells you crystals heal depression also selling them? Interest often clouds perception.
- **What exactly is being claimed?** If someone says he talks to the dead, that is unremarkable; lots of people do that. As Hotspur says in Shakespeare's *I Henry IV* when Glendower claims he can summon the dead: "Why so can I, or so can any man; but will they come when you do call for them?" Some say that Nostradamus predicted the terrible events of 9/11. Did he? In what words, exactly?
- **Can the claim be tested?** This can help determine its plausibility. The pyramids were built by the gods of Atlantis, one might say; they used teleportation to move the stones. It's difficult to design or even imagine a test for that one.

GUIDELINES

- **Defer to simpler explanations.** If crop circles can be made by ordinary people, why invoke supernatural "vortices" or aliens to account for them? This is sometimes expressed as "Occam's razor," which advised that "one should not increase, beyond what is necessary, the number of entities required to explain anything."
- **Insist on exceptional levels of proof for extraordinary claims.** "I saw them" is not solid proof of unicorns in the garden. Nor is a grainy video proof of an alien autopsy.
- **Imagine alternative explanations for phenomena.** If one comes across mutilated cattle, could there be a cause other than aliens practicing dissection? If people feel pain relief after using magnets, is the placebo effect at work?
- **Remember that fraud is common.** Maybe Uri Geller can bend spoons with his mind, or maybe he's good at sleight of hand.
- **Remember that people can delude themselves.** Even a trained investigator might think he sees a face in a photo of Mars. Some scientists did, for awhile. Also, the placebo effect is really a form of self-delusion, and it's common.
- **When possible, devise tests.** In some cases this can be done informally, and in others, the apparatus of a double-blind study may be needed. One ought to at least ask if such tests have been done to bolster extraordinary claims.

No doubt you will add tools of your own as you read, research, discuss, and reflect on subjects presented in this book. Obviously, a skeptical habit of mind can prove useful in arenas that have little to do with the paranormal and like subjects. Certain books come to mind in this regard. *Everything You Know is Wrong*, edited by Russ Kick, and *Lies My Teacher Told Me*, by James Loewen, do a lot of debunking in the areas of American history and culture in general. Tales of the health dangers posed by power lines or of the health benefits of wine and chocolate could be usefully questioned, just as it would be good to ask whether "organic" food differs significantly from its less expensive counterparts across the aisle. A skeptical consumer might wonder if "organic" always certifies the same thing. One such question could lead to another and another, which might not be good news for a culture based on consumerism. Nor would a critical approach to claims be welcomed by "spin artists" who direct political campaigns, or administrations whose policies are glossed over with fanfare, images, and slogans. On the other hand, imagine the policy speeches of a political figure who knew he had to reckon with well-trained, experienced skeptics. The work that you do in reading this book can be fruitful for many years to come. The skills you develop now will certainly be tested in the future. By way of welcome, let me recommend to you an excellent web site devoted to reason: http://skepdic.com/news/.

The Burden of Skepticism
CARL SAGAN

Carl Sagan's résumé could fill many pages. A professor of astronomy at Cornell University, Sagan wrote hundreds of papers, and his books include the Pulitzer Prize winning Dragons of Eden, *and* Demon Haunted World: Science as a Candle in the Dark, *which won the Los Angeles Times* Book Prize for Science and Technology. *Sagan also hosted the PBS series* Cosmos *and co-wrote, with his wife, Ann Druyen, the screenplay for a movie version of his novel,* Contact. *Sagan was also a vital force in the SETI project that radio scans space for signals from other intelligent beings. It has so far yielded no positive findings, but Sagan's backing and his imaginative writings suggest that skepticism is compatible with wonder and with the most exciting kinds of research. The following essay presents Sagan's sense of skepticism, its nature, value, and place in our culture.*

———————— ✦ ————————

What is Skepticism? It's nothing very esoteric. We encounter it every day. When we buy a used car, if we are the least bit wise we will exert some residual skeptical powers—whatever our education has left to us. You could say, "Here's an honest-looking fellow. I'll just take whatever he offers me." Or you might say, "Well, I've heard that occasionally there are small deceptions involved in the sale of a used car, perhaps inadvertent on the part of the salesperson," and then you do something. You kick the tires, you open the doors, you look under the hood. (You might go through the motions even if you don't know what is supposed to be under the hood, or you might bring a mechanically inclined friend.) You know that some skepticism is required, and you understand why. It's upsetting that you might have to disagree with the used-car salesman or ask him questions that he is reluctant to answer. There is at least a small degree of interpersonal confrontation involved in the purchase of a used car and nobody claims it is especially pleasant. But there is a good reason for it—because if you don't exercise some minimal skepticism, if you have an absolutely untrameled credulity, there is probably some price you will have to pay later. Then you'll wish you had made a small investment of skepticism early.

Now this is not something that you have to go through four years of graduate school to understand. Everybody understands this. The trouble is, a used car is one thing but television commercials or pronouncements by presidents and party leaders are another. We are skeptical in some areas but unfortunately not in others.

For example, there is a class of aspirin commercials that reveals the competing product to have only so much of the painkilling ingredient that doctors recommend most—they don't tell you what the mysterious ingredient is—whereas *their* product has a dramatically larger amount (1.2 to 2 times more per tablet). Therefore you should buy their product. But why not just take two of the competing tablets? You're not supposed to ask. Don't apply skepticism to this issue. Don't think. Buy.

Such claims in commercial advertisements constitute small deceptions. They part us from a little money, or induce us to buy a slightly inferior product. It's not so terrible. But consider this:

5   I have here the program of this year's Whole Life Expo in San Francisco. Twenty thousand people attended last year's program. Here are some of the presentations: "Alternative Treatments for AIDS Patients: it will rebuild one's natural defenses and prevent immune system breakdowns—learn about the latest developments that the media has thus far ignored." It seems to me that presentation could do real harm. "How Trapped Blood Proteins Produce Pain and Suffering." "Crystals, Are They Talismans or Stones?" (I have an opinion myself.) It says, "As a crystal focuses sound and light waves for radio and television"—crystal sets are rather a long time ago—"so may it amplify spiritual vibrations for the attuned human." I'll bet very few of you are attuned. Or here's one: "Return of the Goddess, a Presentational Ritual." Another: "Synchronicity, the Recognition Experience." That one is given by "Brother Charles." Or, on the next page, "You, Saint-Germain, and Healing Through the Violet Flame." It goes on and on, with lots

of ads about "opportunities"—ranging from the dubious to the spurious—that are available at the Whole Life Expo.

• • •

If you were to drop down on Earth at any time during the tenure of humans you would find a set of popular, more or less similar, belief systems. They change, often very quickly, often on time scales of a few years: But sometimes belief systems of this sort last for many thousands of years. At least a few are always available. I think it's fair to ask why. We are *Homo sapiens*. That's the distinguishing characteristic about us, that *sapiens* part. We're supposed to be smart. So why is this stuff always with us? Well, for one thing, a great many of these belief systems address real human needs that are not being met by our society. There are unsatisfied medical needs, spiritual needs, and needs for communion with the rest of the human community. There may be more such failings in our society than in many others in human history. And so it is reasonable for people to poke around and try on for size various belief systems, to see if they help.

For example, take a fashionable fad, channeling. It has for its fundamental premise, as does spiritualism, that when we die we don't exactly disappear, that some part of us continues. That part, we are told, can reenter the bodies of human and other beings in the future, and so death loses much of its sting for us personally. What is more, we have an opportunity, if the channeling contentions are true, to make contact with loved ones who have died.

Speaking personally, I would be delighted if reincarnation were real. I lost my parents, both of them, in the past few years, and I would love to have a little conversation with them, to tell them what the kids are doing, make sure everything is all right wherever it is they are. That touches something very deep. But at the same time, precisely for that reason, I know that there are people who will try to take advantage of the vulnerabilities of the bereaved. The spiritualists and the channelers better have a compelling case.

Or take the idea that by thinking hard at geological formations you can tell where mineral or petroleum deposits are. Uri Geller makes this claim. Now if you are an executive of a mineral exploration or petroleum company, your bread and butter depend on finding the minerals or the oil: so spending trivial amounts of money, compared with what you usually spend on geological exploration, this time to find deposits psychically, sounds not so bad. You might be tempted.

10   Or take UFOs, the contention that beings in spaceships from other worlds are visiting us all the time. I find that a thrilling idea. It's at least a break from the ordinary. I've spent a fair amount of time in my scientific life working on the issue of the search for extraterrestrial intelligence. Think how much effort I could save if those guys are coming here. But when we recognize some emotional vulnerability regarding a claim, that is exactly where we have to make the firmest efforts at skeptical scrutiny. That is where we can be had.

Now, let's reconsider channeling. There is a woman in the State of Washington who claims to make contact with a 35,000-year-old somebody, "Ramtha"—she, by the way, speaks English very well with what sounds to me to be an Indian accent. Suppose we had Ramtha here and just suppose Ramtha is cooperative. We could ask some questions: How do we know that Ramtha lived 35,000 years ago? Who is keeping track of the intervening millennia? How does it come to be exactly 35,000 years? That's a very round number. Thirty-five thousand plus or minus what? What were things like 35,000 years ago? What was the climate? Where on Earth did Ramtha live? (I know she speaks English with an Indian accent, but where was that?) What does Ramtha eat? (Archaeologists know something about what people are back then.) We would have a real opportunity to find out if his claims are true. If this were really somebody from 35,000 years ago, you could learn a lot about 35,000 years ago. So, one way or another, either Ramtha really is 35,000 years old, in which case we discover something about that period—that's before the Wisconsin Ice Age, an interesting time—or he's a phony and he'll slip up. What are the indigenous languages, what is the social structure, who else does Ramtha live with—children, grandchildren—what's the life cycle, the infant mortality, what clothes does she wear, what's her life expectancy, what are the weapons, plants, and animals? Tell us. Instead, what we hear are the most banal homilies, indistinguishable from those that alleged UFO occupants tell the poor humans who claim to have been abducted by them.

Occasionally, by the way, I get a letter from someone who is in "contact" with an extraterrestrial who invites me to "ask anything." And so I have a list of questions. The extraterrestrials are very advanced, remember. So I ask things like, "Please give a short proof of Fermat's Last Theorem." Or the Goldbach Conjecture. And then I have to explain what these are, because extraterrestrials will not call it Fermat's Last Theorem, so I write out the little equation with the exponents. I never get an answer.

On the other hand, if I ask something like "Should we humans be good?" I always get an answer. I think something can be deduced from this differential ability to answer questions. Anything vague they are extremely happy to respond to, but anything specific, where there is a chance to find out if they actually know anything, there is only silence.

The French scientist Henri Poincaré remarked on why credulity is rampant: "We also know how cruel the truth often is, and we wonder whether delusion is not more consoling." That's what I have tried to say with my examples. But I don't think that's the only reason credulity is rampant. Skepticism challenges established institutions. If we teach everybody, let's say high school students, the habit of being skeptical, perhaps they will not restrict their skepticism to aspirin commercials and 35,000-year-old channelers (or channelees). Maybe they'll start asking awkward questions about economic, or social, or political, or religious institutions. Then where will we be?

Skepticism is dangerous. That's exactly its function, in my view. It is the business of skepticism to be dangerous. And that's why there is a great reluctance to teach it in the schools. That's why you don't find a general fluency in skepticism in the media. On the other hand, how will we negotiate a very perilous future if we don't have the elementary intellectual tools to ask searching questions of those nominally in charge, especially in a democracy?

I think this is a useful moment to reflect on the sort of   15
national trouble that could have been avoided were skepticism more generally available in American society. The Iran/Nicaragua fiasco is so obvious an example I will not take advantage of our poor, beleaguered president [Reagan] by spelling it out. The Administration's resistance to a Comprehensive Test Ban Treaty and its continuing passion for blowing up nuclear weapons—one of the major drivers of the nuclear arms race—under the pretense of making us "safe" is another such issue. So is Star Wars. The habits of skeptical thought CSICOP encourages have relevance for matters of the greatest importance to the nation. There is enough nonsense promulgated by both political parties that the habit of evenhanded skepticism should be declared a national goal, essential for our survival.

• • •

I want to say a little more about the burden of skepticism. You can get into a habit of thought in which you enjoy making fun of all those other people who don't see things as clearly as you do.

This is a potential social danger present in an organization like CSICOP. We have to guard carefully against it.

It seems to me what is called for is an exquisite balance between two conflicting needs: the most skeptical scrutiny of all hypotheses that are served up to us and at the same time a great openness to new ideas. Obviously those two modes of thought are in some tension. But if you are able to exercise only one of these modes, whichever one it is, you're in deep trouble.

If you are only skeptical, then no new ideas make it through to you. You never learn anything new. You become a crotchety old person convinced that nonsense is ruling the world. (There is, of course, much data to support you.) But every now and then, maybe once in a hundred cases, a new idea turns out to be on the mark, valid and wonderful. If you are too much in the habit of being skeptical about everything, you are going to miss or resent it, and either way you will be standing in the way of understanding and progress.

On the other hand, if you are open to the point of gullibility and have not an ounce of skeptical sense in you, then you cannot distinguish the useful ideas from the worthless ones. If all ideas have equal validity then you are lost, because then, it seems to me, no ideas have any validity at all.

20   Some ideas are better than others. The machinery for distinguishing them is an essential tool in dealing with the world and especially in dealing with the future. And it is precisely the mix of these two modes of thought that is central to the success of science.

Really good scientists do both. On their own, talking to themsleves, they churn up huge numbers of new ideas and criticize them ruthlessly. Most of the ideas never make it to the outside world. Only the ideas that pass through rigorous self-filtration make it out and are criticized by the rest of the scientific community. It sometimes happens that ideas that are accepted by everybody turn out to be wrong, or at least partially wrong, or at least superseded by ideas of greater generality. And, while there are of course some personal losses—emotional bonds to the idea that you yourself played a role inventing—nevertheless the collective ethic is that every time such an idea is overthrown and replaced by something better the enterprise of science has benefited. In science it often happens that scientists say, "You know that's a really good argument; my position is mistaken," and then they actually change their minds and you never hear that old view from them again. They really do it. It doesn't happen as often as it should, because scientists are human and change is sometimes

painful. But it happens every day. I cannot recall the last time
something like that has happened in politics or religion. It's very
rare that a senator, say, replies, "That's a good argument. I will
now change my political affiliation."

• • •

I would like to say a few things about the stimulating sessions on
the search for extraterrestrial intelligence (SETI) and on animal
language at our CSICOP conference. In the history of science there
is an instructive procession for major intellectual battles that turn
out, all of them, to be about how central human beings are. We
could call them battles about the anti-Copernican conceit.
    Here are some of the issues:

- *We are the center of the Universe. All the planets and the stars
  and the Sun and the Moon go around us.* (Boy, must we be
  something *really* special.) That was the prevailing belief—
  Aristarchus aside—until the time of Copernicus. A lot of people liked it because it gave them a personally unwarranted
  central position in the Universe. The mere fact that you were
  on Earth made you privileged. That felt good. Then along
  came the evidence that Earth was just a planet and that those
  other bright moving points of light were planets too.
  Disappointing. Even depressing. Better when we were central
  and unique.
- *But at least our Sun is at the center of the Universe.* No, those
  other stars, they're suns too, and what's more we're out in the
  galactic boondocks. We are nowhere near the center of the
  Galaxy. Very depressing.
- *Well, at least the Milky Way galaxy is at the center of the
  Universe.* Then a little more progress in science. We find there
  isn't any such thing as the center of the Universe. What's more
  there are a hundred billion other galaxies. Nothing special
  about this one. Deep gloom.
- *Well, at least we humans, we are the pinnacle of creation. We're
  separate. All those other creatures, plants and animals, they're
  lower. We're higher. We have no connection with them. Every
  living thing has been created separately.* Then along comes
  Darwin. We find an evolutionary continuum. We're closely
  connected to the other beasts and vegetables. What's more,
  the closest biological relatives to us are chimpanzees. *Those*
  are our close relatives—*those* guys? It's an embarrassment.
  Did you ever go to the zoo and watch them? Do you know

what they do? Imagine in Victorian England, when Darwin produced this insight, what an awkward truth it was.

There are other important examples—privileged reference frames in physics and the unconscious mind in psychology— that I'll pass over.

25   I maintain that in the tradition of this long set of debates— every one of which was won by the Copernicans, by the guys who say there is not much special about us—there was a deep emotional undercurrent in the debates in both CSICOP sessions I mentioned. The search for extraterrestrial intelligence and the analysis of possible animal "language" strike at one of the last remaining pre-Copernican belief systems:

• *At least we are the most intelligent creatures in the whole Universe.* If there are no other smart guys elsewhere, even if we *are* connected to chimpanzees, even if we *are* in the boondocks of a vast and awesome universe, at least there is still something special about us. But the moment we find extraterrestrial intelligence that last bit of conceit is gone. I think some of the resistance to the idea of extraterrestrial intelligence is due to the anti-Copernican conceit. Likewise, without taking sides in the debate on whether other animals—higher primates, especially great apes—are intelligent or have language, that's clearly, on an emotional level, the same issue. If we define humans as creatures who have language and no one else has language, at least we are unique in that regard. But if it turns out that all those dirty, repugnant, laughable chimpanzees can also, with Ameslan or otherwise, communicate ideas, then what is left that is special about us? Propelling emotional predispositions on these issues are present, often unconsciously, in scientific debates. It is important to realize that scientific debates, just like pseudoscientific debates, can be awash with emotion, for these among many different reasons.

Now, let's take a closer look at the radio search for extraterrestrial intelligence. How is this different from pseudoscience? Let me give a couple of real cases. In the early sixties, the Soviets held a press conference in Moscow in which they announced that a distant radio source, called CTA-102, was varying sinusoidally, like a sine wave, with a period of about 100 days. Why did they call a press conference to announce that a distant radio source was varying? Because they thought it was an extraterrestrial civilization of immense powers. That is worth calling a press conference for. This was before even the word "quasar" existed. Today we know that CTA-102 is a quasar. We don't know very well what quasars are: and there is more than one mutually exclusive explanation for them in the scientific literature. Nevertheless, few seriously consider that a quasar, like CTA-102, is some galaxy-girdling extraterrestrial civilization, because there are a number of alternative explanations of their properties that are more or less consistent with the physical laws we know without invoking alien life. The extraterrestrial hypothesis is a hypothesis of last resort. Only if everything else fails do you reach for it.

Second example: British scientists in 1967 found a nearby bright radio source that is fluctuating on a much shorter time scale, with a period constant to ten significant figures. What was it? Their first thought was that it was something like a message being sent to us, or an interstellar navigational beacon for spacecraft that fly the spaces between the stars. They even gave it, among themselves at Cambridge University, the wry designation LGM-1—Little Green Men, LGM. However (they were wiser than the Soviets), they did not call a press conference, and it soon became clear that what we had here was what is now called a "pulsar." In fact it was the first pulsar, the Crab Nebula pulsar. Well, what's a pulsar? A pulsar is a star shrunk to the size of a city, held up as no other stars are, not by gas pressure, not by electron degeneracy, but by nuclear forces. It is in a certain sense an atomic nucleus the size of Pasadena. Now that, I maintain, is an idea at least as bizarre as an interstellar navigational beacon. The answer to what a pulsar is has to be something mighty strange. It isn't an extraterrestrial civilization, it's something else: but a something else that opens our eyes and our minds and indicates possibilities in nature that we had never guessed at.

Then there is the question of false positives. Frank Drake in his original Ozma experiment, Paul Horowitz in the META (Megachannel Extraterrestrial Assay) program sponsored by the Planetary Society, the Ohio University group and many other groups have all had anomalous signals that make the heart palpitate. They think for a moment that they have picked up a genuine signal. In some cases we have not the foggiest idea what it was; the signals did not repeat. The next night you turn the same telescope to the same spot in the sky with the same modulation and the same frequency and band pass everything else the same, and you don't hear a thing. You don't publish that data. It may be a malfunction in the detection system. It may be a military AWACS plane flying by and broadcasting on frequency channels that are supposed to be reserved for radio astronomy. It may be a diathermy machine down the street. There are many possibilities. You don't immediately declare that you have found extraterrestrial intelligence because you find an anomalous signal.

And if it were repeated, would you then announce? You would not. Maybe it's a hoax. Maybe it is something you haven't been smart enough to figure out that is happening to your system. Instead, you would then call scientists at a bunch of other radio telescopes and say that at this particular spot in the sky, at this frequency and bandpass and modulation and all the rest, you seem to be getting something funny. Could they please look at it and see if they got something similar? And only if several independent observers get the same kind of information from the same spot in the sky do you think you have something. Even then you don't know that the something is extraterrestrial intelligence, but at least you could determine that it's not something on Earth. (And that it's also not something in Earth orbit; it's further away than that.) That's the first sequence of events that would be required to be sure that you actually had a signal from an extraterrestrial civilization.

30   Now notice that there is a certain discipline involved. Skepticism imposes a burden. You can't just go off shouting "little green men," because you are going to look mighty silly, as the Soviets did with CTA-102, when it turns out to be something quite different. A special caution is necessary when the stakes are as high as here. We are not obliged to make up our minds before the evidence is in. It's okay not to be sure.

I'm often asked the question, "Do you think there is extraterrestrial intelligence?" I give the standard arguments—there are a lot of places out there, and use the word *billions,* and so on. And then I say it would be astonishing to me if there weren't extraterrestrial intelligence, but of course there is as yet no compelling evidence for it. And then I'm asked, "Yeah, but what do you really think?" I say, "I just told you what I really think." "Yeah, but what's your gut feeling?" But I try not to think with my gut. Really, it's okay to reserve judgment until the evidence is in.

• • •

After my article "The Fine Art of Baloney Detection" came out in *Parade* (Feb. 1, 1987), I got, as you might imagine, a lot of letters. Sixty-five million people read *Parade.* In the article I gave a long list of things that I said were "demonstrated or presumptive baloney"—thirty or forty items. Advocates of all those positions were uniformly offended, so I got lots of letters. I also gave a set of very elementary prescriptions about how to think about baloney—arguments from authority don't work, every step in the chain of evidence has to be valid, and so on. Lots of people wrote back, saying, "You're absolutely right on the generalities; unfortunately that doesn't apply to my particular doctrine." For example, one letter writer said the idea that intelligent life exists outside the earth is an excellent example of baloney. He concluded, "I am as sure of this as of anything in my experience. There is no conscious life anywhere else in the Universe. Mankind thus returns to its rightful position as center of the Universe."

Another writer again agreed with all my generalities, but said that as an inveterate skeptic I have closed my mind to the truth. Most notably I have ignored the evidence for an Earth that is six thousand years old. Well, I haven't ignored it; I considered the purported evidence and *then* rejected it. There is a difference, and this is a difference, we might say, between prejudice and postjudice. Prejudice is making a judgment before you have looked at the facts. Postjudice is making a judgment afterwards. Prejudice is terrible, in the sense that you commit injustices and you make serious mistakes. Postjudice is not terrible. You can't be perfect of course; you may make mistakes also. But it is permissible to make a judgment after you have examined the evidence. In some circles it is even encouraged.

I believe that part of what propels science is the thirst for wonder. It's a very powerful emotion. All children feel it. In a first grade classroom everybody feels it; in a twelfth grade classroom almost nobody feels it, or at least acknowledges it. Something happens between first and twelfth grade, and it's not just puberty. Not only do the schools and the media not teach much skepticism, there is also little encouragement of this stirring sense of wonder. Science and pseudoscience both arouse that feeling. Poor popularizations of science establish an ecological niche for pseudoscience.

If science were explained to the average person in a way that 35
is accessible and exciting, there would be no room for pseudoscience. But there is a kind of Gresham's Law by which in popular culture the bad science drives out the good. And for this I think we have to blame, first, the scientific community ourselves for not doing a better job of popularizing science, and second, the media, which are in this respect almost uniformly dreadful. Every newspaper in America has a daily astrology column. How many have

even a weekly astronomy column? And I believe it is also the fault of the educational system. We do not teach how to think. This is a very serious failure that may even, in a world rigged with 60,000 nuclear weapons, compromise the human future.

I maintain there is much more wonder in science than in pseudoscience. And in addition, to whatever measure this term has any meaning, science has the additional virtue, and it is not an inconsiderable one, of being true.

For Discussion and Writing

1. Explain whether you agree with Sagan about the dangers of the Whole Life Expo.
2. Sagan playfully suggests that the aliens people claim to be in contact with should answer some tough questions, something about "Fermat's last theorem" or the "Goldbach conjecture." He never hears answers or even discussion about these from those "in contact with extraterrestrials." What questions would you pose? Why?
3. Why, in Sagan's view, is skepticism dangerous? He mentioned this in the context of 1980s politics. How might it be dangerous in his sense in our own era?
4. How would you react to a positive signal in response to SETI efforts? That is, if SETI recorded a definite signal originating in space, what, if anything, would change in your worldview?
5. Consider Sagan's standard answer to the question, "Do you think there is extraterrestrial intelligence?" How would you characterize his answer? How would your own answer compare to his? In what sense does his answer reflect a commitment to the methods and habits of science?

CHAPTER 1

Urban Legends

Don't you wish you had a job like mine? All you have to do is think up a certain number of words! Plus, you can repeat words! And they don't even have to be true!

—DAVE BARRY

Who never doubted, never half believed. Where doubt is, there truth is—It is her shadow.

—AMBROSE BIERCE

Back in the 1990s, a terrible fire ravaged the Oakland Hills. Wind, fuel, and rough terrain made this blaze a catastrophe, destroying homes and taking lives. The most bizarre loss of life in the inferno was, however, a drowning. The day after the last flames had been extinguished, a fire crew driving through the smoky streets came upon a grove of blackened trees. "Wait up, fellas," the crew caption called. "There's something up in that tree over there." The men stopped and went to investigate, and sure enough, there was a charred shape in the top limbs of the burnt tree. They soon got a ladder truck over to aid them, and picked a blackened human corpse from the upper limbs. The firefighters speculated that the man had panicked and climbed the tree in hopes of escaping the blaze, but the coroner determined the poor guy had in fact died by drowning. How? It took some time to identify the man and to verify with his family that on the first day of the fire he had been scuba diving out in the San Francisco Bay. Apparently, a fire-fighting helicopter had been scooping water out of the bay and dumping it *on burning homes in the hills. On one run it had scooped the diver up as he was surfacing after using up his air supply, and he was lifted, air tanks, mask, flippers and all, from the Bay, then dumped onto a burning hillside. He drowned in the huge water basket before he even hit the tree.*

That's one version of a strange tale that made its way around the country some time ago. Part of it is true. There was a terrible fire in the Oakland Hills in the nineties, and fire crews do often use water-toting helicopters to fight blazes. The rest is a fascinating lie. The tale combines spectacular irony with near-universal fears of death by drowning or by fire, and has just enough realistic detail in it to make it credible to some people. This story, like those about stolen kidneys, alligators in city sewers, the vanishing hitchhiker, the killer who leaves his arm behind—well, the artificial hook at the end of his stump, anyway—all these are lies. The softer sounding term we use is *urban legend,* and a huge variety of such legends has swamped our culture. They intrigue and entertain us; some appear in expanded form in movies and television shows. For our purposes, what matters most is that in their initial telling they are very widely believed. For example, a story will surface about criminals operating in the parking lot of big malls; the bad guys spray their victims with ether disguised as perfume. This account will hit the Internet and appear in hundreds of thousands of inboxes in a few days. The tale gets retold as something that happened to someone's friend—direct testimony in such tales is rare—and a low-grade alarm grips the gullible. We don't want to be remiss in our duties to friends so we send the warning along to everyone we know who might be dumb enough to fall for the dangerous ruse. "If you go to the mall (on a given day that may cover half of the country's population) and some guy approaches you asking if you'd like to sample a designer perfume he's selling on the cheap, beware. It's likely ether, and when you get close to him, he'll spray it right in your face and when you come to you won't have a purse, a car, or any chance of being a virgin bride." This story will surely ring true if you've ever heard of purse snatchings and other kinds of assault in the parking lots of shopping centers. Fear isn't an analytical state of mind. Mere rumors and possibilities serve as proof enough. Better get those emails out to friends and family right now. If you happened to be wide awake and feeling skeptical when you heard of the ether/perfume attacks, you might ask some questions. Who is telling me this happened? That is, am I hearing from an actual victim, a witness, or someone more remote from the alleged attack? If eyewitness accounts can prove unreliable, how much more doubtful is an account by someone repeating what he read in a mass email forwarded from a stranger about an incident that happened to a friend's friend? Then you might go on to ask technical questions. Can ether sprayed in the open air overcome someone? You might be so skeptical as to ask where the crime took place, and then search for newspaper accounts in a database like LexisNexis. If you can't get specifics about the crime from your source, you could just browse a popular online site devoted to urban legends to see if anyone has debunked this story. If you were the least bit skeptical, you could readily find the problems in this story.

There isn't much harm in such tales, so why bother to debunk them? The value of doing just that can only be appreciated if you think cumulatively. Here's an analogy. If you happen to toss your cold latte into your local river, what's the harm? If your friends imitate you, there's still only a slight impact on the water. If your actions inspire a company to dump sludge, and if that in turn seems to authorize a spreading use of the river as a sewer, real damage will be done. You have to think cumulatively. You have to learn to sum effects, a habit of mind that will change the way you see the world. Urban legends are only one silly form of falsehood among many others that in fact plague our culture. Chronic falsehood may wear away at trust in public life, and habitual, uncritical acceptance of tall tales can breed fearfulness and dimwitted reactions of the sort that clog your email inbox.

The essays in this section present various legends along with issues that any reasonable person might raise. Jan Brunvand's "Lights Out!—A Faxlore Phenomenon" traces the history of an urban legend that claimed some gangs in America initiated members in a murderous ritual. Brunvand, who is one of the best-known writers on such tales, admits that finding the precise origin of the tale is impossible but careful investigating has turned up interesting information. In "French Follies," L. Kirk Hagen reviews a book by French writer Thierry Meyssan which claims that the 9/11 attacks on this country did not involve any terrorists but were in fact orchestrated by our CIA. In a lighter vein, Samuel Sass's "A Patently False Patent Myth—Still!" examines the venerable legend that a patent office official once resigned his position because he thought there was nothing left to invent.

In debunking this tale, Sass turns up other interesting and truly incredible claims that have a long history in our culture. The last essay in this section deals with campus-based urban legends, some of which are no doubt familiar to you already. There is a positive side to all the falsity we find in urban legends. A skeptical stance in the face of such tales will develop our skeptic's toolkit. We can instill a habit of forming questions appropriate to specific claims. We sharpen our listening and reading skills as we zero in on details that suggest falsehood. Our "b.s. detectors" become more finely attuned. We may even acquire a bit of diplomacy as we gently debunk our friends' nonsense.

Lights Out!—A Faxlore Phenomenon
JAN BRUNVAND

Jan Brunvand, professor emeritus in English at the University of Utah, has written nearly a dozen books on urban legends and folklore, including The Mexican Pet *(1986),* Curses! Broiled Again *(1989), and* The Truth Never Stands in the Way of a Good Story *(2000). In the following essay, Brunvand presents a tale that circulated widely in the 1990s about a gang initiation rite involving hoodlums, headlights, and murder. Brunvand's analysis notes similarities between this tale and other stories that circulated via fax and photocopying.*

———————— ✦ ————————

On Saturday August 14, 1993, a small news item—about six column inches—debunking a "faxed warning about gang initiation," appeared in the *Memphis Commercial Appeal*. The headline was "Officials Deny Faxing Gang Warnings," and the subhead read, "Untrue documents promote hysteria." The documents were described as "heavily faxed" and claimed to be official police bulletins. They stated, "This is the time of year for gang initiation," and described the specific threat as follows:

> One of the methods used this year will be for gang members to drive with their lights off at night. When you blink your lights or flash your high beams, they will follow you home and attempt to murder you.

At a press conference, officials of Memphis and of Shelby County, Tennessee, said that these "fax driven rumors criss-crossed the county this week," that police were inundated with calls about them, but that no local law-enforcement office had sent out the faxes, nor was there any evidence for such gang initiation practices. Although it is clear in this news item that the "Lights Out!" rumor was already in active circulation, this is the earliest example I have located. The next time I encountered the rumor was in an e-mail message from Chicago sent on September 9, and the next *published* report I found was in a suburban Chicago newspaper on September 11, four weeks after the Memphis report. But soon the "Lights Out!" rumor emerged in many cities and became a matter of national concern. The flap continued through autumn 1993 and even into the new year in some places. The rumor was driven nationwide largely by facsimile transmissions and thus provides a unique example of a faxlore phenomenon, likely the trend of the future in the circulation of urban rumors and legends.

I collected three kinds of information about "Lights Out!": (1) copies of the warnings themselves, (2) letters from people reporting on the warnings, and (3) further news stories.

My September 9 e-mail report came from someone at the University of Chicago who forwarded a memo credited to the Security Division of the First National Bank of Chicago. The first line, "Beware," was followed by two exclamation points; the capsule description of the initiation ritual, said to be planned for "the Chicagoland area," was followed by the bare elements of an illustrative story: "To date, two families have already fallen victim to this senseless crime." The memo concluded with an appeal for readers to "inform your friends and family not to flash their car lights at anyone!" This early example of the "Lights Out!" warning displays typical features of all subsequent versions: it uses somewhat sensational language, repeats the basic rumor (naming it as "Lights Out!"), and provides a validating reference (i.e., the bank's memo format); it also localizes the supposed criminal plans, alludes in a vague way to specific cases, and recommends a course of action.

Later versions of the warning—usually computer-written and often laser-printed—tend to have more exclamation points (sometimes coming before as well as after sentences), to have more words or whole lines printed in all caps or underlined (sometimes double-underlined, and sometimes both all caps and underlined), and often to have handwritten additions like *This is not a joke*," or "*Be careful out there*," or "*Urgent!*" A few examples were hand-lettered and photocopied or were retyped on a company's letterhead (including the City of Detroit Water and Sewage Department). Most examples that I collected had been faxed; others were e-mailed, sent by post-office mail, or posted as hardcopy memos on bulletin boards.

Dates on these warnings range from early September to early December 1993, most coming in mid-September. Other cities mentioned in them are St. Louis, Detroit, Dallas, Atlanta, Norfolk (Virginia), New York, Baltimore, Los Angeles, Sacramento, and Honolulu. (Articles in the press added Memphis, Toledo, Columbus, Pittsburgh, Philadelphia, Washington, D.C., Minneapolis, Little Rock, Tulsa, Houston, San Antonio, Lubbock, Denver, Salt Lake City, San Jose, and San Francisco. Letters from readers added cities in New Jersey, Florida, Missouri, and the Northwest. Clearly, the "Lights Out!" rumor was flying coast to coast.) The institutions circulating the fliers were banks, businesses, law firms, universities, military posts, hospitals, and day-care centers. Several of the warning notices contain routing stamps or slips indicating that they were circulated throughout a whole office or company.

About mid-September the warnings began to name "Grady Harn of the Sacramento Police Department" as the source of the information. Also, the weekend of September 25 and 26 was pinpointed as "Blood [or Bloods'] Initiation Weekend," when, supposedly, gangs, including the notorious Bloods Gang, would hold their murderous initiation.[1] A few of the fliers, although unsigned, made first-person reference to "my stepfather" or to another relative who had "called me" with this important information. Some fliers admitted that "this information has not been confirmed," but most fliers still advised readers not to flash their lights at anyone, just in case. One person sending me a printed flier added in a note: "One of our supervisors [at work] stood up and read this to us." After the supposed "Bloods' Weekend" came and went without incident, the fliers—now minus the dates—continued to appear, mostly in fax machines.

During the 1993 autumn semester at Indiana University at Kokomo a folklore class studied the "Lights Out!" rumor. The instructor, Susanne Ridlen, forwarded a packet of the twenty items resulting from the project, and these display the variations of the story in one community and of the means by which it was transmitted.

10   The Kokomo students documented transmission of "Lights Out!" via word of mouth, telephone (including long-distance calls), on both commercial and CB radio, via e-mail, fax, printed memos (distributed in schools and workplaces), and in publications.

Several Kokomo versions combined "Lights Out!" with other car-related legends (Brunvand 1981: 19–46; 1984: 50–68; 1986: 49–67; 1989: 89–128), and some people claimed that the gang initiations included the cutting off of feet or ears. The specific gangs involved were said to be the Crypts [*sic*] and the Bloods, groups said to be moving to Kokomo either south from Chicago or north from Indianapolis. Other versions claimed an origin of the information from Mississippi, where such initiations supposedly had occurred. Motorists would be targeted either if they blinked (or "flickered") their lights *or* if they honked at a gang car driving without lights. Police were said to be warning motorists—via gas-station attendants—not to flash their lights. Despite this, two (or three) people, according to the Kokomo rumors, had already died.

A story in the *Kokomo Tribune* on October 14, ("Police Shoot Hole in Gang Initiation Rumor") described "Lights Out!" as a baseless rumor that was thought to have reached Kokomo from Jackson, Mississippi, on September 19 in a message broadcast on CB radio. Both Indiana and Illinois state police gang-crimes units were quoted in the news story as denying the rumor.

(Similarly, the Salt Lake City Police Department on September 24 issued a news release calling the "Lights Out!" story "unfounded . . . unsubstantiated and without merit." Many police departments across the nation issued similar denials.)

The letters (including e-mail, mail, and faxed correspondence) that I received from readers of my books commenting on the "Lights Out!" rumor add to the sketchy story a few more details that must have circulated orally, since they do not appear in the printed fliers. These letters were dated from mid-September 1993 to April 11, 1994, and came from people who knew or suspected that the story was false. Most letters reported a chain of informal communication of the story—i.e., a co-worker whose girlfriend, a nurse, had heard about someone working on the other shift at the hospital or at a different hospital who had treated victims of the ritual. The initiations, according to some writers, "were supposed to test the mental toughness" of gang recruits. Sometimes the gang recruits would trace the offending cars via their license plates. The police were not publicizing the crimes, according to rumors, in order to lull gangs into a false sense of security in hopes that they could be caught in the act. A letter dated March 29, 1994, from New Cumberland, Pennsylvania, reported a variation in the story: "Cars Full of Satan Worshippers Driving Around Without Their Headlights." The writer had overheard his secretary warning her sister about the threat, and she had heard it from the driver of her van pool, who had heard it from a friend who saw a sign warning people about it in a store window.

A Seattle reader in a letter dated September 24 (the Friday before "Bloods' Weekend") mentioned that on Thursday the twenty-third the flier appeared at her workplace and "to my distress, every one of my twelve co-workers fell for it . . . despite my insistence that it couldn't possibly be true." Meanwhile, in Salt Lake City in my own department at the university, here's what happened—or *nearly* happened—on the same days. On the twenty-third, a reader from Fort Lauderdale, Florida, faxed me a letter saying he was also faxing a copy of a memo that he suspected was based on a rumor; page 2 of the fax transmission was the "Lights Out!" warning itself, typed on the letterhead of a Florida Jewish community center. The secretary of my department pulled page 1 of the message and put it into my mailbox without reading it beyond the address. Page 2—the warning memo—however, she read with alarm and then took it with her on Friday to a full departmental meeting; or, not *quite* a full meeting, since I myself, as a partial retiree, had decided to skip town that afternoon. The secretary intended to read the notice to the assembled faculty in order to alert them not to flash their lights when driving home, but she was dissuaded from doing so by my colleague, folklorist Margaret Brady. Brady convinced her that the warning was just "one of those legends that people are always sending Jan." Our secretary still felt the story might be true, since her own daughter had also heard about it in Salt Lake City a few days earlier.

15   The news stories about "Lights Out!" may be taken in chronological order, insofar as dates can be determined from the clippings.

As mentioned earlier, the first clipping I have is from the *Memphis Commercial Appeal* of August 14. The second is from the *Daily Southtown*, a suburban Chicago paper, on September 11 ("Police Say Area Story of Gang Rite Is Hoax"). The lead reads: "It's a great story—just like most so-called 'urban legends.'" Besides describing the same "anonymous handbills," this news story quotes police officials who deny it and adds that it sounds like something that might happen "in the frozen wastelands of Russia." The news story also suggests the possibility of copycat crimes, and it concludes with the threat of prosecution against spreaders of the tale. Every facet of this fairly obscure little news item turns out to be typical of what most papers wrote.

Four days later, on September 15, Mary Schmich, a *Chicago Tribune* columnist, wrote about the rumor, calling it "urban faxlore." Schmich identified the Black Gangster Disciple Nation

as the Chicago street gang blamed for the outrage, but she emphasized that the rumor was unsubstantiated and strongly denied by
Chicago police. Schmich listed radio stations, colleges, hospitals,
churches, and video stores as places where the warning had
appeared. Because she had phoned me to discuss the rumor,
Schmich was able to cite the earlier Memphis example of the
story and also to compare "Lights Out!" to other urban lore about
crime and violence. (Mary Schmich said that she was calling me
at the suggestion of folklorist Alan Dundes of U.C. Berkeley,
whom she had called earlier. He had not yet heard about the
warnings but thought that I might have.)

At this point my phone began ringing off the hook, and I was
preparing to leave on an extended trip; so I put a message on my
answering machine saying, in effect, "No interviews, please."
I decided to stay out of the spotlight and see what reporters might
make of the rumor on their own, or with the help of other folklorists whom they might contact.

Shortly after taking this vow of silence I started to see results:
on September 18 two papers ran stories—the Little Rock *Arkansas
Democrat-Gazette* ("Gang Initiation Rumor Baseless, LR Police
Say") and the *San Jose Mercury News* ("Cops Try to Arrest Rumor
of Gang Rite"). The enterprising Arkansas reporter located three of
the Brunvand books and compared "Lights Out!" to other urban
lore, including an earlier local outbreak of "The Mutilated Boy"
legend (Brunvand 1984: 78–92; 1986: 148–156). The even more
enterprising San Jose reporter managed to get a Memphis Police
spokesman and Alan Dundes on the phone. From Tennessee she
learned that the story was known in Knoxville and Chattanooga as
well; from Dundes (who now had heard the story and had a comment ready for it) she picked up the term *faxlore* and also the ideas
that a fear of teenagers—especially gang members—was reflected
in the story and that it might be inspired by acts of violence against
tourists in Florida. In an unusual twist, the *Mercury News* withheld
details of the warnings, fearing, they said, to suggest copycat
crimes. This article also referred to the speed with which the
rumor had blanketed Silicon Valley, where thousands of people are
linked to e-mail and to computer bulletin boards.

In Salt Lake City (where I also dodged the press) another gang   20
rumor was flying—that gangs were planning to rape a cheerleader
as part of an initiation. Although police and school authorities
denied the rumor, a September 18 article in the *Deseret News*
reported widespread concern among students and parents especially
on the more affluent east side of the Salt Lake Valley. One television

station was criticized for publicizing the story, even though the broadcast had made it clear that the rumors were unconfirmed.

Meanwhile, back in Chicago, on September 21, the student newspaper of the University of Illinois branch there was debunking the story again. One version of the warning photocopied on a state police letterhead was described as having a typeface that did not match the rest of the letterhead, a clue to its unreliability.

On September 22, the *Houston Post,* the *Houston Chronicle,* and the *Toledo Blade* ran articles on the rumor. The *Post* article ("Scary Gang Rumor Has Its Fax All Wrong") was pretty standard, except for calling the warning "an electronic chain letter" and "an urban myth[!]" (Maybe I should have answered the phone after all.) The *Chronicle* article ("HPD Tries to Stop Rumor About Gang Rites") had a novel touch—a color photograph of a grinning police chief holding up one of the fliers; the "Dragnet"-inspired caption read, "Just a phony fax, ma'am." The chief was quoted as saying, "I'd rather deal with the gangs than talk to any more hysterical people on the phone."

A sidelight of the Texas circulation of the rumor was revealed September 23 in a column in the *San Antonio Express-News.* Columnist Roddy Stinson, who a week earlier had dubbed his own city "the wide-eyed booby capital of the nation" for panicking over the "Lights Out!" urban legend (Stinson's term), now gave the booby prize to Houston, where the story had circulated earlier.

During "Bloods' Weekend" itself—September 25 and 26—the newspaper stories increased: I have clippings from papers in central New Jersey, San Francisco, Los Angeles, Salt Lake City, Minneapolis, and Pittsburgh. The New Jersey story mentions dozens of calls to police from fearful people, spurred by warnings traced to the Johnson & Johnson headquarters in New Brunswick and also circulated in area colleges and high schools and in a large insurance company. The San Francisco article ("Rumors Fly on Computer Networks") also names hospitals as hotbeds of the story, but emphasizes computer rather than faxed transmission. Alan Dundes is quoted anew, this time with a different slant on the story. "There is an element of the car, which represents power, mobility, and sex," the Berkeley professor comments, adding that the rumor was probably fueled by recent shootings of foreign tourists in Florida.

25   The *L.A. Times* article of September 24 is the first publication to mention the mysterious Grady Harn of the Sacramento Police Department, who is named on many fliers; the *Times* checked with Sacramento and found that no one of that name serves on

the police force there. Another innovation in the *Times* story is an unattributed claim that "the warnings are the work of a computer hacker who used facsimile telephone numbers to disseminate the messages." The fliers are described as "clumsily worded," which suggests, perhaps, poor social or communicative skills of the assumed hacker. Finally, the *L.A. Times* mentions that these phony warnings are "the latest examples of what sociologists call an urban myth." Although Los Angeles gang investigators are quoted in the story, the reporters who wrote the piece did not attempt to interview any gang members themselves.

Both Salt Lake City newspapers now covered the story, each relating it to the earlier rumors about gang intentions to rape cheerleaders. One county sheriff in Utah said he had not been able to get off the phone for more than 30 seconds at a time while fielding calls about "Lights Out!" from citizens and from the press. In a technically garbled explanation of how the story may have started, a police official suggested that "the hoax note was faxed into a billboard computer system."

Probably "Bloods' Weekend" was when the Associated Press circulated an article debunking "Lights Out!" that was widely reprinted and quoted. (I do not have a dated copy of the AP release.) The AP story quoted Ralph Rosnow and Gary Fine, coauthors of a book on rumor and gossip. Fine voiced the opinion that "*gang* in this particular rumor is a code word for poor, young black men."

The Minneapolis news article of September 25 again described the suspected villain in the case as a "hacker," but the paper associated "hacking" with *faxing* messages rather than with using computerized e-mail or a computer bulletin board. Articles published in Pittsburgh on September 25 and 27 added little to the picture except for speculating that the rumor came from "an unidentified originator in California."

In an interesting juxtaposition, the *Baltimore Sun* on September 27 ran a long story debunking the "Blue Star Acid" rumor (Brunvand 1984:162–169; 1989: 55–64), which had cropped up there again recently with a sidebar story on "Lights Out!" The Baltimore version was that members of "the Los Angeles–based gang the Bloods were randomly shooting motorists as part of a nationwide initiation campaign."

At last the rumor was mentioned in the national press. In the September 27 issue of *U.S. News & World Report*, a column by John Leo mentioned "Lights Out!" in passing as "a new bit of urban folklore." The column was mostly devoted to comments on the shootings of foreign tourists in Florida. *Newsweek*, in a brief notice headlined

30

"Big Fax Attack," mentioned Houston, Los Angeles, and Atlanta as sites of the rumor. In a syndicated column of September 29, William Raspberry of the *Washington Post* mentioned the rumor, although he indicated that just "people" (gangs were not mentioned) were driving with their lights off, hoping to entice victims to flash their headlights at them and thus become targets for violence.

The last weekend of September the magazine section of the *Dallas Observer* ran a detailed account titled "Anatomy of a Rumor: How the Gang-Initiation Story Terrified Dallas." The author called it "something of a minor urban myth in several cities," and he did a creditable job of tracking local versions back to individuals who had picked it up while traveling, on the phone, via fax, and so on. According to the *Observer*, one Dallas business-man said he was handed the warning "when he boarded an American Airlines return flight from Tampa."

From October to mid-December only a few further news stories appeared; the cities that were late to catch the rumor were Denver; Philadelphia and Allentown, Pennsylvania; Columbus, Ohio; and Lubbock, Texas. With Lubbock, on December 14, my clipping file bottoms out. The Denver story was mainly about rumors of gang rapes at a mall, with "Lights Out!" mentioned only in passing. The *Philadelphia Inquirer* story was unrestrained in calling the rumor "a big, fat, stinking, Pinocchio-nose kind of lie," but added, "and everybody believes it." Ralph Rosnow, who teaches at Temple University, was again quoted. The *Allentown Morning Call* story mentioned that the rumor had been retyped on Thomas Jefferson University security letterhead; both Patricia Turner, a professor at U.C. Davis, and Alan Dundes were quoted in this story, evidently from original interviews by the Allentown writer. Turner made some interesting observations about the theme of the "demonized outsider" threatening a Good Samaritan on the road. Dundes repeated some of his earlier remarks, and he too touched on the "Good Samaritan" theme.

In Columbus, "Lights Out!" got only a short paragraph in a story that was primarily about another rumor—that groups are trying to raise funds to buy firearms for the homeless. Similarly, in Lubbock, Texas, "Lights Out!" rated only a short mention in a full-page feature story about "Those pesky rumors." The only unusual touch here was the remark of a local police sergeant about how he deals with the panicky public in such cases; he said, "I just try to sound authoritative and reassuring." By mid-December, then, the story was effectively dead in the nation's media, although a few individuals continued to write me letters about it.

Unexpectedly, "Lights Out!" emerged one more time in the national media in "Traps," a new CBS-TV police drama, in which George C. Scott plays Joe Trapcheck, a former homicide investigator who comes out of retirement to serve as a consultant in his old department. In the premiere episode, aired on Thursday, March 31, 1994, he has joined the "Headlight Killer Taskforce," which is working to solve a series of shootings that occurred after people gave a "courtesy blink" to a car driving with its headlights out. Curiously, the episode also included another piece of urban folklore, where a photocopy machine is used to fool a suspect into revealing needed information; he is told that he's actually hooked up to a new type of polygraph (Brunvand 1993:139–145).

Reviewing the "Lights Out!" phenomenon, briefly, as *folklore,*   35
it seems evident that although modern technology and communications facilitated the rapid dissemination of the rumor over an extremely broad area, the variations that developed were similar to those typically caused by oral transmission alone. Details were added and altered; the story was localized; authorities were invoked to support the story; supposed actual cases were cited, and so on. "Lights Out!" was similar to other recent rumors and legends, including "Blue Star Acid" (also fax- and photocopy-delivered), "The Assailant in the Backseat" and other car horror stories, "The Attempted Abduction" and other mall-crime stories, and the like. *Faxlore* is a catchy term, but it is not clear that it should imply any essentially different kind of modern tradition.

Despite the sensational tone of the warnings, their informal channels of distribution, their poor English usage, and their lack of any specific verification, their message was taken to heart by many Americans. Thousands of people must have duplicated and distributed the fliers for them to have penetrated so widely. I believe the folklorists and sociologists who commented on "Lights Out!" were right in identifying themes like teenage and gang crimes, racism, urban problems, and attacks on foreign motorists as topics underlying the "Lights Out!" hysteria. (I'm not sure, however, where the sex, mentioned by Alan Dundes, comes in.) A well-known gang name, the Bloods, lent itself perfectly to intensifying the hysteria, as did another name, the Cryps (when misunderstood as "Crypts"). In Chicago, a gang with the very word "Black" in its name—the Black Gangster Disciple Nation—fed into this same racial fear, and in Kokomo the idea that the warning had come from Mississippi implies the same stereotype.

Press reports reveal other views of the rumor flap. Journalists tended to confuse terms like *myth, rumor, legend, chain letter,* and *hoax,* as well as to ignore the technical differences between fax, e-mail, and computer bulletin boards or computer newsgroups. Several newspapers mentioned copycat crimes, although none of the papers ever reported any actual "Lights Out!" crimes *or* copycats. In hope of determining the precise origin of the rumor—something folklorists seldom seek or find—journalists focused upon (indeed, may have *invented*) the *hoaxing hacker* character, presumably someone from California. No evidence for the existence of such a hoaxer was ever presented. An idea proposed by both law-enforcement and newspaper sources is that the originator of the story should be found and prosecuted. Despite having this serious plan in mind, newspapers felt free to pun shamelessly in the wording of their stories and headlines: "just the fax," "a fax attack," "has its fax all wrong," "guns down the rumor," and others.

One persistent fear that both the general public and newspapers responded to was the idea of dangerous gang activity entering one's own community from some outside source, usually a nearby larger city that is thought to be awash with gang crimes. It still amazes me (as mentioned above) that no investigative reporter seems to have bothered to have contacted any local gang members to ask about initiation rituals in general and about "Lights Out!" or other car-related customs in particular.

Finally, I re-emphasize one theme of the warnings pointed out in only a single news article among the reports I collected. This is the "Good Samaritan" theme mentioned by Turner and Dundes. Flashing one's headlights at a car driving toward you at night without its lights on is a simple, common act of courtesy and safety. It's something most drivers have been taught to do, either by a driver's education teacher or simply by customary example from other drivers. (I'll be so bold as to call this a folk custom.) Some of the warning fliers allude to this custom by referring to it as a "courtesy flash." (I'll concede, however, that light flashing may also imply negative criticism in the minds of some drivers who flash or are flashed at.) Another strong message of "Light Out!" then, is that something you, as a driver, have learned to do as a good and socially useful thing may, in this crime-ridden modern world, have become an act of aggression toward another driver who represents an outsider to your standards of behavior—perhaps a younger person of a different race who belongs to a street gang—and this outsider will go so far as to murder you for daring to be courteous. In other words, the "Lights Out!" rumor says, "Forget about being a courteous driver, because *it might kill you!*"

Note

1. Folklorist Ed Kahn of Berkeley, California, pointed out to me the similarity to the much-feared "Michelangelo" computer virus, supposedly set to strike DOS-based machines worldwide on March 6 (the Renaissance master's birthdate), 1992. Like the "DataCrime" (or "Friday the 13th") virus of 1989, this threat proved to be much less destructive than predicted.

References

Brunvand, Jan Harold. 1981. *The Vanishing Hitchhiker: American Urban Legends and Their Meanings*. New York: W. W. Norton.

———. 1984. *The Choking Doberman and Other "New" Urban Legends*. New York: W. W. Norton.

———. 1986. *The Mexican Pet: More "New" Urban and Some Old Favorites*. New York: W. W. Norton.

———. 1989. *Curses! Broiled Again! The Hottest Urban Legends Going*. New York: W. W. Norton.

———. 1993. *The Baby Train and Other Lusty Urban Legends*. New York: W. W. Norton.

For Discussion and Writing

1. What are some of the newspapers named in this account, and how did they respond to stories about this gang ritual? What other official voices does Brunvand present?
2. How do emails figure in the circulation of this legend? What details do various email versions of the story present? What steps were taken by sources to lend the tales an official appearance?
3. Some of the versions specifically name gangs—Bloods and Crypts (*sic*)—as participants in the violent rituals. What does this add to the tale's acceptance by the public? If you were telling this tale, what details would you include to make it credible?
4. Brunvand refers to many newspaper accounts and police department memos that denied the veracity of the stories. What can you conclude about the popular attitude toward the tale from the repeated measures taken to debunk it?
5. Write a brief analysis of the tale's circulation. That is, what made it so believable? Consider the simple courtesy at the heart of the tale—flashing another motorist a warning. Consider the alleged villains, those young gang members. What fears and prejudices does the tale play upon?

French Follies: A 9/11 Conspiracy Theory Turns Out to Be An Appalling Deception

L. KIRK HAGEN

L. Kirk Hagen is a professor in the Arts and Humanities department of the University of Houston–Downtown. In the following article, Hagen reviews a book by Thierry Meyssan entitled L'Effroyable Imposture. *Hagen argues that Meyssan's spurious claims about the forces behind the 9/11 attacks constitute an appalling deception in their own right. The piece copied here appeared in* Skeptic *in 2002.*

✦

For some years now, many American liberals have been dismayed by the odd collection of "progressive" ideas emanating from France. The final decades of the 20th century may have been good overall for liberalism in France, with 14 years of socialist presidential leadership. But those same years ironically proved to be fertile ground for some decidedly irrational, illiberal, and un-Frenchlike ideas. From literary critic Jacques Derrida—the man sometimes cited as one of the most influential thinkers of the century—we learned that the Einsteinian constant is not a constant or a center, but the very concept of variability. It is an insight for which physicists will be forever grateful, I am sure. From psychoanalyst Jacques Lacan we found out that the erect penis is equivalent to the square root of -1. These and countless similar examples of pseudo-intellectual nonsense were documented in Alan Sokal and Jean Bricmont's scathing *Impostures Intellectuelles*, published in Paris in 1997.

Now, just when we thought we had heard the worst, a new book from the French Left on the 9/11 attacks outdoes them all. Its title is *L'Effroyable Imposture;* its author one Thierry Meyssan, whom the French press describes as a "left-wing activist" and leader of the Voltaire Network, a non-profit electronic data bank dedicated to "the struggles for liberties and secularism." Meyssan's leftist bona fides are indeed evident throughout the book. He uses the awkward but politically correct *etats-unien* rather than *américain* to refer to things and people from the United States. Thus on page 24 he talks about "secret clashes that are tearing apart the United-Statesian ruling class" (Do radicals still talk like that?). Nonetheless the book's publisher assures us that Meyssan is an investigative journalist, and that all of the information in his book can be independently verified.

That's good to know, because Meyssan reveals that no terrorists were involved in the 9/11 attacks, that no airplane crashed into the Pentagon on 9/11, and that the whole affair was a hoax orchestrated by—who else—a cabal of right-wing CIA rogues. To date, the French press has been ambivalent about this. Many have dismissed the book as a crackpot conspiracy rant, while others have been content to summarize it noncommittally. A few think there just might be something to it. The French public, meantime, has gulped it all down like a new Beaujolais. *L'Effroyable Imposture* rose to the top of the best seller list and sold out within hours of its appearance last April.

It is unlikely that Meyssan's success will be repeated on this side of the Atlantic, however. For one thing, the book will be seen as deeply offensive to Americans, for fairly obvious reasons. For another, it lacks the elements that even the most cynical reader has come to expect from books in this genre. Unlike the JFK conspiracies, *L'Effroyable Imposture* is not even marginally plausible. Unlike the Roswell conspiracies, it is not even marginally entertaining. Rather Meyssan has written a thoroughly ridiculous book that succeeds only in trivializing one of the new century's greatest human tragedies. For the record, let's review the major questions that Meyssan raises anyway.

WHY DO WE SEE NO DEBRIS OF AN AIRPLANE IN THE PHOTOGRAPHS TAKEN OF THE PENTAGON ON 911?

No debris, no plane, right? The Pentagon was therefore struck by   5
an air launched cruise missile. Come to think of it, who remembers seeing debris from Timothy McVeigh's so-called "Ryder Van" in front of the Murrah Building back in 1995? The only evidence of a van I remember was part of an axle found a few blocks from the detonation site: The only debris of a jet I recall in the case of American Airlines Flight 77 is a piece of the fuselage, lying in the lawn in front of the Pentagon, plainly visible in a widely-circulated AP photo. Could it be that we don't see more debris in the photos because the Boeing 757, like the Ryder Van, was literally blown to bits? The French daily *Le Monde* consulted aeronautics experts,

and lo and behold, they confirmed exactly that someone there figured out that jet fuel is volatile, especially when 11,000 gallons strike steel-reinforced concrete walls at 340 mph.

HOW COULD AUTHORITIES HAVE LOST TRACK OF A JET AS IT FLEW FOR SOME 300 MILES OVER OHIO?

Here Meyssan demonstrates a scandalous disregard for facts. American Airlines Flight 11 struck the World Trade Center at 8:45 a.m. The assumption at the time was that this was an accident. Indeed it was widely reported that a small, private plane was involved. It became obvious that a concerted attack was under way only when United Airlines Flight 175 struck the south tower at 9:03 a.m. American Flight 77 then struck the Pentagon at 9:43 a.m. Surely terrorists, unlike Meyssan, would have understood that forty minutes is just barely enough time for the FAA to account for all aircraft along the Eastern Seaboard—one of the busiest air corridors in the world—and to coordinate, an appropriate response with the military. American Flight 11 and United Flight 175 were among 200 planes that left Logan International Airport in Boston between 7:00 a.m. and 9:00 a.m. on September 11. How many others were departing from or traveling to JFK International, LaGuardia, Reagan National, Dulles International, or Baltimore/Washington, not to mention the myriad regional airports in the vicinity? It is remarkable that the FAA acted as quickly as it did. As early as 9:17 a.m. it closed all airports in the New York City area, and by 9:40 a.m. halted all air traffic nationwide. Controllers had been monitoring Flight 77 as it approached Washington, and had even warned the White House. Tragically, they lost radar and radio contact as the plane approached its target, but that is hardly proof of a CIA plot.

HOW COULD FLIGHT 77 HAVE ESCAPED SURFACE TO AIR MISSILE BATTERIES AT THE PENTAGON?

If this seems incomprehensible to Meyssan, it may be that he is working the stereotype of Americans as trigger-happy cowboys who would not think twice about shooting down a civilian airliner and asking questions later. Meyssan apparently has given no thought to the consequences of a mistaken and unauthorized attack on a civilian plane. Seven months after 9/11 a Frontier Airlines jet accidentally wandered into restricted airspace above the White House, in full view of the press corps. Mercifully, that plane was not shot down either. During the past decade, aircraft have violated no-fly zones in Washington ten times per year on average. None has ever been destroyed by a surface-to-air missile.

WHAT ABOUT THE NEW YORK ATTACKS?

Unfortunately for Meyssan, the photographic evidence of planes striking the World Trade Center towers is massive and irrefutable. But then no self-respecting conspiracy buff has ever let something as trifling as irrefutability stand in the way of a good story. You see, American Airlines Flight 11 and United Airlines Flight 175 were remotely commandeered by the conspirators, who had placed beacons in the towers ahead of time. On page 32, Meyssan tells us that signals from the beacons were recorded by amateur radio operators. He offers no citation or proof. So much for independent verification.

Besides, if the conspirators had the technical savvy to remotely commandeer two jet liners for the attack on New York, why not just commandeer a third for the attack on the Pentagon? Anyone with the genius to pull off this massive deception would have known that other geniuses, like Meyssan, would quickly see through their charade down in Washington. Meyssan has no explanation for this, but I assume he will get back to us. We are just as anxious to hear what he has to say about the real fate of American Flight 77, which if we believe his account left Dulles International Airport at 8:10 on September 11 with 59 people on board, and then vanished into thin air, coincidentally about time eyewitnesses mistakenly thought they saw a commercial airliner fiting Flight 77's description crash into the Pentagon. All we get from Meyssan about this is a rhetorical question, on page 24. "What became of Flight 77? One of many questions the American Administration must answer." How's that for chutzpath? The Administration has offered an answer. It is Meyssan who has none.

The rest of the book is a careless pastiche of ruses common to   10
conspiracy theories. Meyssan passes off rumor and speculation as fact. He draws far-reaching conclusions from the flimsiest of premises, even when those premises are contradictory. He finds sinister motives behind mundane actions. His book is padded

with quotations—they routinely run on for more than a page—but he is careful to leave out anything that doesn't support this thesis.

Meyssan quotes a CNN interview in which General Wesley Clarke says "We've known for some time that some group has been planning [an attack]. Obviously, we didn't do enough [to prepare for one]." From this Meyssan concludes (page 24) that Clarke is referring not to foreign aggressors but to right-wing militia groups. That is simply false. There is no mention of any militia in that interview. By the way, what else does that CNN story say, just two sentences after this quote? "Witnesses described a commercial airplane crashing into the Pentagon, the world's largest office building. 'I saw the tail of a large airliner. . . . It plowed right into the Pentagon,' said an Associated Press Radio reporter. 'There is billowing black smoke.'"

On page 17 Meyssan suggests that terrorist pilots would have been too skillful to have hit the side of the Pentagon instead of the roof, where their attack would have done more damage. On page 32, he suggests that terrorist pilots would have been too amateurish to have guided planes into the World Trade Centers. Either way, he acknowledges that the latter attacks took place in the morning of a work day rather than at night or on a weekend. He acknowledges too as many as up to 40,000 persons were supposed to be in the towers on 9/11. He concludes nonetheless (page 36) that the attacks were not intended to cause a large scale loss of human life.

Given Meyssan's obsession with secularism, it is no surprise that religion plays a major supporting role in this conspiracy. On pages 79–80 he mentions the disgraceful accusations made by Jerry Falwell and Pat Robertson that gays, lesbians, abortiontists and pagans were responsible for the attacks. Those comments alone suffice to convince Meyssan that George W. Bush had assumed the mantle of "spiritual head of America and the civilized world." As proof, he points out that just days after the attacks French President Chirac and Prime Minister Jospin attended an ecumenical service in Paris and sang "God Bless America." (*God Bless America*, get it?), which Meyssan identifies as the unofficial U.S. national anthem. Meyssan is more sympathetic towards Islamic fundamentalism. On page 54 he assures us that no Arab Kamikazes were on board the doomed airliners because the Koran prohibits suicide. Apparently that explains the utter absence of suicide bombings by extremists elsewhere in the world.

Some of Mesyssan's tales are hilarious. On page 38 he pretends to have caught George W. Bush in a lie. During a public meeting in Florida (December 4, 2001), the President recalled how he first learned about the attacks during his visit to an elementary school. "I was sitting outside the classroom waiting to go in, and I saw an airplane hit the tower—the TV was obviously on" Aha! The only known videotape of the first plane striking the North Tower was made by the Naudet brothers, and was not available until much later. Meyssan therefore concludes that Bush had seen "secret images which were transmitted to him without delay in the secure communication room that had been set up at the elementary school before his visit." Ergo, the US intelligence community knew what was going to happen in advance.

In order to accept this version of events, you have to believe   15
that George W. Bush is not a politician prone to misstatement. Detractors of the President have, perhaps begrudgingly, acknowledged his patience and tolerance in pursuing the war on terrorism. Yet as far as I know, no one has accused Bush of oratorical prowess. Bush apologists insist that the President is vulnerable to slips of the tongue when he is tired or speaking impromptu, as he was during that Florida meeting. Indeed the comment that so excites Meyssan occurs at the end of a long question and answer session, and when you listen to the audio version, Bush does sound like he is running out of gas. His comments are full of classic Bushisms. The President makes his own attempt at political correctness by referring to Muslim women as "women of cover." He speaks of an "initial leg of a strategy" to revitalize the airline industry. Twice he mentions his efforts to "route out terror" (sic) when he meant to say "root out terror."

And then there is this comment from the President, which inexplicably escapes Meyssan's investigative eye: "We provided a significant amount of loans and grants for the airline industry to make sure the airplanes, which were directly hit by the attacks, continue to *fly*." *Airplanes* directly hit by attacks, Mr. President? We had not heard of that until now. Obviously a plane was shot down! Flight 77 Mystery solved!

Or maybe the President meant to say *airlines* directly hit by the attacks instead of *airplanes*. For that matter, Bush's reference to seeing a plane hit the Trade Center is ambiguous because he has left out the word *that*. He may have meant. "I saw an airplane [that] hit the tower" (sinister interpretation) or "I saw [that] an airplane hit the tower" (innocent interpretation). French grammar does not permit a similarly ambiguous sentence, so you have to choose one interpretation or the other when translating. Needless to say, Meyssan opts for the first.

The only real mystery here is what Meyssan thought he would accomplish by concocting such an improbable story. Halfway through the book his conspiracy fodder is pretty much spent, and the remainder is little more than a summary of anecdotes and news stories which to Meyssan's mind support this diabolical plot. His final chapter *La Conjuration* is a rehash of the Bay of Pigs episode with only a half-hearted attempt at establishing a link to 9/11.

But then Meyssan's motivation was probably not journalistic in the first place. One cannot read this book without suspecting that it was meant to express solidarity with America's adversaries. Maybe that's why Meyssan found it important to present his theory, bolstered with a new round of absurdities, to the Arab League in Abu Dhabi in April 2002. If *L'Effroyable Imposture* was meant as a political screed, Meyssan is even more misguided than he lets on. The plausible culprits for the 9/11 attacks—Al Qaeda and their Taliban patrons—are about as far removed from leftist values as anyone can get. They are anti-democratic, anti-secular, unabashedly homophobic, and they openly endorse one of the cruelest forms of gender apartheid in the world. Surely Meyssan understands that his efforts to get them off the hook, coupled with his comical neglect of fact and reason, will only undermine the ideology he espouses. In fact, I am beginning to suspect that some darker conspiracy may be afoot. Could it be that as early as the 1960's some right-wing *agents provocateurs* began infiltrating the French Left posing as intellectuals? Could it be that once their deep cover was firmly established they initiated a compaign of buffoonery as a means of discrediting liberals? Perhaps that is why the neo-fascist Jean-Marie Le Pen was able to snatch victory from a clearly disoriented left wing back in May, just a month or so after Meyssan's book hit the shelves.

20   In case you're wondering, the English translation of *L'Effroyable Imposture* is "The Appalling Deception." What an interesting choice of words.

For Discussion and Writing

1. Hagen repeats a question that Meyssan raised: Why isn't there any airplane debris in photos taken just after the 9/11 attack on the Pentagon? He then claims that photo evidence contradicts that. How reliable do you think photographic evidence is for either claim?

2. How does Hagen reply to the charge that authorities could not have lost track of a jet flying for a distance of nearly 300 miles?

3. Meyssan claims that no jet ever struck the Pentagon. What does he say actually happened to American Airlines Flight 77?
4. List some reasons why someone might believe that "the real story" behind the 9/11 attacks is being covered up by the U.S. government. Think about lies that government officials have told. In your view, to what degree does general mistrust of government officials contribute to belief in conspiracy theories?
5. Photographic evidence says, in effect, "seeing is believing." Discuss and evaluate the place of this proverbial wisdom in our age.

A Patently False Patent Myth—Still

SAMUEL SASS

The U.S. Patent Office has dates from the late eighteenth century when Thomas Jefferson helped to create a system for patent support. It is part of our national history, and, in fact, is the surprising source of a persistent urban legend. The author of this article, Samuel Sass, worked for General Electric as a librarian. His article, which first appeared in Skeptical Inquirer, *was recently updated; in addition to debunking a patent office legend, it also presents the role of uncritical media in furthering the legend.*

———————— ✦ ————————

For close to a century there has periodically appeared in print the story about an official of the U.S. Patent Office who resigned his post because he believed that all possible inventions had already been invented. Some years ago, before I retired as librarian of a General Electric Company division, I was asked by a skeptical scientist to find out what there was to this recurring tale. My research proved to be easier than I had expected. I found that this matter had been investigated as a project of the D.C. Historical Records Survey under the Works Projects Administration. The investigator, Dr. Eber Jeffery, published his findings in the July 1940 *Journal of the Patent Office Society.*

Jeffery found no evidence that any official or employee of the U.S. Patent Office had ever resigned because he thought there was nothing left to invent. However, Jeffery may have found a clue to the origin of the myth. In his 1843 report to Congress, the then-commissioner of the Patent Office, Henry L. Ellsworth, included the following comment: "The advancement of the arts, from year to year, taxes our credulity and seems to presage the arrival of that period when human improvement must end." As Jeffery shows, it's evident from the rest of that report that Commissioner Ellsworth was simply using a bit of rhetorical flourish to emphasize that the number of patents was growing at a great rate. Far from considering inventions at an end, he outlined areas in which he expected patent activity to increase, and it is clear that he was making plans for the future.

When Commissioner Ellsworth did resign in 1845, his letter of resignation certainly gave no indication that he was resigning because he thought there was nothing left for the Patent Office to do. He gave as his reason the pressure of private affairs, and stated, "I wish to express a willingness that others may share public favors and have an opportunity to make greater improvements." He indicated that he would have resigned earlier if it had not been for the need to rebuild after the fire of 1836, which had destroyed the Patent Office building. In any case, the letter of resignation should have put an end to any notion that his comment in the 1843 report was to be taken literally.

Unfortunately, the only words of Commissioner Ellsworth that have lived on are those about the advancement of the arts taxing credulity and presaging the period when human improvement must end. For example, the December 1979 *Saturday Review* contained an article by Paul Dickson titled "It'll Never Fly, Orville: Two Centuries of Embarrassing Predictions." He lists a pageful of "some of the worst wrong-headed predictions." Ellsworth's rhetorical sentence is included with such laughable statements as that said by Napoleon to Robert Fulton: "What sir, you would make a ship sail against the wind and currents by lighting a bonfire under her decks? I pray excuse me. I have no time to listen to such nonsense."

5   If in the case of Commissioner Ellsworth there was at least a quotation out of context on which the "nothing left to invent" story was based, a more recent myth attributing a similar statement to a commissioner who served a half-century later is totally baseless. This news story surfaced in the fall of 1985, when full-page advertisements sponsored by the TRW Corporation appeared in a number of leading periodicals, including *Harper's* and *Business Week.*

These ads had as their theme "The Future Isn't What It Used to Be." They contained photographs of six individuals, ranging from a baseball player to a president of the United States, who had allegedly made wrong predictions. Along with such statements as

"Sensible and responsible women do not want to vote," attributed to President Cleveland, and "There is no likelihood man can ever tap the power of the atom," attributed to physicist Robert Millikan, there is a prediction that was supposedly made by Commissioner of the U.S. Patent Office Charles H. Duell. The words attributed to him were: "Everything that can be invented has been invented." The date given was 1899.

Since I was certain that the quotation was spurious, I wrote to the TRW advertising manager to ask its source. In response to my inquiry, I received a letter referring me to two books, although I had specifically asked for the *primary* and not secondary sources. The books were *The Experts Speak*, by Christopher Cerf and Victor Navasky, published in 1984 by Pantheon, and *The Book of Facts and Fallacies*, by Chris Morgan and David Langford, published in 1981 by St. Martin's Press.

When I examined these two volumes I found that the 1981 Morgan and Langford work contained Commissioner Ellsworth's sentence about the advancement of the arts taxing our credulity, although the quote was somewhat garbled. It also contained the following comment by the authors: "We suppose that at just about any period in history one can imagine, the average dim-witted official will have doubted that anything new can be produced; the attitude cropped up again in 1899, when the director of the U.S. Patent Office urged President McKinley to abolish the office, and even the post of director," since "everything that can be invented has been invented." The authors do not give the name of the commissioner whom they call "director," but it was Charles H. Duell who held that office in 1899. They don't offer any documentation to support that alleged statement, and they would have had a tough time finding any.

It's easy enough to prove that Duell was not the "dim-witted official" so glibly referred to. One need only examine his 1899 report, a document of only a few pages, available in any depository library. Far from suggesting to the president that he abolish the Patent Office, Duell quotes the following from McKinley's annual message: "Our future progress and prosperity depend upon our ability to equal, if not surpass, other nations in the enlargement and advance of science, industry and commerce. To invention we must turn as one of the most powerful aids to the accomplishment of such a result." Duell then adds, "May not our inventors hopefully look to the Fifty-sixth Congress for aid and effectual encouragement in improving the American patent system?" Surely these words are not those of some kind of idiot who

believes that everything has already been invented. Other information in that report also definitely refutes any such notion.
Duell presents statistics showing the growth in the number of
patents from 435 in 1837 to 25,527 in 1899. In the one year
between 1898 and 1899 there was an increase of about 3,000. It's
hardly likely that he would expect a sudden and abrupt ending to
patent applications.

10   The other book cited by the advertising manager of TRW, Inc.,
The Experts Speak, by Cerf and Navasky, offers a key to how myths
are perpetuated. This volume, published three years after the
Morgan and Langford work, contains the spurious Duell quote,
"Everything that can be invented has been invented," and prints it
as though it had formed part of the commissioner's 1899 report to
President McKinley. However, unlike the earlier work, *The Experts
Speak* contains source notes in the back. The source given reads
as follows: "Charles H. Duell, quoted from Chris Morgan and
David Langford, *Facts and Fallacies* (Exeter, England, Webb &
Bower, 1981), p. 64." Unlikely as it is for the head of the U.S.
Patent Office to have said something so silly, evidently it did not
occur to Cerf and Navasky to question that statement. They simply copied it from the earlier book. One can expect that in the
future there will be more copying because it is easier than check-
ing the facts.

          The irony is that the subtitle of *The Experts Speak* is "The
Definitive Compendium of Authoritative Misinformation." One
can only wonder how much more misinformation is contained in
this nearly 400-page compendium. On the title page the book is
described as a "joint project of the *Nation* magazine and the
Institute of Expertology." Whatever this institute may be, on the
theory that the *Nation* is a responsible publication, I wrote to
Mr. Navasky, who is editor of that magazine and coauthor of the
book, to ask if he could tell me where and when Commissioner
Duell made the stupid statement attributed to him. I did not
receive a reply.

ADDENDUM TO ORIGINAL ARTICLE

The earliest appearance of the patent myth in print that I am
aware of is the October 16, 1915, issue of *The Scientific American*.
It contains the following item: "Someone poring over the old files
in the United States Patent Office in Washington the other day
found a letter written in 1833 that illustrates the limitations of the

human imagination. It was from an old employee of the Patent Office, offering his resignation to the head of the department. His reason was that as everything inventable had been invented the Patent Office would soon be discontinued and there would be no further need of his services. . . . "

As in all "urban legends," the details are vague. Neither "the old employee" who is supposed to have resigned nor the "someone poring over the old files" is identified. The fact is that when the Patent Office burned to the ground in 1836, all records were destroyed so that even if that 1833 letter had ever existed it could not have been seen "the other day" in 1915.

With the imaginative addition later of the names of Commissioners Ellsworth and Duell, the myth kept cropping up sporadically for decades but then received a major boost twenty years ago by the publication of the Morgan and Langford book in 1981 and the Cerf and Navasky book three years later. The 1985 TRW ad, which made use of the misinformation in these volumes, helped spread it more widely.

A particularly discouraging aspect of the repetition of this   15
fable is that it is repeated by individuals who have research and fact-checking facilities at their disposal. For instance, in his book *The Road Ahead*, published in 1995, Bill Gates relates the myth as fact. He was chided for that in the February 1996 issue of *Scientific American* in these words: "If Bill Gates's grasp of the past is any guide, readers should take his visions of the future with a dose of skepticism." In view of the fact that eighty years earlier *The Scientific American* had made the same mistake it's encouraging to know that the editors felt compelled to correct Gates.

Two other prominent individuals who failed to take a second look are Carol Browner, former Administrator of the Environmental Protection Agency, and Hugh Downs, radio and television journalist. The former repeated the myth in an October 2000 talk to the National Press Club, and Downs stated in his July 17, 1996, "Perspective" radio commentary spiel that in "a handwritten note" Commissioner Duell had urged President McKinley to abolish the Patent Office because "Everything that can be invented has been invented." He was evidently so pleased with himself for being a purveyor of that news that the ended by telling his audience, "Remember that you heard it here first, on radio."

It would be the height of optimism to believe that efforts to debunk this myth will cause it to disappear. It's too good a story and lends itself too readily to those who are eager to make a point and to whom facts and truth are secondary.

For Discussion and Writing

1. Who first investigated the claim that a patent officer had resigned because he believed everything had already been invented?
2. What was the remark that may have prompted the original legend? Sass refers to a 1940 article in the *Journal of the Patent Office Society*. Find out if this journal is still published. How would you get a copy of the 1940 article if you wanted to see exactly what Sass refers to?
3. When Sass first saw advertisements that alluded to the patent office legend, what did he do? Examine the steps he took and the questions he asked. What can you learn about the art of debunking from this?
4. The author refers to two texts that TRW cited in support of their own role in advancing this tale. Sass says that *The Experts Speak* offers a key to how myths are perpetuated. Explain this.
5. In his addendum, Sass notes that the 1915 patent legend article in *The Scientific American* was vague in its details. What details did he cite, and how vague were they? Evaluate the role of media in the spread of this urban legend, noting all the "players" and their contribution to the myth. Besides the aid of uncritical media, why else does this story appeal to audiences?

Big Lies on Campus: Exam Scams
RICHARD ROEPER

Richard Roeper, co-host of the television show "Ebert and Roeper," is a columnist for the Chicago Sun-Times *and the author of prolixly entitled* Urban Legends: The Truth Behind All Those Deliciously Entertaining Myths That Are Absolutely, Positively, 100% Not True. *In the following collection of campus tales, Roeper recounts several hoary tales that have circulated around American campuses for years.*

◆

At Urban Legend University, there's a constant battle going on between lazy but clever students who are trying to scam their way through exams by any means necessary, and savvy world-wise professors who attempt to thwart these students with some creative solutions of their own. Each of the following stories is so delicious you'll wish they were true—and, as always, it's impossible to make the claim that none of these incidents ever took place.

There's certainly no shortage of students and alumni who will swear one or more of these episodes have occurred at their school, whether that school is Ohio State, Yale, North Carolina, USC, Texas A&M, Grambling, Brown, Case Western or Slippery Rock. Amazing how such incredible tales are seemingly cloned through the years.

THE STOLEN EXAM

There's a scene in *Animal House* where the under-achieving Delta boys purloin the carbon of a final exam from a garbage can. Only problem is, the dreaded Omegas are onto the game, and they've switched the real final for a phony version, leaving the Deltas hopelessly unprepared for the big test.

That was the one and only moral lesson in *Animal House*, thank God.

In the urban legend of the stolen exam, it's the teacher who   5
puts a roadblock in the thieving student's attempt to cheat his way to glory. On the day before the test, the student meets with the professor, who tells him he needs to get an "A" on the final or he'll fail the course. The student starts to make his case for leniency, but the professor is called away from the office for a moment. Filled with anxiety, the student paces around the room and pokes around—and that's when he comes across a stack of tests. The final exams, just sitting out in the open! He quickly snatches one copy and jams it into his coat, just before the professor returns to the office.

"Now where were we?" says the professor.

"I was just leaving," the student replies. "Gotta study for the big test!"

His instructor is confused. Why did the kid's mood change so quickly! If he thinks one night of studying hard is going to adequately prepare him for an exam, let him dream.

The next morning, the instructor counts the tests and realizes one is missing. He had at least a dozen students visit him the day before, and there's no way of knowing which one had the gall to steal a copy of the test—or is there?

Chuckling to himself, the professor takes out a pair of scissors   10
and carefully slices a half-inch from the bottom of each remaining copy of the test. When the students turn in their papers at the end of the test, only one literally sticks out—the stolen exam.

Even though the student scored a 96 on the test, he was flunked by the professor, and he didn't utter a peep of protest about it.

THE OPEN-BOOK EXAM

The instructor of a particularly difficult class in Freshman English tells her students she's going to cut them a big break for the final: it's going to be "open-book." As a matter of fact, she says, students may use "anything you can carry into the classroom" to help them with the test.

Nearly everybody in the class takes this to mean they can come in with books, reference guides, handwritten notes, etc. But one smart-ass freshman football player takes the professor's words literally. After all, she's the one who always says you must choose your words carefully—and she did say "anything you can carry," didn't she? So on the day of the exam, he shows up carrying a nerdy little graduate student under his arm.

"And just what do you think you're doing?" says the professor over the titters of the class.

15   "You said we could use anything we could carry into the classroom," replies the student. "I'm carrying Dilbert, and he'll be taking the test for me."

Trapped by her own words, the professor has no choice but to allow the graduate student to take the exam for the football player, who winds up with an "A" for the course.

THE STACK OF BLUE BOOK EXAMS

This happened in one of those big, impersonal classes you have to take your freshman year, with about 300 other people all packed into some gigantic lecture hall where the teacher has to use a microphone and an overhead projector just to communicate with everyone.

For the final exam, the teacher handed out blue books to the students and told them they had exactly two hours to answer as many of the 200 multiple choice questions as possible. He set a timer to go off in 120 minutes and said that when the buzzer went off, everyone had to stop writing immediately, with no exceptions. Violate this rule and you'd receive an automatic "F."

Two hours later, the alarm sounded, and the professor commanded everyone to drop their pencils and drop off their blue books on the way out. Everyone began filing out—except one frantic kid who kept scribbling away, desperately trying to pencil in a few more answers even though time had expired.

20   "You there!" the teacher called out. "If you don't stop writing immediately, you're going to be flunked!"

"I just need a minute more, just one minute!" the student pleaded as he continued to write in the blue book.

At that point, it really didn't matter what he said; by this time, the teacher had already doomed the kid to an automatic "F." Most of the class had already turned in their exams by the time the troublemaker finally gathered his things and clomped down the stairs.

"You might as well keep that exam as a souvenir, because you've already failed this course," said the instructor.

"You've got to be kidding me!" the student cried. "I was only one minute late. What difference does it make?"

The teacher was unmoved. "Rules are rules. If I let you have   25
an extra minute I'd have to let everyone have an extra minute, wouldn't I?"

"Do you know who I am?" said the student. "Do you know what my name is?"

"No I don't, and I couldn't care less," replied the teacher.

"Good!" said the student—and with that he jammed his blue book right in the middle of the stack before dashing out of there.

• • •

I've included this story because I've heard it at least 20 times over the last decade, but to me, there's a gaping flaw in the telling. Okay, the teacher doesn't know the names of all the students in the overcrowded class, so he wouldn't be able to identify the student by name as he's a grading the tests. But once he was finished with the grading process, couldn't he require all students to show up, with student IDs, to claim their exams? All he'd have to do is make a face identification of the culprit, hang on to that particular exam and change the grade to an "F."

Most urban legends, even the ones that defy logic, have a nice   30
little airtight quality about them; that's why they survive through myriad retellings. This one should fade—not because it's implausible, but because of the obvious way in which the teacher could have nailed the student, thus negating the twist.

THE LETTER HOME TO MOM

Once again, the ubiquitous blue book plays a part in an exam scam classic:

Our unprepared student freaks out when he's confronted with a complicated essay question that will count for 100 percent of the test. He has no idea what to say—this is the one portion of the textbook he didn't study! To make matters worse, the professor has given each student *two* blue books, indicating that he expects a long and detailed answer.

And then a light bulb goes off. The student starts writing in a blue book—but he's not answering the question, he's writing a letter to his mother. "I really think I did well on the essay," he writes. "I finished ahead of everyone else in the class so I figured I'd write to you, dear mother. I don't want to get up and leave early—it'll seem like I'm showing off. Anyway, let me tell you about this class. I'm so lucky to have had this teacher! He's by far the smartest and most inspirational teacher I've ever had . . ."

At the end of the class, the student turns in the letter to mom and then runs back to his dorm room, where he opens the textbook for the class and uses it as a reference guide as he composes a thoughtful and comprehensive answer to the essay question. He then mails that blue book to his mother in Boston.

That night the professor rings the student and says, "I don't know how to tell you this, but we have a big problem."

35   "You're kidding me," says the student. "To be honest with you, I thought I aced the test."

"You very well might have, for all I know," says the teacher. "I haven't seen your answers."

"I don't understand."

"I've got a letter to your mother here instead of your essay. Does that make any sense to you?"

"Oh no!" says the student, trying his best to sound shocked. "That means I must have mailed the test to my mom. This is the most embarrassing thing that's ever happened to me." The student says he'll call his mother right away and instruct her to send the envelope straight to the professor; that way, the teacher will know the story is legitimate.

40   Sure enough, an envelope arrives at the professor's office a few days later, and he opens it to find the student's test, which of course contains a beautifully written essay. Not only does the professor give the kid an "A," he sends the other booklet to the student's mother with a note attached telling her what a pleasure it was having the lad in his class.

THE FLAT TIRE EXCUSE

Three smart (and incredibly cocky) fraternity brothers were so confident they'd ace their chemistry final that they went on a weekend road trip before the exam, which was scheduled for

Monday at 10 a.m. They spent all weekend partying with some girls from a nearby school and never once even bothered to pick up a book, even though the final was going to count for 50 percent of their grade.

Problem was, they overslept Monday morning. By the time they made it back to campus it was noon, and they knew the professor would be busy collecting exam booklets from the other students. Suddenly the "A's" or "B's" they counted on receiving for the class were looking like "D's" at best! Depression set in. What to do?

"I've got the plan!" said one of the brothers as they crossed the quad and headed for the classroom. "We'll tell the professor we were doing a charity thing—like a dance marathon—and we overslept this morning because we were so tired from dancing, and as we were racing back to campus, we got a flat tire and it took forever to get the thing fixed."

The three charmers told the story to their stupid professor, who fell for it hook, line, and sinker.

"All right boys, I'm not going to penalize you for your good   45
intentions, even though you should have given yourselves more time to return to campus," he said. "I'll see you here bright and early tomorrow morning. You'll have two hours to take the exam." The frat boys exchanged knowing glances on the way out the door. Any teacher who falls for that deserves to get taken for a ride. The boys spent the rest of the day studying to reassure themselves, and their cocky swagger had returned by the next morning, when they entered the empty classroom.

"There's nobody in either of the adjoining classrooms, so each of you gets your own room," said the professor. "Not that I'd accuse you boys of cheating or anything, but we'll play it on the safe side."

These guys didn't care, as they weren't *cheaters* or anything; they were just resourceful types who had figured out a way to buy a little time from their unsophisticated instructor.

In the separate classrooms, each young man tackled the exam. The first question was worth 5 points, and was a breeze. At about the same time, each of the boys flipped to the second page, where they found the following message:

"Question #2 (worth 95 points): Which tire went flat?"

The cries of anguish could be heard through the building.   50
Of course, the boys never discussed which tire supposedly went flat.

For Discussion and Writing

1. Present brief versions of any of these tales that you have heard. Discuss the variations that your classmates report.
2. In your opinion, what is there about "The Stolen Exam" tale that appeals to an audience? In what sense does this tale, or any of the others, have a hero?
3. Campus life revolves around academic routines familiar to any college student. What are some of these routines, and how do the legends exploit them?
4. Have you heard the legend about colleges automatically giving A's to anyone whose roommate commits suicide? Look on the Internet for stories about roommates. Discuss ways that a skeptical person might investigate such tales. Why do you suppose most of such stories are not generally questioned? If it isn't too hard to track down the truth, why do some tales persist?

Urban Legends: Research and Writing Possibilities

1. Before the term "urban legend" became popular, there were "old wives' tales." These were bits of lore that seemed to circulate endlessly in our culture. They were generally brief assertions: If you swim within an hour after you eat, you'll get cramps and drown; chewing gum takes years to pass through the digestive system; the average American has more than 5 pounds of undigested red meat in his intestines; if a woman's carrying low, it's a boy; if a woman's carrying high, it's a girl. Collect at least a dozen of these, put them into a survey, and give the survey to 20 or so people outside of class. If possible, interview the respondents afterward to see what they base their beliefs on. Report your findings along with your assessment of your subjects' critical skills and skeptical stance.
2. Some urban legends are born almost as soon as news of a spectacular event hits the media. After Hurricane Katrina, for example, there were tales of government plots to deliberately blow up levees protecting New Orleans. If you search online under TWA Flight 800 you could find items like this excerpt found online at http://www.whatreallyhappened.com/RANCHO/CRASH/TWA/twa.html.

> The government of the United States, despite the embarrassment of having been caught in court rigging lab tests and lying in its reports, still officially attributes the disaster to a spark in the center fuel tank, while government spokespeople insist that the witnesses who saw a missile hit the jumbo jet are all drunks.

A well-known former press secretary claimed to have proof of a missile strike bringing the plane down. It turned out that his evidence came from Internet sites, which as we know can be unreliable. Investigate and analyze the claims surrounding such an event, determining what a reasonable person might conclude about the matter.

3. Not too long ago, a frightening story of stolen organs was making the rounds. Usually the tale presented a hapless guy in a hotel bar who is drinking alone when a beautiful woman approaches him and strikes up a conversation. They have a few drinks together, she invites him up to her room, and the next thing he knows he's waking up in a tub of ice, staring at a note pinned to the wall instructing him to call 911. The operator only has to hear a little of his tale—she know's what's happened. His kidneys have been stolen. Find a version of this story, or repeat it if you've heard it. Compare it to other such tales that have circulated around South America. (There is even a book entitled *Organ Theft Legends* by Veronique Campion-Vincent.) What common threads can you find in your comparison? What fears do the tales prey on? When did the different tales begin to be reported?

4. The "Lights Out" legend focuses on gangs. Find several more tales that involve gangs and analyze them to determine what fears they prey on. There's definitely a racial component to some of these legends. Consider how this contributes to anxiety about minorities in America. Discuss the hold of such legends on the popular imagination and whether that hold will yield to reason.

5. Find several legends about dead celebrities who aren't actually dead, and about celebrities who are dead but who keep appearing (sort of like Elvis). Do the legends suggest why a celebrity might fake his or her death? Why do you suppose the public clings to beliefs that some people are not dead? For example, Jerry Mathers, the "Beaver" in the fifties television show *Leave it to Beaver*, was rumored to have died in Vietnam.

CHAPTER 2

The Media and Public Gullibility

One of the most striking differences between a cat and a lie is that a cat has only nine lives.

—MARK TWAIN

He who joyfully marches in rank and file has already earned my contempt. He has been given a large brain by mistake, since for him the spinal cord would suffice.

—ALBERT EINSTEIN

The evidence of opinion polls varies a little in numbers, but overall it would seem that most Americans believe in some sort of paranormal phenomena. According to one Gallup poll, nearly a third of Americans think that aliens probably have visited our planet, even though there isn't a shred of evidence to support that belief, and many people think aliens have not only visited earth but have abducted people while they were here. Harvard psychiatrist (and alien enthusiast) John Mack published a study that suggests about 4 million people in the United States have been abducted by aliens. There are a few therapists who actually specialize in treating alien abduction victims, which in itself is reasonable, but when the therapists write books "documenting" the experiences of "actual" kidnap victims, a line of some sort has been crossed. (See *Secret Life: Documented First-Hand Accounts of Alien Abduction*, by David M. Jacobs.)

If aliens don't interest you, maybe a message from a dead relative would. Psychics bank on our grief and desire to hold on to our dead. In the past, they have waited in shaded rooms and offices for clientele to show up for word from beyond. More recently, the psychic entrepreneur has found his way to television. "Crossing Over" features John Edward, who does what debunkers call "cold readings." In a studio filled with eager, supportive men and women, Edward fires questions at a preselected audience member. "I'm getting something about a dear one who passed recently, something about the chest or nearby, the cause of death . . ." he might say. The target says, "Um, that could be Uncle Jack." The psychic welcomes this progress, which the audience sees as remarkable. If anyone stopped to think about it, they might recall a number of close people who have died recently. Heart attacks and lung cancer kill plenty of people, and if Uncle Jack died from a brain tumor, well that's near the chest, too. Edward fills out a picture that seems amazingly accurate, unless you consider all the wrong guesses he makes along the way.

If you don't want to hear from the dead, maybe you would like to be on better terms with your cat. Pet psychics can help you and Tabitha communicate because they can tell exactly what's on your cat's mind. "She hates that you moved her litter box, and you need to stop making fun of her when she tries to get into the fishbowl." In fact, a pet psychic's session with a turtle or a cow is very similar to a cold reading. Leading questions put to the animal's owner help pet psychics fill in a surprisingly detailed picture.

When we aren't talking to house pets or the recently dead, we take in popular accounts of extraordinary lost civilizations. How many times have you seen a TV show about Atlantis? Every year or so there's either a replay of a classic "inquiry" into the age-old mystery, or a new investigator finds the lost city. Almost. Some rubble just offshore somewhere holds the key. Viewers get the feeling this investigator is about to uncover brochures and furniture from the Atlantis Chamber of Commerce. It never happens. Attention soon turns to Noah's Ark, which some explorer has reason to believe is beached at 5000 meters. Satellite photos show an unexplained, mysterious shape lying up there in the rocks and snow. With financing and other support the ark may be reached in a year or so. It isn't. Public weariness with disappointments like this threatens to harden into rational thought, until Bigfoot shows up in a stunning new home video which airs on television and becomes the basis for a popular book that "Good Morning America" and other "news and entertainment" shows feature.

An outside observer might suspect Americans are ill-educated. Yet the majority of Americans are literate, most are high school graduates, and a fair number go on to college. Every state in the union funds a public university. The United States has private institutions that draw students from around the world. It could be that nothing in public or higher education counters the stream of paranormal books, TV shows, and movies. Who is watching all the television programs based on paranormal material? A partial list of such shows in production as of 2005 includes "Crossing Over with John Edward," "Joan of Arcadia," "The Dead Zone," "Haunted History," "Mysterious World," "Out There," and so on. Some of these are presented as investigative, others as pure entertainment. All of them hose our culture with a stream of unreal events.

It isn't as if the media manufacture nonsense just to keep viewers happy and dumb, although an uncritical audience may suit them well. Still, networks and newspapers require an audience and some have been known to repeat sensational falsehoods. A lie that might die quietly in neglect takes on life as it airs repeatedly. Think of the little industry that has kept rumors about aliens and Roswell, New Mexico, alive for decades. Initial newspaper reports convinced readers that something extraordinary had happened there on or about July 4, 1947. Something did crash near Roswell in 1947—it was likely an experimental weather balloon. More than 30 years after that event, a book on the subject was published, and now Roswell has made its way into popular UFO legend. Movies like *Independence Day* play off the tale, big publishing houses support the fiction by signing experts and witnesses as authors, and web sites connected to the tale flourish. Hoaxers even fob off a video of an alien autopsy.

The essays in this section take a critical look at media handling of paranormal stories. In an addendum to a National Science Foundation report entitled "Science Indicators 2000: Belief in the Paranormal or Pseudoscience," Melissa Pollak outlines public attitudes toward belief in the paranormal, and the role the media play in that belief. Shari Waxman's "Mind Over Media" argues that news shows tend to legitimize the paranormal generally, something that may take no more than a tag line such as "a Harvard-trained scientist now says there may be something to communicating with the dead." We might not find out what Harvard taught that scientist, although basic logic would reject the argument from authority here. In "That's Entertainment! TV's UFO Coverup," Philip J. Klass claims that television documentaries about UFOs often simply ignore evidence that contradicts

UFO witness accounts. "Stupid 'Pet Psychic' Tricks," by Bryan Farha, attacks a popular TV show that features a woman who claims she can communicate with pets. Farha suggests the pet psychic take the well-known "Million Dollar Challenge" from the James Randi Educational Foundation. If she passes a controlled test of her abilities, she wins a million dollars. In "Bone (Box) of Contention: The James Ossuary," Joe Nickell demonstrates that television isn't the only medium that has spread fantastic tales to eager and gullible audiences. The readings all insist that the burden of proof is on those who make extraordinary claims. It's useful to keep such a standard at hand.

Science Indicators 2000: Belief in the Paranormal or Pseudoscience
THE NATIONAL SCIENCE BOARD

Established by Congress in 1950, the National Science Board oversees the National Science Foundation and advises Congress and the president on matters relating to science. Melissa Pollak, the primary author of the report that follows, has worked for the NSF since 1980. She wrote the 2000, 2002, and 2004 Indicators chapters of the NSB reports. The piece that follows asks and answers a few leading questions about Americans' beliefs in the paranormal.

───────── ✦ ─────────

SCIENCE AND TECHNOLOGY: PUBLIC ATTITUDES AND PUBLIC UNDERSTANDING
Belief in the Paranormal or Pseudoscience[1]

- Belief in the paranormal: How common is it?
- Do the media have a role in fostering belief in the paranormal?
- What is being done to present the other side?

Does it matter if people believe in astrology, extrasensory perception (ESP), or that aliens have landed on Earth? Are people who check their horoscopes, call psychic hotlines, or follow stories about alien abductions just engaging in harmless forms of entertainment? Or are they displaying signs of scientific illiteracy?

Concerns have been raised, especially in the science community, about widespread belief in paranormal phenomena. Scientists (and others) have observed that people who believe in the existence of paranormal phenomena may have trouble distinguishing fantasy from reality. Their beliefs may indicate an absence of critical thinking skills necessary not only for informed decisionmaking in the voting booth and in other civic venues (for example, jury duty[2]), but also for making wise choices needed for day-to-day living.[3]

Specific harms caused by paranormal beliefs have been summarized as:

- a decline in scientific literacy and critical thinking;
- the inability of citizens to make well-informed decisions;
- monetary losses (psychic hotlines, for example, offer little value for the money spent);
- a diversion of resources that might have been spent on more productive and worthwhile activities (for example, solving society's serious problems);
- the encouragement of a something-for-nothing mentality and that there are easy answers to serious problems, for example, that positive thinking can replace hard work; and
- false hopes and unrealistic expectations (Beyerstein 1998).

For a better understanding of the harms associated with pseudoscience, it is useful to draw a distinction between science literacy and scientific literacy. The former refers to the possession of technical knowledge. Scientific literacy, on the other hand, involves not simply knowing the facts, but also requires the ability to think logically, draw conclusions, and make decisions based on careful scrutiny and analysis of those facts (Maienschein 1999; Peccei and Eiserling 1996).

The amount of information now available can be over- 5 whelming and seems to be increasing exponentially. This has led to "information pollution," which includes the presentation of fiction as fact. Thus, being able to distinguish fact from fiction has become just as important as knowing what is true and what is not. The lack of this ability is what worries scientists (and others), leading them to conclude that pseudoscientific beliefs can have a detrimental effect on the well-being of society.[4]

BELIEF IN THE PARANORMAL: HOW COMMON IS IT?

Belief in the paranormal seems to be widespread. Various polls have shown that

- As many as one-third of Americans believe in astrology, that is, that the position of the stars and planets can affect people's lives (Harris 1998, Gallup 1996, and Southern Focus 1998). In 1999, 7 percent of those queried in the NSF survey said that astrology is "very scientific" and 29 percent answered "sort of scientific." Twelve percent said they read their horoscope every day or "quite often"; 32 percent answered "just occasionally."[5]
- Nearly half or more believe in extrasensory perception or ESP (Gallup 1996; Southern Focus 1998). According to one poll, the number of people who have consulted a fortuneteller or a psychic may be increasing: in 1996, 17 percent of the respondents reported contact with a fortuneteller or psychic, up from 14 percent in 1990 (Gallup 1996).[6]
- Between one-third and one-half of Americans believe in unidentified flying objects (UFOs). A somewhat smaller percentage believes that aliens have landed on Earth (Gallup 1996; Southern Focus 1998).

Other polls have shown one-fifth to one-half of the respondents believing in haunted houses and ghosts (Harris 1998; Gallup 1996; Sparks, Nelson, and Campbell 1997), faith healing (Roper 1994, *USA Today* 1998), communication with the dead (Gallup 1996), and lucky numbers. Some surveys repeated periodically even show increasing belief in these examples of pseudoscience (*USA Today* 1998).

Belief in most—but not all—paranormal phenomena is higher among women than men. More women than men believe in ESP (especially telepathy and precognition), astrology, hauntings, and psychic healing. On the other hand, men have stronger beliefs in UFOs and bizarre life forms, for example, the Loch Ness monster (Irwin 1993). In the NSF survey, 39 percent of the women, compared with 32 percent of the men, said astrology is "very" or "sort of" scientific; 56 percent of the women, compared with 63 percent of the men, answered "not at all scientific."[7]

Not surprisingly, belief in astrology is negatively associated with level of education.[8] Among those without high school diplomas, only 41 percent said that astrology is "not at all scientific." The comparable percentages for high school and college graduates are 60 percent and 76 percent, respectively.

DO THE MEDIA HAVE A ROLE IN FOSTERING BELIEF IN THE PARANORMAL?

Scientists and others believe that the media—and in particular, the entertainment industry—may be at least partially responsible for the large numbers of people who believe in astrology, ESP, alien abductions, and other forms of pseudoscience. Because not everyone who watches shows with paranormal themes perceives such fare as merely entertaining fiction, there is concern that the unchallenged manner in which some mainstream media portray paranormal activities is exacerbating the problem and contributing to the public's scientific illiteracy.[9] In recent years, studies have been undertaken to determine whether televised depictions of paranormal events and beliefs influence television viewers' conceptions of reality (Sparks 1998). Although the results of these studies are tentative and require replication, all of them suggest that the way television presents paranormal subjects does have an effect on what viewers believe. For example,

- Those who regularly watch shows like *The X-Files, Unsolved Mysteries*, and *Sightings* were significantly more likely than those who did not watch these programs to endorse paranormal beliefs (Sparks, Nelson, and Campbell 1997).[10]
- Shows about paranormal phenomena, including UFOs, without disclaimers are more likely than those with disclaimers to foster belief in the paranormal (Sparks, Hansen, and Shah 1994; Sparks and Pellechia 1997).
- Some fans of *The X-Files* find the show's storylines "highly plausible," and also believe that the government is currently conducting clandestine investigations similar to those depicted on the series (Evans 1996).

WHAT IS BEING DONE TO PRESENT THE OTHER SIDE?

The Committee for the Scientific Investigation of Claims of the Paranormal (CSICOP) is a nonprofit scientific and educational organization started in 1976 by scientists (including several Nobel laureates), members of the academic community, and science writers. Members of CSICOP, frequently referred to as skeptics, advocate the scientific investigation of paranormal claims and the dissemination of factual information to counter those claims.

CSICOP's mission includes taking advantage of opportunities to promote critical thinking, science education, and the use of reason to determine the merits of important issues.[11]

The Council for Media Integrity, an educational outreach and advocacy program of CSICOP, was established in 1996. Its objective is to promote the accurate depiction of science by the media. The Council, which includes distinguished international scientists, academics, and members of the media, believes it is necessary to counteract the entertainment industry's portrayal of paranormal phenomena because:

- television has such a pervasive impact on what people believe;
- an increasing number of shows are devoted to the paranormal, and they attract large audiences;
- a number of shows use a documentary style to promote belief in the reality of UFOs, government coverups, and alien abductions;
- opposing views are seldom heard in shows that advocate belief in the paranormal; and
- some shows contribute to scientific illiteracy by promoting unproven ideas and beliefs as real, instilling a distrust of scientists[12] and fostering misunderstanding of the methods of scientific inquiry.

To promote media responsibility—particularly within the entertainment industry—and to publicize irresponsibility—the Council established two awards[13]:

- The "Candle in the Dark Award" is given to television programs that have made a major contribution to advancing the public's understanding of science and scientific principles. The 1997 and 1998 awards went to two PBS programs: *Bill Nye The Science Guy* and *Scientific American Frontiers*.
- The "Snuffed Candle Award" is given to television programs that impede public understanding of the methods of scientific inquiry. The 1997 and 1998 winners were Dan Akroyd, for promoting the paranormal on the show *Psi-Factor*, and Art Bell, whose radio talk-show promoted belief in UFOs and alien abductions.

In its efforts to debunk pseudoscience, the Council also urges   15
TV producers to label documentary-type shows depicting the
paranormal as either entertainment or fiction, provides the media
with the names of expert spokespersons, asks U.S. newspapers to
print disclaimers with horoscope columns, and uses "media
watchdogs" to monitor programs and encourage responsibility on
the part of television producers.

Finally, various skeptics groups and renowned skeptic James
Randi have long-standing offers of large sums of money to anyone
who can prove a paranormal claim. Randi and members of his
"2000 Club" are offering more than a million dollars. So far, no
one has met the challenge.

Notes

1. Pseudoscience has been defined as "claims presented so that they
   appear [to be] scientific even though they lack supporting evidence
   and plausibility." In contrast, science is "a set of methods designed
   to describe and interpret observed and inferred phenomena, past or
   present, and aimed at building a testable body of knowledge open to
   rejection or confirmation" (Shermer 1997). Paranormal topics
   include yogic flying, therapeutic touch, astrology, fire walking,
   voodoo, magical thinking, Uri Geller, placebo, alternative medicine,
   channeling, Carlos hoax, psychic hotlines and detectives, near-death
   experiences, UFOs, the Bermuda Triangle, homeopathy, faith healing, and reincarnation (Committee for the Scientific Investigation of
   Claims of the Paranormal).
2. Because of several well-publicized court cases, considerable attention has been focused on the role of science in the courtroom and
   the ability of judges and juries to make sound decisions in cases
   involving highly complex, science- or technology-based evidence.
   (See Angell 1996 and Frankel 1998.)
3. A fairly common example that reflects a dearth of critical thinking
   skills is the number of people who become victims of get-rich-quick
   (for example, pyramid) schemes.
4. According to James Randi, "acceptance of nonsense as mere harmless aberrations can be dangerous to us. We live in an international
   society that is enlarging the boundaries of knowledge at an unprecedented rate, and we cannot keep up with much more than a small
   portion of what is made available to us. To mix our data input with
   childish notions of magic and fantasy is to cripple our perception of
   the world around us. We must reach for the truth, not for the ghosts
   of dead absurdities" (Randi 1992).

5. In the 1996 Gallup Poll, 18 percent of respondents said they read an astrology column regularly.

6. At the First Amendment Center's forum on science and the media, one of the participants cited what he called the "most frightening" results of a poll of students in Columbia's graduate school of journalism: 57 percent of the student journalists believed in ESP; 57 percent believed in dowsing; 47 percent in aura reading; and 25 percent in the lost continent of Atlantis (J. Franklin cited in Hartz and Chappell 1997).

7. In an earlier NSF survey, 6 percent of the female—compared with 3 percent of the male—respondents reported changing their behavior because of an astrology report.

8. A survey of 1,500 first-year college students found that 48.5 percent of arts—and 33.4 percent of science—students considered both astronomy and astrology scientific (De Robertis and Delaney 1993).

9. Examples of pseudoscience that receive a considerable amount of coverage in the mainstream media are unproven health-related therapies. Also, as Carl Sagan pointed out, almost every newspaper has an astrology column, but not many have even a weekly column devoted to science.

10. This result could simply mean that people who believe in the para normal are more likely than others to watch such programs. However, the findings are consistent with the conclusions of earlier experiments conducted by the same researcher (Sparks 1998).

11. CSICOP's official journal the SKEPTICAL INQUIRER is a vehicle for disseminating and publicizing the results of scientific studies of paranormal claims.

12. According to one study, scientists are portrayed more negatively than members of any other profession on prime-time entertainment shows. They are more likely to be killed or to kill someone. In fact, the study found that 10 percent of the scientists on fictional TV shows get killed and 5 percent kill someone (Gerbner 1987).

13. The award titles were inspired by Carl Sagan's book, *The Demon-Haunted World: Science as a Candle in the Dark* (Sagan 1996).

Selected Bibliography

Angell, M. 1996. *Science on Trial: The Clash of Medical Evidence and the Law in the Breast Implant Case*. New York: W.W. Norton & Company, Inc.

Beyerstein, B.L. 1998. The sorry state of scientific literacy in the industrialized democracies. *The Learning Quarterly* 2, No. 2:5–11.

The Committee for the Scientific Investigation of Claims of the Paranormal (CSICOP). Information available from www.csicop.org.

De Robertis, and Delaney, 1993. A survey of the attitudes of university students to astrology and astronomy. *Journal of the Royal Astronomical Society of Canada* 87, No. 1:34–50.

Evans, W. 1996. Science and reason in film and television. The SKEPTICAL INQUIRER (January/February).

Gallup News Service Poll. 1996. (September). Results are based on telephone interviews with 1,000 adults, age 18 and older, conducted September 3–5, 1996. For results based on the total sample of adults, one can say with 95-percent confidence that the margin of sampling error is plus or minus 3 percentage points.

Gerbner, G. 1987. Science on television: How it affects public conceptions. *Issues in Science and Technology* (spring):109–15.

The Harris Poll #41. 1998. Large majority of people believe they will go to Heaven; Only one in fifty thinks they will go to Hell: Many Christians and non-Christians believe in astrology, ghosts, and reincarnation. New York: Louis Harris & Associates, Inc. (August 12). This poll was conducted by telephone within the United States July 17–21, among a nationwide cross-section of 1,011 adults. The results have a statistical precision of plus or minus 3 percentage points.

Hartz, J., and R. Chappell. 1997. *Worlds Apart: How the Distance Between Science and Journalism Threatens America's Future.* Nashville, Tennessee: Freedom Forum First Amendment Center.

Maienschein, J., and students. 1999. Commentary: To the future. Argument for scientific literacy. *Science Communication* (September): 101–13.

Peccei, R., and F. Eiserling. 1996. Literacy for the 21st Century. *Los Angeles Times* (February 26).

Randi, J. 1992. It's time for science to take a stand against popular superstitions. *Time* (April 13).

The Roper Center for Public Opinion Research. 1994.

Sagan, C. 1996. *The Demon-Haunted World: Science as a Candle in the Dark.* New York: Random House.

Shermer, M. 1997. *Why People Believe Weird Things: Pseudoscience, Superstition, and Other Confusions of Our Time.* New York: W.H. Freeman and Company.

Southern Focus Poll. 1998. Conducted by The University of North Carolina at Chapel Hill, Institute for Research in Social Science (Spring). Available from www.irss.unc.edu. The Southern Focus Poll is sponsored by the Institute for Research in Social Science and the Center for the Study of the American South. Each fall and spring, a random sample of approximately 800 adult Southerners (residents of the states of Alabama, Arkansas, Florida, Georgia, Kentucky, Louisiana, Mississippi, North Carolina, Oklahoma, South Carolina, Tennessee, Texas, and Virginia) and 400 non-Southerners are interviewed by telephone. For more information, see www.irss.unc.edu/irss/ researchdesservices/resdesservices.html.

Sparks, G.G. 1998. Paranormal depictions in the media: How do they affect what people believe? SKEPTICAL INQUIRER (July/August): 35–9.

Sparks, G.G., T. Hansen, and R. Shah, 1994. Do televised depictions of paranormal events influence viewers' beliefs? SKEPTICAL INQUIRER 18:386–95.

Sparks, G.G., and M. Pellechia, 1997. The Effect of news stories about UFOs on readers' UFO beliefs: The role confirming or disconfirming testimony from a scientist. *Communication Reports* (summer).

Sparks, G.G., C.L. Nelson, and R.G. Campbell. 1997. The relationship between exposure to televised messages about paranormal phenomena and paranormal beliefs. *Journal of Broadcasting & Electronic Media* 41 (summer): 345–59.

USA Today Poll. 1998. Conducted by Yankelovich Partners (April 20). In Nisbet, M. New poll points to increase in paranormal belief. Available from www.csicop.org/articles/poll/index.html. One thousand people were surveyed in 1997 (8,709 in 1976); the poll has a margin of error of plus or minus 3.5 percent.

For Discussion and Writing

1. According to the first section of the report, what is the harm in public beliefs in paranormal claims? Discuss one area of concern, such as jury duty. How could our culture's preoccupation with pseudoscience and aliens be linked to this?

2. What separates "science literacy" from "scientific literacy"? How literate are you in either sense? What, if anything, can you point to as having helped you gain a little scientific literacy?

3. Lots of people read their horoscopes. Perhaps you have. Discuss your experience with horoscopes. In what sense can it be said that astrology is not at all scientific?

4. Scan the newspapers for a few days, and consult a television programming guide for the week. How much of the content refers to or presents paranormal or mysterious subjects? If you can, watch a program on UFOs, Bigfoot, or some such topic and evaluate its skeptical content, if there is any.

5. Who were some winners of the Council for Media Integrity's "Snuffed Candle Award"? In your view, to what degree do TV shows influence public beliefs? What do you base your answer on?

Mind Over Media: How the News Legitimizes the Paranormal and Why It Matters

SHARI WAXMAN

Shari Waxman is a writer in New York. In the following article, she considers the role of various media in making the paranormal seem credible. Psychics and seers are, she notes, handled with kid gloves and often with no hint that their claims may be dubious or fraudulent.

✦

Scientists are "mad," "dangerous," "useless" twits, often plagued, and ultimately destroyed, by their insistence on reason. At least this is how skeptic William Evans believes they are portrayed by the entertainment industry. That is, if they are not deemed entirely irrelevant. On television shows like the *X-Files*, for example, in which "the paranormal is portrayed as, well, normal," it is the scientists who are the aliens.[1]

In the six years since Evans' article, the television and film industries have continued to rely heavily on paranormal themes.[2,3] At the same time, the percentage of Americans that hold paranormal beliefs has been rising sharply. In 2000, a Gallup poll reported that 34% of women and 27% of men believed in ghosts; by 2001 the percentages had increased to 43% and 34%, respectively.[4]

Though Evans' concerns are warranted (exposure to science fiction has been associated with an increased likelihood of paranormal beliefs[5,6]), science fiction is, after all, only fiction. Anyone who sees crop circles in their front lawn after watching the movie *Signs* is surely not blameless. Non-fiction media, on the other hand, begin with a premise of truth. In the news genre there is little excuse for ghosts and the afterlife, psychics and seers, pseudoscientists and parapsychologists. So why are purveyors of the paranormal and their alleged happenings popping up in places where we normally expect to find hard news?

NEWS AS ENTERTAINMENT

When questioned about the *Travel Channel's* lean away from travel and adventure documentaries and toward paranormal-themed documentaries, senior vice president, Steve Cheskin, said, "I [was] at *Discovery* 15 years, six of those at *The Learning Channel.* I learned about what works in ratings. The word 'mystery' is a good word; 'secrets' is a good word. [They imply] that you're going to deliver something [viewers] didn't know before."[7] If it is true that mysteries of the unknown draw audiences, then science and reason are likely to ruin the effect.

Perhaps that is why investigations of paranormal phenomena— 5 phenomena that can be readily debunked—are often left unresolved. According to Michael Shermer, author of *Why People Believe Weird Things,* people may believe that "if *they* cannot explain something, it must be inexplicable and therefore a true mystery of the paranormal."[8] The apparent stumping of investigative journalists can only strengthen this reaction.

Science: The Fantasy Killer

To introduce an NBC *Dateline* report on John Edward, host Stone Phillips said:

> Celebrated psychic John Edward says he can communicate with the dead. That the dearly departed are still with us. A Harvard trained scientist says there may be something to his claims. Now we're about to see Edward in action, claiming to channel the dead at the request of the living. Listen carefully, this medium has a message. Will you believe it?[9]

The emotionally provocative language used here not only hinders reason,[10] it creates a mood of mystery and intrigue that all but precludes scientific perspectives. William Evans notes that television and movies often bypass reason altogether, without "acknowledg[ing] that skepticism is an understandable first response to fantastic claims and wondrous events."[11] Incredibly, his complaint also applies to news programs. Maintaining a vaudevillian one—like that established by Phillips—may require that practical reasoning be omitted. No one wants to be debriefed after a magic show.

On October 31st, 2002, *The New York Times* ran a profile on four ghostbusters from the Atlantic Paranormal Society. Their services include the detection and flushing out of ghosts (hence the expression "spirit plumbers"). Though the hygienists of the underworld admit, without irony, that ghost complaints rise whenever a scary movie is shown in theatres, scientific and skeptical perspectives on hauntings were not included in the article.[12] (Incidentally, this was not *The New York Times'* first article on the how-to's of ghosthunting.[13])

CBS also chose to sacrifice science—perhaps for entertainment's sake—in their *48 Hours* investigation of an alleged haunted house in Vicksburg, Mississippi. Parapsychologists explained to *48 Hours* how they are able to detect ghosts:

> The fields break down filtering mechanisms in the brain, and allow us to perceive a level of reality that's there all the time. There is a natural Earth source underneath the house that's creating a powerful magnetic field. (The house) might be described as kind of a storage battery for these energies, and people who go into this house are exposing themselves to those energies . . . that is what's triggering these experiences.[14]

10   Pseudoscientists are expected to use such scientific sounding nonsense to feign credibility.[15] That *48 Hours* failed to probe or challenge these statements presents the more serious problem of media willingness to accept the misleading lingo. The following passage— excerpted from ABC's *Downtown 20/20* investigation of Francis Bennett, founder of the New York Ghost Chapter—highlights the issue:

> Using infrared video cameras, electromagnetic field meters and thermoscan meters, which measure changes in temperature, Bennett and her team document the presence of ghosts. It is an endeavor she insists is based on science and she's earning her Ph.D. from a Florida Institute called Celestial Visions.[16]

What is required to earn a Ph.D. from the Celestial Visions program in Metaphysical Arts is a mystery worth investigating although, apparently, not to *Downtown 20/20*. Challenging the expertise of their expert could, after all, just confuse the matter (i.e., ruin the fantasy). That *Downtown 20/20* did not include a neurological hypothesis of paranormal experiences (one is that the phenomenon results when a sensitive temporal lobe is exposed to normal magnetic fields[17]) is also understandable. Practical explanations of ghostly encounters would surely weaken the awe-inducing tenor of the report.

If Katie Couric Believes It . . .

Are stories about UFOs on *Good Morning America* more damaging than stories of UFOs on *The X-Files?* It is not an unreasonable hypothesis, as newsworthiness implies at least some validity. The actual endorsement of strange beliefs by trusted news anchors— for instance, that "psychic medium" John Edward is actually a psychic medium—only makes matters worse. Not only have programs including NBC's *Today Show* and *Dateline*, CNN's *Larry King Live*, and CBS's *Early Show* provided Edward with open forums for self-promotion, they have done so with maddening reverence.

Most interviews of Edward have focused on the man—how he developed his mediumship, what drives him—rather than on the validity of his claims. In her interview of Edward for NBC's *Today Show* (November 21, 2000), Katie Couric says, "Tell me when you first realized you had this power." The premise—that Couric believes in his powers—is neither remitted nor qualified during the interview. This is only moderately irresponsible compared to Couric's later question: "So before *starting to help other people* (my emphasis) did you try to communicate with your own loved ones who had died?" The question implies that Edward helps people.

Media coddling of those who claim paranormal powers is not harmless. According to Hy Ruchlis, author of *Clear Thinking* (1990): "All frauds do damage to the fabric of human knowledge. In addition to destroying trust, fraudulent 'facts are counterproductive. Problems are not likely to be correctly or even adequately resolved with lies."[18] Those who provide the stage for the proliferation of "fraudulent facts" aid this process. (Indeed, in an attempt to quantify the consequences of Edward's media exposure, one journalist found a strong positive relationship between Edward's television appearances and his book sales.[19])

When Paula Zahn interviewed Edward for CNN's *American Morning* (May 10, 2002) she concluded the interview by wishing him "Continued good luck." In effect she wished Edward continued success in his financial and emotional manipulation of the people who trust him.

CONSEQUENCES

Even if news of supernatural phenomena provides an escape from news of terrorist threats and international conflicts, good intentions and alleged therapeutic benefits do not mitigate potential

15

damages. In fact, the current atmosphere of fear and uncertainty may only exacerbate these consequences. Ruchlis recalls that:

> There was a resurgence of superstitious beliefs during the 1960s, associated with disillusionment in "science" for creating nuclear weapons that threatened the globe with total destruction. It was also a time when an unpopular war in Vietnam was actively resisted by many young people . . . . They also turned against "science". . . (and) reacted to the rationality of science by turning to its opposite, superstitions like astrology. . . . They also unwisely rejected the objectivity, rationality, and powerful way of thinking that have enabled scientists to investigate thoroughly and solve a wide variety of difficult problems.[20]

Ultimately, the legitimization of pseudoscientific research and paranormal phenomena by trusted news sources cannot occur without the simultaneous de-valuation of science and reason. If the trend continues, the American public will be left with two disconcerting options: (1) They can learn to distrust the information provided by mainstream news sources, or (2) They can learn to readily accept scientifically baseless claims as provided by mainstream news sources. The implications are profound.

References

Evans, W. 1996. "Science and Reason in Film and Television." *Skeptical Inquirer*, 20. http://www.csicop.org/si/9601/media.html

Television shows, such as Psi Factor, Millenium, Profiler, Buffy the Vampire Slayer, and The Dark Side; movies, such as The Sixth Sense, The Others, K-Pax, A. I., and What Lies Beneath.

Variety: Ghostly Grosses. 2001. *Box Office News*, October 29.

Ebenkamp, B. 2000. "They're Giving Ghosts of a Chance."*Brandweek*, November 13; Ebenkamp, B. 2001. "Ghosts, Goblins, Ghouls, Gallup." *Brandweek*, June 18.

Sparks, G. G., C. L. Nelson, and R. G. Campbell. 1997. "The Relationship Between Exposure to Televised Messages About Paranormal Phenomena and Paranormal Beliefs." *Journal of Broadcasting and Electronic Media*, 41, 345–358.

National Science Foundation. 2000. "Science and Technology: Public Attitudes and Public Understanding." Science and Engineering Indicators 2000. http://www.nsf.gov/sbe/srs/seind00/access/c8/c8c5.htm

Mcadams, D. D. 2000. "Trips to the Other Side."*Broadcasting & Cable*, July 31.

Shermer, M. 2002. *Why People Believe Weird Things*. Henry Holt and Company: New York, 52.

NBC News, Dateline. Aired November 17, 2000.

Ibid., 55.

Evans, W. 1996.

Leland, J. 2002. "Don't Say Ghostbusters; Say Spirit Plumber." *New York Times*, October 31, F1, F11.

Mittlebach, M. & M. Crewdson. 1999. "In Pursuit of Spirits Doing Time in the Afterlife." *New York Times*, October 29.

CBS News.com. 1999. 48 Hours Investigates, August 8. http://www.cbsnews.com/stories/1999/08/05/48hours/main57180.shtml

Shermer, M. 2002, 49.

ABC News.com: 2001. "Downtown Goes Ghosts Hunting." June 18. http://more.abcnews.go.com/sections/downtown/2020/downtown_010618_ghostbuster.html.

Lockman, D. 2002. "Galvanizing Ghosts: Geometric Fields May Be the Culprit." *Psychology Today*, May–June.

Ruchlis, H. 1990. *Clear Thinking: A Practical Introduction*. Prometheus Books: New York, 29.

Nisbett, M. "Talking to Heaven through Television: How the Mass Media Package and Sell Psychic Medium John Edward." Committee for the Scientific Investigation of Claims of the Paranormal. http://www.csicop.org/genx

Ruchlis, H. 1990, 49.

For Discussion and Writing

1. Think of a few instances in movies and the like in which scientists are portrayed negatively. What is the usual basis of such portrayals? How are science villains like those in *James Bond* movies any different from typical villains?

2. Look at Stone Phillips' introduction to the episode on John Edward. In what sense is his language provocative? How is it slanted? When he asks, "Will you believe it?", how is he setting up an hour's entertainment?

3. What questions might a reasonable skeptic ask of the parapsychologists quoted in the *48 Hours* episode? Imagine some questions, and imagine answers designed to evade charges of fakery and lying.

4. How, according to the author, did Katie Couric's remarks lend credibility to Edward? Why would she phrase her questions in the way that she did? What do they suggest about her own belief in Edward's psychic powers?

5. Waxman declares that "the legitimization of pseudoscientific research . . . by trusted news sources cannot occur without the simultaneous de-valuation of science and reason." Do you agree? Explain your position.

That's Entertainment! TV's UFO Coverup

PHILIP J. KLASS

Philip Klass, who died in 2005, was a founding member of CSICOP. He spent many years investigating UFOs, although his training was in electrical engineering. He worked to debunk UFO claims and identify sightings in a, well, down to earth manner. Among his publications are several books, including UFOs—Identified *(1968),* The Real Roswell Crashed-Saucer Coverup *(1997),* UFO Abductions: A Dangerous Game *(1989), and* Bringing UFOs Down to Earth *(1997). In the article that follows, Klass links public belief in demonstrable falsehoods with TV coverage that is more focused on entertaining than informing.*

--- ✦ ---

Don't be surprised or shocked if you discover that a good friend—a well-educated, intelligent person—believes in UFOs, or that he or she suspects that the U.S. government recovered a crashed extraterrestrial craft and ET bodies in New Mexico and has kept them under wraps for nearly half a century. Don't be surprised if your respected friend, or a member of your own family, is convinced that ETs are abducting thousands of Americans and subjecting them to dreadful indignities.

The really surprising thing is that you do not believe in crashed saucers, alien abductions, and government coverup if you spend even a few hours every week watching TV. There are many TV shows that promote belief in the reality of UFOs, government coverup, and alien abductions. And they attract very large audiences—typically tens of millions of viewers. Often they are broadcast a second, possibly even a third time.

TV has become the most pervasive means of influencing what people believe. That explains why companies spend billions of dollars every year on TV advertising to convince the public that Brand X beer tastes best, that you should eat Brand Y cereal, and that a Brand Z automobile is the world's best.

According to a recent survey reported in Business Week magazine, our children spend nearly twice as much time watching TV as they do in school.

5   Consider the problem that TV created for the Audi 5000 automobile and the claim that the car would suddenly accelerate and

crash into the front of an owner's garage when the automatic transmission was in neutral. The Audi 5000 was introduced in 1978, and during the next four years only thirteen owners complained of a mysterious sudden acceleration incident. Then, in November 1986, CBS featured the alleged Audi 5000 problem on its popular 60 Minutes show. During the next month, some fourteen hundred people claimed that their Audi 5000s had experienced sudden acceleration problems (P. J. O'Rourke, *Parliament of Whores*, Atlantic Monthly Press, 1991, pp. 86–7). Subsequent investigation by the National Transportation Safety Board revealed that the problem was the result of driver error—stepping on the accelerator when they intended to step on the brake.

Here's another example: several years ago, a man who claimed he had found a hypodermic needle in a Pepsi-Cola can became an instant celebrity when he appeared on network TV news to describe his amazing discovery. Within several weeks, roughly fifty other persons around the country claimed they too had discovered hypodermic needles in Pepsi-Cola cans. Investigation showed all these reports were spurious.

TV's brainwashing of the public on UFOs occurs not only on NBC's *Unsolved Mysteries* and Fox network's *Sightings*, but also on more respected programs such as CBS's *48 Hours* and ones hosted by CNN's Larry King.

Why pick on the TV networks? Cannot the same criticism be leveled at the print media? No. Generally, even cub reporters know that when writing an article on a controversial subject they should try to present both sides of the issue. If they fail to do so, their older and wiser managing editors will remind them. An article may devote 60 or 70 percent of its content to pro-UFO views, but with TV the pro-UFO content typically runs 95 percent—or higher.

TV news programs do try to offer viewers an even-handed treatment of controversial subjects. Thus it is not surprising that many viewers assume they are getting an equally balanced treatment in TV shows that follow the news, such as *Unsolved Mysteries* and *Sightings*. This is especially true when the show is CBS's *48 Hours*, hosted by news anchor Dan Rather.

This "schizophrenic" policy would be less troubling if such   10
TV programs were required to carry a continuous disclaimer, such as "This program is providing you with a one-sided treatment of a controversial issue. It is intended solely to entertain you," or at least if such a disclaimer were voiced by the host at the beginning and the end of such a program. But alas, at best there is

only a brief disclaimer which typically says: "The following is a controversial subject."

Consider a typical NBC *Unsolved Mysteries* show dealing with the Roswell "crashed-saucer" incident. The show, which aired Sept. 18, 1994, included an appearance by me. Prior to the taping of my interview, I gave the producer photocopies of once top-secret and secret Air Force documents that had never before been seen on TV and that provided important new evidence that a flying saucer had not crashed in New Mexico.

These documents, dating back to late 1948, revealed that if an ET craft was recovered from New Mexico in July 1947, nobody informed top Pentagon intelligence officials who should have been the first to know. One of these top-secret documents, dated December 10, 1948, more than a year and a half after the alleged recovery of an ET craft and "alien" bodies, showed that top Air Force and Navy intelligence officials then believed that UFOs might be Soviet spy vehicles.

When the hour-long *Unsolved Mysteries* show aired, I appeared for only twenty seconds to discuss the early history of the UFO era. Not one of the once top-secret and secret documents, which disproved the Roswell myth, or my taped references to these documents, was used.

On October 1, 1994, the famed Larry King aired a two-hour special program on the TNT cable network. Its title was "*UFO Coverup? Live From Area 51.*" (Area 51 is part of an Air Force base in Nevada where new aircraft and weapons are tested. UFO believers allege that one can see alien spacecraft flying over the area and that the government has secret dealings and encounters with aliens there.)

15   Approximately one hour—half the two-hour program—was broadcast live from Nevada. For this hour, four pro-UFO guests were allowed to make wild claims, without a single live skeptic to respond. To give viewers the illusion of "balance," the show included pre-taped interviews with Carl Sagan and with me. Sagan appeared in five very brief segments, averaging less than fifteen seconds each, for a total of one and one-quarter minutes. I appeared in four brief segments for a total airtime of one and a half minutes.

So during the two-hour show, the audience was exposed to less than three minutes of skeptical views on UFOs, crashed saucers, and government coverup. And because Sagan and I were taped many weeks earlier, neither of us could respond to nonsense spouted by the four UFO promoters who appeared live for an hour.

Some weeks earlier, when I went to the studio for my taped interview for this Larry King show, I handed producer Tom Farmer photocopies of the same once top-secret and secret documents I had given to *Unsolved Mysteries.* Once again I stressed that these documents had never before appeared on any television show. Yet not one of these documents was shown during the two-hour program.

Near the end of the program, Larry King summed up the situation in the following words: "Crashed saucers. Who knows? But clearly the government is withholding something. . . ." In fact, it was Larry King and his producer who were withholding the hard data that would show that the government is not involved in a crashed-saucer coverup.

Larry King ended the program with these words: "We hope that you learned a lot tonight and that you found it both entertaining and informative at the same time."

If you were looking for a truly "informative" program on   20
UFOs, you'd expect to find it on the *Science Frontiers* program broadcast on The Learning Channel, right? Wrong!

Last spring, The Learning Channel's *Science Frontiers* program aired a one-hour program titled "*UFO.*" Not one of the many "UFO experts" interviewed on the program was a skeptic. The British producer sent a film crew to Washington—where I live—to interview pro-UFOlogist Fred Whiting, who was given nearly three minutes of airtime. Whiting assured the viewers: "There is indeed a coverup." But I was not invited to be interviewed.

In early 1994, I received a phone call from a producer of the CBS show *48 Hours*, saying they were producing a segment on the Roswell crashed saucer and would like to come down from New York in mid-April to interview me.

In late March 1994, I visited Roswell in connection with a new crashed-saucer book that was making its debut there. Not surprisingly, the CBS film crew from *48 Hours* was on hand and they did a brief interview with me. In an effort to inform the viewers of the 1948 top-secret document, I pulled it out of my pocket and held it up in front of the CBS camera. And I promised to provide the producer with more such documents, never before shown on TV, when they came to Washington for the more lengthy interview.

CBS never came to Washington for my interview. And when the show later aired, with Dan Rather as its host, CBS opted not to include any of the brief interview with me in Roswell—holding up the once top-secret document.

Young children, and their parents, will experience similar   25
"brainwashing" when they visit Disney World's new "Tomorrowland" in Orlando. A new dynamic exhibit is called "Alien Encounters and Extra-TERRORestrial Experience." To encourage parents and

children to visit the new UFO exhibit, in mid-March 1995 Walt Disney Inc. broadcast a one-hour TV show on ABC titled "Alien Encounters from New Tomorrowland."

The show began by showing several brief home-video segments of bogus "UFOs" while the narrator intoned: "This is not swamp gas. It is not a flock of birds. This is an actual spacecraft from another world, piloted by alien intelligence. . . . Intelligent life from distant galaxies is now attempting to make open contact with the human race. Tonight we will show you the evidence."

The Disney show included the Roswell crashed-saucer case with considerable emphasis on government coverup. At one point, the narrator noted that Jimmy Carter had had a UFO sighting prior to becoming president. The narrator added: "Later, when he assumed the office of president . . . his staff attempted to explore the availability of official investigations into alien contacts."

Then, as the camera rapidly panned a typewritten document, it zoomed in on the words "no jurisdiction," and the narrator said: "As this internal government memo illustrates, there are some security secrets outside the jurisdiction even of the White House." The implication was that even the president did not have access to UFO secrets.

In reality, the memo was an FBI response to a White House inquiry about FBI involvement in investigating UFOs. The memo said that the FBI had "no jurisdiction" to investigate UFO reports and referred the White House to the Air Force. But the camera panned and zoomed so fast no viewer could read the memo.

30   Near the end of the program the narrator said: "Statistics indicate a greater probability that you will experience extraterrestrial contact in the next five years than the chances you will win a state lottery. But how do you prepare for such an extraordinary event? At Tomorrowland in Disney World, scientists and Disney engineers have brought to life a possible scenario that helps acclimate the public to their inevitable alien encounters."

More recently, Walt Disney Inc. has purchased the ABC television network. I won't be surprised if Disney and ABC use UFOs to attract more viewers.

For the tiny handful of those who produce TV and radio shows dealing with claims of the paranormal who truly want to provide their audience with both sides, the Committee for the Scientific Investigation of Claims of the Paranormal (CSICOP) is an invaluable resource in providing the names of experienced skeptics. The same is true for print-media reporters. If TV shows on UFOs are 95 percent "loaded" to promote belief, without CSICOP they would be 100 percent loaded.

For Discussion and Writing

1. The author claims it would be surprising if you, his readers, didn't believe in crashed saucers and alien abductions. Do you believe in such things, or in a government coverup of such events? If so, what role does evidence play in your belief (or the beliefs of friends) concerning these subjects?
2. Klass seems to equate beer and other advertising subjects with UFO beliefs. Explain his connection. How does the story about the Audi 5000 fit in with his larger subject?
3. What is the author's objection to the 1994 NBC *Unsolved Mysteries* presentation of the Roswell crash story? NBC did not mention top-secret documents that cast doubt on tales of dead aliens. Explain why you think networks should or should not debunk such tales. If you were an NBC executive, how might you explain your decision to omit evidence that solved these "mysteries"?
4. What was Larry King's contribution to legends of a government coverup of UFO information? Why do you think King chose not to present documents never before shown on television?
5. Discuss the cumulative effects, as you see them, of media presentations that promote belief in UFOs. What other stance might media take in programming about aliens etc.?

Stupid "Pet Psychic" Tricks: Crossing Over with Fifi and Fido on the Animal Planet Network

BRYAN FARHA

Bryan Farha has written essays that are critical of the extraordinary claims of psychics and others, among them "Blundered Predictions in 2004: A Sylvia Browne Review," and "Number Manipulation: The Not 'So Spooky' Tim McVeigh." He is a professor in the Department of Behavioral Studies and Counseling Psychology at Oklahoma City University, and has appeared on the National Geographic Channel program Is It Real? *to provide a skeptical perspective on claims of telepathic communications between humans and animals. The following essay shows, pointedly, some alternative explanations for apparently successful communications between a psychic and various animals.*

———————— ✦ ————————

If David Letterman wants to expand his "Stupid Pet Tricks" segment on the *Late Show* to include stupid pet psychic tricks, I believe we have a winner. Move over James Van Praagh and John Edward, there's a new television show in town. The Animal Planet cable network has launched *Pet Psychic*, which is hosted by England-born Sonya Fitzpatrick. During Sonya's introductory bio on each telecast, she claims to be able to hear the thoughts of all animals in her vicinity. On the show, Sonya "reads" the thoughts of a variety of animals, asking the pets questions, and claiming to get answers from the critters. She then communicates the answer to the pet owner, who feels comforted after the alleged telepathic communication. Sometimes questions are requested by animal owners, who are often interested in finding out reasons for peculiar pet behaviors. And she's multi-talented, also "crossing over" to communicate with pets that have died.

Further, Sonya also professes ability to function as a pet psychic detective. For example, there is a $4,000 reward for information leading to the conviction of the person or persons who abused a cat named "TLC." The abused cat "told" Sonya that the guilty person was a thin male with dark hair who didn't like cats. One member of the veterinary staff who treated TLC said of Sonya's psychic detective work that the staff was "shocked" at her accuracy and that "any kind of skepticism fades away." Excuse me, but this is where skepticism enters.

Let's look at some "Stupid Pet Psychic Tricks" used by Sonya Fitzpatrick to make her appear psychic. All are taken from a single program, which aired on July 1, 2002.

PREDICTION BASED ON PRIOR KNOWLEDGE

"Tony" the Llama. Sonya made a house call to a ranch outside her current residence of Houston for this alleged telepathic experience. She accurately pointed out that Tony had some behavioral issues and that he was a problem llama. The fact that the owner confirmed this made the statements seem very impressive.

Stupid Pet Psychic Trick: Immediately before her psychic vision   5
of the llama's behavioral problems, Tony jerked and flailed notice-
ably while being observed by Sonya and the owner. After seeing this
unruly behavior, just how psychic was it to predict that the llama had
disciplinary problems? Anyone could have had the same psychic
vision after observing a child who misbehaved like this, even before
being told of such a problem. Yet the owner seemed impressed, and
probably many in the television audience were as well.

Percy and Bogie. It was never established which one was
which, but referring to one of the dogs, this dialog took place
between Sonya and the pet's owner.

Sonya: When did he have some medication?
Owner: He's had an ear infection.
Sonya: Yah—he [dog] says that was bad. He says he's had that
on and off.

Stupid Pet Psychic Trick: Notice Sonya only makes this last comment after already hearing the owner say the dog had an ear infection. If Sonya can communicate with animals, why didn't she just
ask the dog initially what the medication was for and report the
answer to us before the owner did? But she asked a general question
about medication and got a specific answer from the pet's owner,
and wants us to believe that the dog told her the experience was bad?

"Bonnie" the Dog. This dog kept growling and snarling before
Sonya said anything. Therefore, Sonya's first comment about the
dog's behavior was, "she's a talker."

Stupid Pet Psychic Trick: How hard is it to convince an owner
of this given the free prior knowledge of snarling and growling?

MAKING THE OBVIOUS SEEM TELEPATHIC

Two Cats. Sonya asked the owner if one of the cats crawls under   10
things. The amazed owner confirmed this and said they both go
under the covers with her.

Stupid Pet Psychic Trick: What's amazing about this? What cat
doesn't crawl under things? And it didn't have to be the covers.
Don't most cats crawl under desks, tables, sofas, beds, and any
other available space? The owner was impressed enough to
believe one of the cats told Sonya she'd prefer it if the owner
would buy a second litter box—one for each cat.

"Bonnie" Again. Sonya states, "she's [Bonnie] asking me why
is it that you [owner] don't want her on you sometimes?"

Stupid Pet Psychic Trick: The owner's answer is the same that most of us would give—because sometimes we've got other things we need to do like cook, work on the computer, etc. Maybe this category should have been labeled, "Duh."

Crossing Over Willie. Willie was a diseased Golden Retriever. His owner had arranged to have him euthanized by a veterinarian. Sonya had a vision—which the owner confirmed—that Willie used to scratch behind his cars. Really? A dog scratching behind his ears? Shocking.

MAKING IT FIT

15   *"Joy" Who Crossed Over.* Joy is a cat who ran away without apparent cause and supposedly died. In an effort to find out why Joy ran away, this dialog ensued:

> Sonya: When did you [owner] change a floor in your house? [no response]. Or a carpet?
> Owner: We just cleaned our carpet.

Sonya goes on to say that Joy ran away because they cleaned the carpet. But if Sonya can communicate with dead animals, why didn't she just ask the departed cat the question and provide the answer before asking the owner about changing the floor? More important, wasn't Sonya's question really implying that a different floor was installed? When people are asked if they've changed a floor aren't they assuming a new floor was installed? Yet the owner had no problem adjusting what Sonya had said. People who want to believe are going to make any statement fit.

COMFORTING THEMES

Recall the old rule of fortune telling—"tell 'em what they want to hear." Pet owners want to hear things that will make them feel good about their animals. It's especially important for grieving owners to feel comfort when the pet has "crossed over." Sonya made the following comments, all during a single July 1, 2002 show about various pets that had died and were "telepathically" communicating their thoughts to her "He loves you;" "He's with you all the time;" "He comes around you a lot;" "She's around you, darling;" "She didn't suffer;" "She's with you all the time." Sonya told Felicia, the pet owner who was feeling guilty about putting her dog Willie to sleep, that the departed Willie reassured her, "I was ready to go . . . you did the right thing."

CONCLUDING REMARKS

Obviously, Sonya is using old rehashed fortune telling and psychic "tricks" that only appear new when done under the guise of communicating with animals. It's difficult enough for skeptics to verify human psychic claims because of the vagueness of the readings. Since animals don't speak our tongue (sorry, Sonya), verifiability would be even more difficult with pet psychics. But some of her claims do lend themselves to controlled testing—Sonya needs to ask the animals direct and specific questions and then let the owners verify the answers.

I would like to challenge Sonya to take the Million Dollar Psychic Challenge from the James Randi Educational Foundation. If she's not interested in the money, she can donate the earnings to her favorite animal charity. Television is about money, too, and surely this type of programming sells. It just doesn't seem as if it belongs on the *Animal Planet*—an otherwise good network. If Sonya won't contact James Randi, maybe she'll contact David Letterman.

For Discussion and Writing

1. What do you think is so appealing about the possibility of "hearing an animal's thoughts"? What exactly do you think Sonya Fitzpatrick means by that phrase?

2. One believer in Fitzpatrick's ability claimed to be so impressed with her accuracy that he lost all skepticism. Farha notes that "this is where skepticism enters." What do you think he means? When exactly should skepticism arise in this context?

3. Evaluate what the author characterizes as "Stupid Pet Psychic Tricks" in the article. What role do observation and generalizing seem to play in Fitzpatrick's successes?

4. Compare Fitzpatrick's leading questions with those of John Edward. What do you see? Study the behavior of a friend's pet and try to "read" its thoughts. Can you be convincing?

Bone (Box) of Contention: The James Ossuary

JOE NICKELL

The tale of this antique ossuary would probably have a modest circulation, except for two things: First, it bears an inscription that refers to James, son of Joseph, brother of Jesus. An artifact referring to Jesus is of interest to many people. Second, the media got a hold of it. The Biblical Archaeology Review *published a report supporting the authenticity of the ossuary, the Royal Ontario Museum chose to exhibit the box, and the Discovery Channel did a story on it. Naturally, newspapers carried word of the extraordinary find, although they did not always report the views of Eric Meyers, who thought the inscription on the box was fake. In the piece that follows, Joe Nickell, Senior Research Fellow at CSICOP and author of* Pen, Ink, and Evidence *and* Detecting Forgery, *reviews the controversy around the artifact.*

◆

Supposedly recently discovered, the James ossuary—a limestone mortuary box that purportedly held the remains of Jesus' brother—is the subject of controversy. It has captured the attention of theologians, secular scholars, laity, and journalists around the world. Some have rushed to suggest that the inscription on it is the earliest-known reference to Jesus outside the bible, providing archaeological evidence of his historical existence.

"World Exclusive!" proclaimed *Biblical Archaeology Review*. "Evidence of Jesus Written in Stone," the cover continued; "Ossuary of 'James, Brother of Jesus found in Jerusalem," urged the contents page: "Read how this important object came to light and how scientists proved it wasn't a modern forgery."

Actually, as we shall soon see, the matter is much less clear than such hype would suggest, and there are many questions yet to be answered.

BACKGROUND

The initial report in *Biblical Archaeology Review* (BAR) was written by a French scholar, André Lemaire (2002), who believes both the artifact and its inscription authentic.

Such an ossuary, or "bone box," was used to store bones in 5
Jewish burial practice during the period from the first century b.c.
to the Roman destruction of Jerusalem in 70 a.d. (In this tradition
the corpse would first be interred in a niche in a burial cave. After
about a year, when the remains became skeletonized, the bones
were gathered into a chest, usually made from a hollowed-out
block of limestone fitted with a lid [Figueras 1983, 26]).

Incised on one of the James ossuary's long sides, the inscription consists of a single line of twenty small Aramaic characters.
It reads (from right to left): "Ya'akov bar Yosef akhui diYeshua"—
that is, "Jacob [English James], son of Yosef [Joseph], brother of
Yeshua [Jesus]." Based on the script, Lemaire dates the inscription to some time between 20 b.c. and 70 a.d. And he believes that
the inscription's mention of a father named Joseph plus a brother
named Jesus suggests "that this is the ossuary of the James in the
New Testament," which in turn "would also mean that we have
here the first epigraphic mention—from about 63 c.e.—of Jesus of
Nazareth" (Lemaire 2002, 33).

Lemaire believes the inscription has a consistency and correctness that show "it is genuinely ancient and not a fake." The
box was examined by two experts from the Geological Survey of
Israel at the request of BAR. They concluded that the ossuary had
a gray patina (or coating of age). "The same gray patina is found
also within some of the letters," he wrote, "although the inscription was cleaned and the patina is therefore absent from several
letters." They added, "The patina has a cauliflower shape known
to be developed in a cave environment." The experts also reported
they saw no evidence of "the use of a modern tool or instrument"
(Rosenfeld and Ilani 2002).

Unfortunately, the cleaning of the inscription—an act either
of stupidity or shrewdness—is problematic. It might have
removed traces of modern tooling. And when we are told that the
patina is found "within some of the letters," we should certainly
want to know which ones, since scholars have debated whether
the phrase "brother of Jesus" might be a spurious addition
(Altman 2002; Shuman 2002).

It is even possible for traces of patination in an inscription to
be original when the carving is not. That could happen if—as is
the case of the James ossuary—shallow carving was done over a
deeply pitted surface. The patinated bottoms of remnant pits
could thus remain inside the fresh scribings.

In any case the patina may not be all it is claimed. According 10
to one forgery expert, because patination is expected with age,

"The production of a convincing patina has therefore been of great interest to those engaged in faking or restoration" (Jones 1990). Although false patinas are most commonly applied to metalwork, stone sculptures and artifacts—including fake "prehistoric" flint implements—have been treated to create the appearance of antiquity (Jones 1990). For example, the versatile forger Alceo Dossena (1878–1937) produced convincing patinas on marble (a hard, metamorphic limestone) that gave his works "an incredible look of age" (Sox 1987).

The patina traces of the James ossuary inscription have already been questioned. Responding to the claim that patina was cleaned from the inscription, one art expert notes that genuine patina would be difficult to remove while forged patina cracks off. "This appears to be what happened with the ossuary," he concludes (Lupia 2002).

PROVENANCE

The reason for questioning the patina is that additional evidence raises doubts about the ossuary's authenticity. To begin with, there is the matter of its provenance, which concerns the origin or derivation of an artifact. Experts in the fields of objets d'art and other rarities use the term to refer to a work's being traceable to a particular source. For example, records may show that an artifact came from a certain archaeological dig, was subsequently owned by a museum, and then, when the museum sold off some of its collection, was bought by a private collector.

Provenance matters more with a sensational artifact, and the refusal or inability of an owner to explain how he or she acquired an item is, prima facie, suspicious—a possible indicator of forgery or theft. One of my cases, for instance, concerned a purported manuscript of Lincoln's celebrated Gettysburg Address (actually the second sheet of what was ostensibly a two-page draft, signed by Lincoln). Suspicions were raised when it was reported that the dealer who sold the item wanted to remain anonymous, and my subsequent ultraviolet and stereomicroscopic examination revealed it was a forgery (Nickell 1996).

With the James ossuary, the provenance seems to be, well, under development. In his BAR article, André Lemaire (2002) referred to the "newly revealed ossuary" which he would only say was "now in a private collection in Israel." A sidebar stated that on a recent visit to Jerusalem, "Lemaire happened to meet a certain collector by chance; the collector mentioned that he had some objects he wanted Lemaire to see." One of the objects was the James ossuary (Feldman 2002).

The owner had pleaded with reporters not to reveal his name   15 or address, but he was apparently uncovered by the Israeli Antiquities Authority.

He is Oded Golan, a Tel Aviv engineer, entrepreneur, and collector. Golan explained that he had not wished to be identified due to concerns for privacy.

"It's a character issue," he told the Associated Press (Laub 2002). "I don't like publicity." But Golan received some attention that may have been most unwanted: He came under investigation by the Antiquities Authority's theft unit (Scrivener 2002).

According to Golan, he bought the ossuary in the Old City (old Jerusalem) "in the 1970s," paying a few hundred dollars to an Arab antiquities dealer he can no longer identify (Van Biema 2002; Adams 2002; Wilford 2002). He has said that it was the box's engraving that interested him, yet nothing in the phrase "James, son of Joseph, brother of Jesus" ever "rang a bell" in Golan's mind (Adams 2002). Incredibly, the sensational inscription had to wait three decades before finally being appreciated by André Lemaire.

Many scholars were horrified that the ossuary had apparently been looted from its burial site—not just because looting is illegal and immoral, but because an artifact's being robbed of its context "compromises everything," according to P. Kyle McCarter Jr., who chairs the Near Eastern studies department at Johns Hopkins University. McCarter added, "We don't know where [the box] came from, so there will always be nagging doubts. Extraordinary finds need extraordinary evidence to support them" (Van Biema 2002).

Not only the box's provenance was lost but also, reportedly, its   20 contents which might have helped establish its provenance. "Unfortunately," stated André Lemaire (2002), "as is almost always the case with ossuaries that come from the antiquities market rather than from a legal excavation, it was emptied." I lamented this reported state of affairs to a reporter (Ryan 2002), observing that the bones could have been examined by forensic anthropologists to potentially determine cause of death. James was reportedly thrown from the top of the Temple and stoned and beaten to death (Hurley 2002), so his skeletal remains might show evidence of such trauma.

As it turns out, Lemaire did not mention—perhaps he did not know—that Mr. Golan has a Tupperware container of bone fragments he says were in the ossuary when he acquired it. One piece is as large as one-half inch by three inches, and has raised questions about potential DNA evidence. Yet, according to Time magazine, Golan will not allow the fragments "to be displayed or analyzed" (Van Biema 2002).

FURTHER SUSPICIONS

In addition to the questionable provenance, the exterior appearance of the ossuary also raises suspicions. To view the box, which was on display at the Royal Ontario Museum, I recently traveled to Toronto with several of my Center for Inquiry colleagues. They included Kevin Christopher, who has degrees in classics and linguistics, with whom I had been studying the case (see acknowledgments). We were able to get a good look at the box, and what we observed raised eyebrows.

First of all, I was surprised to see that the ossuary was far from being "unadorned" as Lemaire (2002, 27) reported. He stated that "The only decoration is a line forming a frame about 0.5 inch (1.2 cm) from the outer edges," but he is mistaken. Significantly, on the side opposite the inscribed side are circular designs, badly worn but unmistakably present.

Now, ossuaries are usually decorated on only one side (Royal 2002), presumably the one intended to face out during storage. If a name was added (possibly with an identifying phrase), it was apparently carved after purchase by someone such as a family member (Figueras 1983, 18). A look at a number of ossuaries (Figueras 1983; Goodenough 1953) shows that the name might be engraved on the decorated side if there were space for it; otherwise it might be cut on the top, an end, or the back. Wherever placed, it "probably faced outwards where it could be read" (Altman 2002a).

25   In the case of the James ossuary, there would have indeed been room on the front, yet the scribe elected to carve the inscription on the back. (A possible reason for this will soon become evident.)

Furthermore, the box's decorations—the carved "frame" Lemaire referred to which outlines all four sides, plus the circular designs—are badly worn, whereas the inscription seems almost pristine. That is, the decorations are blurred, partially effaced, and (like much of the surface) pitted. Yet the lettering is entirely distinct and blessed with sharp edges, as if it were of recent vintage. My colleagues and I were all struck with that observation. So was an Israeli engineering professor, Dr. Daniel Eylon, of the University of Dayton, who noted that "sharp edges do not last 2,000 years."

Dr. Eylon applied a technique that is employed in determining whether damage to an airplane part occurred prior to an accident or after it.

Examining photographs of the inscription for scratches accrued over time, he stated: "The inscription would be underneath these scratches if it had been on the box at the time of burial, but the majority of this inscription is on top of the scratches" (Eylon 2002).

The inscription's off-center placement is even in an area of the back that suffers the least damage. Commenting on what is termed biovermiculation—that is, "limestone erosion and dissolution caused by bacteria over time in the form of pitting and etching"—one art historian states: "The ossuary had plenty except in and around the area of the inscription. This is not normal" (Lupia 2002). Indeed, that is one of the first things I had observed in studying the James ossuary. It suggested a forger might have selected a relatively smooth area of the back as a place to carve the small, neat characters.

Early on, the text of the inscription itself raised doubts   30 among experts familiar with Aramaic scripts. They observed that the "James, son of Joseph" portion was in a seemingly formal script while the "brother of Jesus" phrase was in a more cursive style. This suggested "at least the possibility of a second hand," according to one expert (McCarter 2002). Another states, "The second part of the inscription bears the hallmarks of a fraudulent later addition and is questionable to say the least" (Altman 2002b). But the perceived dichotomy in styles may simply signal that the forger was an inexpert copyist or that the effect results from the vagaries of stone carving.

Taken together, the various clues suggest a scenario in which a forger purchased a genuine ossuary that—lacking feet, elaborate ornament, and inscription—cost little. He then obtained an Aramaic rendition of the desired wording, carved it into what seemed a good spot on the blank back, and perhaps added patination followed by "cleaning" to help mitigate against the fresh look of the carving.

Forgers frequently select genuine old artifacts upon which to inflict their handiwork. Examples that I have personally investigated and helped expose include such inscribed works as two

Daniel Boone muskets, the diary of Jack the Ripper, a carte de visite photo of Robert E. Lee, a dictionary with flyleaf notes by Charles Dickens, and many more (Nickell 1990; 1996).

Mounting evidence has begun to suggest that the James ossuary may be yet another such production.

ACKNOWLEDGMENTS

Those making the December 5, 2002, trip to view the ossuary were—in addition to Kevin Christopher (who drove, assisted with research, and offered valuable observations)—Benjamin Radford, Katherine Bourdonnay, and Norm Allen. Also, Paul Kurtz provided encouragement, Barry Karr financial authorization, Tim Binga research assistance, and Ranjit Sandhu word processing, while other CFI staff helped in many additional ways.

References

Adams, Paul. 2002. Ossuary's owner emerges to tell his story. *The Globe and Mail* (Toronto), November 7.

Altman, Rochelle I. 2002a. Final report on the James ossuary. Online at web.israelinsider.com . . . , November 6.

——. 2002b. Quoted in Wilford 2002.

Eylon, Daniel. 2002. Quoted in Wilford 2002.

Feldman, Steven. 2002. The right man for the inscription. Sidebar to Lemaire (2002) signed "S.F.," 30. (Feldman is managing editor of *BAR*.)

Figueras, Pau. 1983. *Decorated Jewish Ossuaries*. Leiden: E. J. Brill.

Goodenough, Erwin R. 1953. *Jewish Symbols in the Greco-Roman Period*, vol. 3. New York: Pantheon Books.

Hurley, Amanda Kolson. 2002. The last days of James. Sidebar to Lemaire (2002) signed "A. K. H.," 32. (Hurley is an assistant editor of *BAR*.)

Jones, Mark, ed. 1990. *Fake? The Art of Deception*. Berkeley: The University of California Press, 258–261.

Laub, Karin. 2002. Ancient burial box isn't for sale, owner says. *Buffalo News*, November 8.

Lemaire, André. 2002. Burial box of James the brother of Jesus. *Biblical Archaeology Review*, 28:6 (November/December), 24–33, 70; sidebar 28.

Lupia, John. 2002. Quoted in Altman 2002a.

McCarter, P. Kyle. 2002. Quoted in Wilford 2002.

Nickell, Joe. 1990. *Pen, Ink and Evidence: A Study of Writing and Writing Materials for the Penman, Collector, and Document Detective*; reprinted New Castle, Delaware: Oak Knoll Press, 2000.

———. 1996. *Detecting Forgery*. Lexington, Ky.: University Press of Kentucky, 45–48, 96, 99–102.

Rosenfeld, Ammon, and Shimon Ilani. 2002. Letter to editor of *Biblical Archaeology Review*, September 17 (reproduced in Lemaire 2002).

Royal Ontario Museum. 2002. James ossuary display text, exhibit of November 15–December 29.

Ryan, Terri Jo. 2002. Baylor religion professors anxious to check out "James" bone box. *Tribune-Herald* (Waco, Texas), November 4.

Scrivener, Leslie. 2002. Expert skeptical about ossuary. *Toronto Star* (www.thestar.com), November 25.

Shuman, Ellis. 2002. "Brother of Jesus" bone-box plot thickens. Online at web.israelinsider.com. . . , November 5.

Sox, David. 1987. *Unmasking the Forger: The Dossena Deception*. London: Unwin Hyman, 8–9, 11, 37, 47, 90.

Van Biema, David. 2002. The brother of Jesus? *Time* magazine. Online at www.time.com. . . , October 27.

Wilford, John Noble. 2002. Experts question authenticity of bone box of "brother of Jesus." *New York Times*, December 3.

For Discussion and Writing

1. The *Biblical Archaeology Review* claimed on its cover that "scientists proved" the box was not a fake. How persuasive is such a claim for you?
2. What is patina, and why does it matter in this controversy? What is provenance? Explain how it plays a role in the tale of the box.
3. Who is Oded Golan? What is his role in the story? Evaluate his explanations. What warning bells do they trigger for you, if any?
4. What role do bacteria play in the author's evaluation of the bone box?
5. Suppose the bone box were actually proven to be authentic. What interest might this hold for Christians or Jews? What, if any, conclusions might be drawn from such an artifact?

The Media and Public Gullibility: Research and Writing Possibilities

1. *If television shows it, it's real.* That seems to be the attitude of some viewers, and maybe this isn't so strange when you consider that the airwaves are filled with shows that "investigate" paranormal stuff. There is actually a "Paranormal TV" web site that advertises such shows as *Mysterious World* and *Haunted History.* They also feature a show called *Ghost Hunters* hosted by two guys named Jason and Grant. One blurb for an episode invites guests to follow along as

> Jason and Grant meet Hester, a plantation employee. She relates to them the haunting tales that guests have reported, including: a wandering slave; seeing children's reflections in a mirror; a Confederate soldier by the pond; and the ghost of a murdered man who died on a staircase trying to reach his wife before he died. During the night, the team puts cameras in the most haunted areas of the plantation.
>
> Jason and Grant pick up a temperature change on the stairs with the thermal imaging camera, which shows something in front of them that they can't explain. On a slave path, the camera catches what appears to be a human torso passing in front of them. (http://paranormal.about.com)

   Write a paper that investigates current television fare presenting paranormal topics. Search through your local television guide to find shows focused on mystery and the paranormal. Visit network web sites to review ads for shows like these. Analyze the language and subjects so that you get a sense of the target audience. Who do you think are the likely viewers? What can you surmise about the audience's critical standards of proof?

2. John Edward, who claims to be able to communicate with dead people, has been presented on television doing just that . . . communicating with dead people. At least that's the idea behind his show, *Crossing Over.* One ad for the show claims "John Edward is an internationally acclaimed psychic medium who can communicate with the world beyond." Skeptics have described his shows as exercises in "cold reading." If you can, watch an episode of *Crossing Over,* but only after finding out about cold reading techniques. You can read an entry defining this term online at http://skeptic.com/coldread.html. Compare this information with Edward's performance and determine if Edward actually displays psychic powers.

3. Does your school library have any books about ghosts? Most are probably scholarly works about ghosts in Victorian imagination or ghosts as

metaphors in literature of one sort or another. But some may be like *Ghosts: True Encounters with the World Beyond*, by Hans Holzer. The back flap of this book promises that Dr. Holzer will not only introduce readers to ghosts, but also explain "why they seek contact with our world." Check out such a text and compare its "findings and evidence" with those from a text about alien abduction. For this latter type of book look into *The Threat* by David M. Jacobs, Ph.D., or any of the many such texts offered on Amazon.com. Do you see similarities between ghost and alien stories? Does either text offer what you consider definitive proof? What is the role of anecdote in convincing readers of the veracity of materials?

4. Have you seen the infamous alien autopsy video that seems to show doctors cutting into an unearthly creature? Fox television showed snippets of a 17-minute video in the 1990s, inviting viewers to make up their own minds about its credibility. If you can find a copy of the video online, view it in its entirety. Read a careful critique of the video, such as the cover story of the November/December 1995 *Skeptical Inquirer*. As of this writing this article can be accessed at http://www.csicop.org/si/9511/mediawatch.html. What flaws did skeptics find in the video? Should Fox network have detected these in advance of its showing? ABC's show *20/20* presented a story on the alien autopsy that was skeptical from the start. Write a paper about which approach to the video "evidence" better serves the public.

5. Do a database search for newspaper articles from the last year or so that deal with reports of ghost sightings. In fact, if you were to enter the term "ghost sightings" in the LexisNexis database searching back in a one-year period you would find hundreds of articles, among them items like "ASU Can Be a Spooky Place," which reports stories of ghosts haunting campuses. Other articles note that in Thailand, after the catastrophic tsunami of 2004, reports of ghosts haunting the beaches and nearby areas were common. Apparitions haunt the pages of newspapers, it seems. Read a couple dozen such accounts, then pick a half-dozen or so from these. You could vary the search term to "alien abduction" or "miraculous apparitions," too. Write an essay about the responsibilities of the press in covering such stories. Keep alert to the role of the stories themselves in the rise of public interest. Does the mere act of reporting fuel belief? Can news accounts be both objective and critical? Are reporters trained to question claims or just to report them? Can journalism survive without appealing to public hunger for tales of extraordinary phenomena?

CHAPTER 3

Alternative Medicine

While a unicorn's presence can be tested with a mere glance, remedies not based on physics cannot be tested at all.
—HOWARD FIENBERG

[Such] marketing targets people worried about the prospect of exposure to lethal biological or chemical weapons. The FTC is aware of no scientific basis for any of the self-treatment alternatives being marketed on the Internet.
—HOWARD BEALES, FTC DIRECTOR OF CONSUMER PROTECTION

For some people, alternative is another word for quackery. You can't blame them, when you consider that the alternative medicine tent covers some fairly bizarre acts, like iridology, whose practitioners claim to be able to diagnose illness by peering into the iris because every human organ has a counterpart in the iris. Urine therapy, also under the tent, recommends that patients drink a bit of their own urine in order to cure various ailments, perhaps excluding nausea. Psychic surgeons have a place in the alternative medicine show. Reiki and many other practices have a space under the tent. To add to the confusion, some creditable therapies like acupuncture and chiropractic are usually classified as alternative healing approaches, although they have large followings and a growing body of research to bolster their claims of effectiveness. The average person will not know which "alternatives" have actually been carefully tested.

It helps to be wary of claims about remedies and procedures, but a patient who hasn't been helped by traditional Western medicine may look for alternatives and might actually get relief from herbs or massages that Western doctors regard as unreliable at best. The patient whose tennis elbow eases up or vanishes altogether after a few acupuncture treatments will swear by that medicine even if there is little research to back up the technique. A desperately ill person may want to believe that his doctor can heal him by manipulating his cranial bones despite the lack of evidence that such manipulation can even be done. Sick people grasp at remedies that the healthy might ridicule. A coffee enema could be just the thing to reverse the ravages of colon cancer. Maybe a strict diet of asparagus and tea made from a home-grown fungus will accomplish what spinal fusion couldn't. Illness and pain tend to banish skepticism. Still, we ought to remember that Western medicine is based on doubt, and it has for centuries progressed according to the methods of Western science. That is, its claims are reviewed publicly and tested repeatedly. If an experiment or study result can't be replicated, it is dismissed from serious consideration. Ideally, a system of testing and peer review will lead to consensus, and this testing and review add a useful, critical habit of thinking to our culture. Without some kind of filter, all claims pass equally into circulation and acceptance.

Even a systematic, critical review of claims will not resolve all controversies, however. Sometimes, questions remain open for years. For example, in the 1970s some scientists claimed, on the basis of dubious research, that fluoridation of water was causing deaths by cancer. They weren't the first researchers to criticize the policy of adding fluoride to public drinking water as a tooth-decay inhibitor. But chance favored these anti-fluoridation efforts so much that spurious claims about fluoride made it into the *Congressional Record*.[1] Fears backed by flawed studies helped to keep fluoride out of some community waters, despite clear evidence that it reduced the incidence of tooth decay. These days, controversy over fluoridation persists, with experts lining up on either side of the issue. A quick Internet search of "fluoridation" will turn up numerous sites that oppose the practice. Looking into more formal publications will bring detailed arguments in favor of fluoridation. One article, whose primary audience is physicians, ends with an interesting word of caution:

> These recommendations are provided only as assistance for physicians making clinical decisions regarding the care of their

patients. As such, they cannot substitute for the individual judgment brought to each clinical situation by the patient's family physician. As with all clinical reference resources, they reflect the best understanding of the science of medicine at the time of publication, but they should be used with the clear understanding that continued research may result in new knowledge and recommendations.[2]

Research is open-ended in this matter, as it is in many critical areas. Doctors are advised to use individual judgment, and that is just as true for us, the lay people who look into alternative medicine. We have to think critically and apply skeptical tools to the claims we hear. That takes some work. Easy answers are the stock-in-trade of con artists and talk show entertainers.

The essays in this chapter present opportunities to hone a reader's skepticism regarding alternative medicine. In "What's That I Smell? The Claims of Aromatherapy," Lynn McCutcheon analyzes the recurrent themes she has found in her examination of books and articles on the subject. The popular attraction to magnetic cures is critiqued by James D. Livingston in "Magnetic Therapy: Plausible Attraction?" Harriet Hall employs a keen judgment and lively humor to take on therapies based on oxygen in "Oxygen Is Good—Even When It's Not There." Her second essay, "Wired to the Kitchen Sink: Studying Weird Claims for Fun and Profit," illustrates weaknesses and oddities found in the alternative "craniosacral therapy." Finally, there is an essay enthusiastically supporting the powers of homeopathy in general. Catherine Guthrie's "Homeopathy Finally Gets Some Respect" presents a contrast in method and belief to the other essays in this section.

Notes

1. A readable account of the general history of fluoridation efforts circa the mid-twentieth century can be found in *Health Quakery* published in 1980 by Consumers Union.
2. AAFT Position Paper: Fluoridation of Public Water Supplies. AFP May 1996, vol. 53, issue 7, pp. 2373–2376.

What's That I Smell? The Claims of Aromatherapy

LYNN MCCUTCHEON

Aromatherapy enjoys quite a popularity these days. A brief search of the market will turn up such titles as The Fragrant Mind *and* Holistic Aromatherapy for Animals. *The views of aromatherapists vary, but most share the belief that simply breathing certain fragrances can have healthful and medicinal benefits. In the following article, published in* Skeptical Inquirer *(May/June 1996), Lynn McCutcheon takes on the claims and methods of aromatherapy. McCutcheon has taught psychology for many years; when this article was published, she was on the adjunct faculty at Florida Southern College.*

— ✦ —

Aromatherapy typically involves putting a few drops of some pleasant-smelling, plant-derived oil in your bath water, sniffing it from an inhaler, or massaging it directly into your skin. I sampled a number of these "essential oils," as they are called, and I was impressed with their unique aromas. So what's the problem with smelling something fragrant while you are bathing or while you are getting massaged? According to John Meisenheimer, who practices dermatology in Orlando, Florida, a tiny percentage of the population is allergic to some essential oils. But for the rest of us, the answer is, "nothing." A small dose of aromatic oil probably won't hurt you a bit, and if you enjoy the smell, that's fine!

The problem lies with the claims made by aromatherapy's most widely known practitioners—claims that are causally confused, ambiguous, dubious, and unsupported by scientific evidence. After reading several books and articles written by the enthusiastic supporters of aromatherapy, I believe that there are some recurrent themes that are worth a closer look.

One such theme is what I call "confused causation." Virtually all aromatherapists claim that if you relax for several minutes in warm bath water to which has been added a few drops of essential oil, you will get out of the tub feeling pleasant. I agree, but what causes the pleasantness? Is it the warmth, the water, the minutes spent resting, the few drops of oil, or some combination thereof? It would be easy to conduct an experiment in order to find out, but for some strange reason aromatherapists haven't seen fit to do this. Instead, they imply that the essential oil is the main cause. Says Meisenheimer: "The amount of essential oil from a few drops placed in your bath that might actually penetrate the stratum corneum [skin] is probably too small to have any meaningful, systemic, physiologic effect."

Other examples of confused causation permeate aromatherapists' writings. Hoffmann (1987, p. 94) claims that chamomile is good for insomnia if taken in a late bath. Is it the lateness or the chamomile that makes you sleepy? For stress, Lavabre (1990, p. 108) recommends relaxation, a better diet, nutritional supplements, more exercise, and a few drops of an oil blend. Heinerman informs us (1988, p. 197) that jasmine oil massaged into the abdomen and groin promotes sexual stimulation. I'll bet it does, with or without the jasmine. On page 301 he suggests that to make unsafe water safe, boil it and add rosemary, sage, or thyme before drinking. The heat probably kills most of the germs. Edwards (1994, p. 135) mentions that many patients in hospitals in England receive massages with essential oils. According to her, "the relaxing and uplifting effect of the oils helps boost the morale of the patients." Isn't it possible that the massage did as much to boost morale as the oils did?

5   One of the favorite tactics employed by aromatherapists is the use of ambiguous claims. Any good psychic can tell you that you never make a specific prediction. You always leave yourself enough room so that whatever the outcome, you can claim success. Judging from what I read, the aromatherapists have mastered this strategy. Here are some of my favorites, followed by my brief commentary.

According to Frawley (1992, p. 155), incense "cleanses the air of negative energies." What are negative energies? The reader is encouraged to get massaged with oil regularly (p. 155) because this "keeps the nerves in balance." How would we know an unbalanced nerve if we saw one? Hoffmann tells us (p. 95) that *ylang ylang* is "supposedly an aphrodisiac." Is it or isn't it? Lavabre declares (p. 114) that benzain resinoid will "drive out evil spirits." I'd love to see that. Presumably spruce oil is an even better essence because it is recommended (p.64) "for any type of psychic work." Why limit yourself to evil spirits? Edwards (p. 134) quotes Visant Lad as saying that "life energy enters the body through breath taken through the nose." Is life energy the same thing as oxygen, and if so, why can't it enter through the mouth? About tea tree oil, Edwards opines (p. 135), "There is hope [it] may play a role in the successful treatment of AIDS." Is it hope or is it evidence? On the same page she tells readers that aromatherapy is good for "restoring harmony and balance between the mind and body." Such a phrase can mean almost anything you wish.

Not all of the claims are hopelessly ambiguous or unlikely to be true. I did a computer search of the psychological literature back to 1967, using the terms *essential oil, aromatherapy*; and the names of 23 common essences. I found that chamomile (Roberts and Williams 1992) can put people in a better mood, and lavender sometimes causes mistakes in arithmetic (Ludvigson and Rottman 1989). Furthermore, several of the odors used by aromatherapists are capable of producing physiological arousal as measured by electroencephalogram (EEG) recordings (Klemm et al. 1992); and emotional changes, as measured by self-report (Kikuchi et al. 1992; Nakano et al. 1992). Peppermint odor appears to be capable of causing very small EEG, electromyogram (EMG), and heart rate changes during sleep (Badia et al. 1990); and some odors can modify artificially induced sleep time in mice (Tsuchiya et al. 1991). There is evidence that specific odors can better enable one to recall information that was learned in the presence of that odor (Smith et al. 1992).

As a whole, these findings stretched to the limit would support only small craft, sailing cautiously near the shores of the aromatic sea. Unfortunately, some aromatherapists have been more than willing to sail boldly into uncharted waters. Consider these claims about specific essential oils, with my comments.

"A few drops of jasmine (Tisserand 1988, p. 87) cures postnatal depression." I didn't find any olfactory research that mentions postnatal depression. "Marjoram oil (Tisserand, p. 37) turns off sexual desire." The few studies I found that mentioned marjoram had nothing to do with sex. Price (1991, p. 93) tells us that juniper berry is "relaxing" and "stimulating" (both?), and she (p. 48) and Valnet (1982, p. 87) recommend lavender for insomnia. The Klemm study showed that lavender was both arousing and unpleasant. Hoffmann (p. 94) claims that *patchouli* is good for anxiety. My computer search of the word *patchouli* turned up nothing. Valnet (p. 70) claims that *ylang ylang* is good for one's sex drive. *Ylang ylang* didn't turn up anything either.

Other claims of dubious validity are common to the writings   10
of aromatherapists—broad claims that are related to the practice

of aromatherapy in general. The following claims are my words, but they represent a synthesis of views expressed by the authors listed.

- *Smell is the most direct route to the brain.* (Avery 1992; Edwards 1994; Green 1992; Raphael 1994). The implication is that smell is superior to the other senses because olfactory information gets to the brain quickest, and since aromatherapy is concerned with smell, it is a superior method of treatment. Olfactory information gets to the brain very quickly, but so does auditory, tactile, and visual information. The differences would certainly be measured in milliseconds, and it would have no practical consequence. The olfactory sense is directly linked to the limbic system—a portion of the brain concerned with emotionality and memories. The aromatherapists make much of this—the smell of ginger evokes memories of grandma's cookies, etc. What they don't tell you is that the sight of grandma's photo or hearing her voice can do the same. All the senses are part of a massive network that links all parts of the brain. Smell enjoys no particular advantage when it comes to access to or speed of access to various parts of the brain.
- *Natural oils are better than synthetic ones.* (Avery 1992; Edwards 1994; Hillyer 1994; Lavabre 1990; Price 1991; Raphael 1994; Rose 1988). Most of these authors felt it unnecessary to explain such a statement, but Lavabre told readers that "natural" molecules work better because they have memory (p. 49). It is possible to make a synthetic preparation identical on a molecular level to the most important compound in an essential oil. John Renner, who has heard many of the bizarre claims made by aromatherapists, told me that if the molecules are the same, "I doubt seriously that your body could tell the difference." Given that essential oils contain several compounds, it seems possible that a natural oil might have more than one active agent. If that is so, then aromatherapists should be spearheading the research effort to determine which chemical compounds are inducing the changes they claim are taking place. Instead, most of them seem all too willing to assume that natural oils are better, and that there is no need to defend this assertion with any rationale or research evidence.
- *Essential oils can help your memory.* (Hoffmann 1987; Lavabre 1990; Price 1991; Valnet 1982). I found no evidence to support this, and none of these authors provided a hint about how they arrived at that conclusion. Psychologist Elizabeth Loftus,

a world-renowned human memory expert, told me in a personal communication that she knows "of no cogent scientific evidence that smells cure amnesia, or that they strengthen memory." There is such a phenomenon as context-dependent learning. It has been shown that it is easier to remember X when you can return to the environment or context in which you learned X. Presumably, the context provides cues that make it easier to recall X. It has further been shown that at least one essential oil can serve as a contextual cue (Smith et al. 1992). If this is the basis for the above-mentioned claim, it is highly misleading. The essence itself is not important, only the fact that it was a significant part of the context in which the original learning took place. In other words, if the essence wasn't present when you learned X then it won't help you recall it later.

- *Scientists are doing a lot of research on essential oils.* (Avery 1992; Price 1991; Rose 1988; Valnet 1982). Statements like this are usually followed by specific claims. The implication is that these claims are supported by scientific research. As we saw earlier, that isn't necessarily true. Whether or not scientists really are doing a lot of research on essential oils is debatable. By comparison with fifty years ago, there is probably more research on essential oils today. By comparison with hearing and vision, research on the consequences of smelling essential oils lags way behind. If there really is a lot of research on the effects of essential oils, why is it that these authors are so reluctant to cite it? Their books and articles rarely list or mention any scientific journal articles. Instead, if there are any references at all they are to books written by other aromatherapists. All of this sounds as though I am strongly opposed to the use of essential oils. I'm not! If it pleases you to put some in your bath water or have a little rubbed on your back once in a while, by all means, go ahead. It is not the odor that arises from these fragrances that is troubling, it is the stench arising from the unwarranted claims made about them.

References

Avery, A. 1992. *Aromatherapy and You.* Kailua, HI: Blue Heron Hill Press.

Badia, P., et al. 1990. Responsiveness to olfactory stimuli presented in sleep. *Physiology and Behavior* 48: 87–90.

Edwards, L. 1994. Aromatherapy and essential oils. *Healthy and Natural Journal*, October, pp. 134–137.

Frawley, D. 1992. Herbs and the mind. In *American Herbalism: Essays on Herbs and Herbalism.* ed. by M. Tierra. Freedom, Calif: Crossing Press.

Green, M. 1992. Simpler scents: The combined use of herbs and essential oils. In *American Herbalism: Essays on Herbs and Herbalism*, ed. by M. Tierra. Freedom, Calif: Crossing Press.

Heinerman, J. 1988. *Heinermans Encyclopedia of Fruits, Vegetables, and Herbs.* West Nyack, N.Y.: Parker Publishing.

Hillyer, P. 1994. "Making $cents with Aromatherapy." *Whole Foods*, February, pp. 26–35.

Hoffmann, D. 1987. Aromatherapy. In *The Herbal Handbook.* Rochester, Vt.: Healing Arts Press.

Kikochi, A., et al. 1992. Effects of odors on cardiac response patterns and subjective states in a reaction time task. *Pychologica Folia* 51: 74–82.

Klemm, W. R. et al. 1992. Topographical EEG maps of human response to odors. *Chemical Senses* 17: 347–361.

Lavabre, M. 1990. *Aromatherapy Workbook.* Rochester, Vt.: Healing Arts Press.

Ludvigson, H., and T. Rottman. 1989. Effects of ambient odors of lavender and cloves on cognition, memory, affect and mood. *Chemical Sense* 14: 325–361.

Nakano, Y., et al. 1992. A study of fragrance impressions, evaluation and categorization. *Psychologica Folia* 51: 83–90.

Price, S. 1991. *Aromatherapy for Common Ailments.* New York: Simon and Schuster.

Raphael, A. 1994. "Ahh! Aromatherapy." *Delicious*, December, pp. 47–48.

Roberts, A., and J. Williams. 1992. The effect of olfactory stimulation on Fluency, vividness of imagery and associated mood: A preliminary study. *British Journal of Medical Psychology* 65: 197–199.

Rose, J. 1988. Healing scents from herbs: Aromatherapy. In *Herbal Handbook.* Escondido, Calif: Bernard Jensen Enterprises.

Smith, D. G., et al. 1992. Verbal memory elicited by ambient odor. *Perceptual and Motor Skills* 74: 339–343.

Tisserand, M. 1988. *Aromatherapy for Women.* Rochester, Vt.: Healing Arts Press.

Tsuchiya, T., et al. 1991. Effects of olfactory stimulation on the sleep time induced by pentobarbital administration in mice. *Brain Research Bulletin* 26: 397–401.

Valnet, J. 1982. *The Practice of Aromatherapy.* London: C.W. Daniel.

For Discussion and Writing

1. According to the author, what's the harm in enjoying pleasant scents? At what point does McCutcheon choose to argue with aromatherapists?
2. What does McCutcheon mean by "confused causation"? Think of a number of examples of this error from other areas of experience. How would you answer the questions McCutcheon raises about confused causation and aromatherapists' claims?
3. What are some of the claims that McCutcheon labels as ambiguous? Find several such claims in the advertisements of a popular magazine like *People* or *Good Housekeeping*. Why is the language in these ads, and in the claims for aromatherapy, ambiguous?
4. The author includes the claim of one practitioner that "life energy enters the body through breath taken through the nose," and then asks If "life energy is the same as oxygen." From a scientific point of view, what is the difference between life energy and oxygen? How is such language unclear?
5. One claim that the author presents skeptically is "Essential oils can help your memory." What do you think of such a claim? How might you test it formally? What kind of results would you expect from a product claiming to help you in this way? What kinds of foods, herbs, or fragrances have you used for medicinal or other benefits? Discuss your experiences.

Magnetic Therapy: Plausible Attraction?

JAMES D. LIVINGSTON

James D. Livingston now teaches in the Department of Materials Science and Engineering at the Massachusetts Institute of Technology, and was for more than 30 years a physicist at General Electric's Corporate Research and Development Center. He is the author of Driving Force: The Natural Magic of Magnets *(Harvard, 1996), a popular science book on the history, legends, science, and technology of magnets. Recently he and his wife, Sherry Penney, co-authored a biography of Martha Wright, an early abolitionist and women's rights advocate. His article "Magnetic Therapy: Plausible Attraction?" appeared in* Skeptical Inquirer *(July/August 1998). Note its formal tone and the manner in which Livingston remains open to possible therapeutic uses of magnetism.*

———————— ✦ ————————

A double-blind study at Baylor College of Medicine, published last November in *Archives of Physical and Rehabilitation Medicine* (Vallbona 1997), concluded that permanent magnets reduce pain in post-polio patients, and the results were heralded in *The New York Times* and on Bryant Gumbel's *Public Eye*. PBS's *Health Week* and *Time* magazine recently reported on the growing use of magnets by champion senior golfers and other professional athletes to relieve pain. Magnetic pain relief products are now sold in many golf shops, and ads for them appear in national golf and tennis magazines. Long a significant component of the health industry in Japan and China, magnetic therapy is becoming a more and more visible part of the alternative-medicine boom in the United States and Europe. Is it all just hokum, as many previously assumed, or is magnetic therapy becoming scientifically respectable?

EARLY HISTORY

For thousands of years, wonder and magic were associated with the mysterious forces exerted by natural magnets—magnetite-rich rocks, today called lodestones. Many trace magnetic therapy back to Paracelsus (1493–1543), a physician and alchemist who reasoned that since magnets have the power to attract iron, perhaps they can also attract diseases and leach them from the body. Charles Mackay, in *Extraordinary Popular Delusions and the Madness of Crowds* (1841), says of Paracelsus that "his claim to be the first of the magnetisers can scarcely be challenged." But Paracelsus was also aware of the important role of the patient's mind in the process of healing (Buranelli 1975). He wrote, "The spirit is the master, the imagination is the instrument, the body is the plastic material. The moral atmosphere surrounding the patient can have a strong influence on the course of the disease. It is not the curse or the blessing that works, but the idea. The imagination produces the effect." Paracelsus was apparently well aware of the placebo effect.

The development in eighteenth-century England of carbon-steel permanent magnets more powerful than lodestones brought renewed interest in the possible healing powers of magnets, and among those interested was Maximilian Hell, a professor of astronomy at the University of Vienna. Hell claimed several cures using steel magnets, but he was rapidly eclipsed by a friend who borrowed his magnets to treat a young woman suffering from a severe mental illness. The friend was Franz Anton Mesmer (1734–1815), and Mesmer's success with the "magnets from Hell" led directly to his widespread promotion of his theory of "animal magnetism." Although he first used actual magnets, he later found he could "magnetize" virtually anything—paper, wood, leather, water—and produce the same effect on patients. He concluded that the animal magnetism resided in himself, the various materials simply aiding the flow of the "universal fluid" between him and the patients.

Mesmer became so successful in Paris that in 1784 King Louis XVI established a Royal Commission to evaluate the claims of animal magnetism, a commission that included Antoine Lavoisier and Benjamin Franklin among its members. They conducted a series of experiments and concluded that all the observed effects could be attributed to the power of suggestion, and that "the practice of magnetization is the art of increasing the imagination by degrees." Thomas Jefferson, arriving in Paris soon after the Commission report, noted in his journal: "Animal magnetism is dead, ridiculed."

Ridiculed, perhaps, but not dead. Mesmer himself faded from public view, but "magnetizing" persisted in various forms. Many early magnetizers evolved into students of hypnosis and developed various forms of hypnotherapy. (The trance induced in many of Mesmer's patients is thought to be what is now called a hypnotic trance, and most dictionaries today list mesmerism as a synonym for hypnotism.) One American who became interested in magnetic healing was Daniel David Palmer, who opened Palmer's School of Magnetic Cure in Iowa in the 1890s. His ideas developed into the system of hands-on therapy known as chiropractic. Others focused on hand gestures without actual touch, an approach recently reborn as "therapeutic touch." Mary Baker Eddy was "cured" by a magnetizer, but she later became convinced that cures could best be achieved through prayer, and founded Christian Science.

Most of these byproducts of mesmerism, like Mesmer himself, 5 ceased to use actual magnets. But the development of electrical technology in the late nineteenth century impressed the general public with the mysterious powers of electric and magnetic fields, and therapeutic magnets had a rebirth, with many "doctors" promoting magnets to relieve pain, enhance sleep, and cure a wide variety of diseases. The most notable of these was Dr. C. J. Thacher, whom *Collier's Magazine* dubbed "King of the magnetic quacks" (Macklis 1993). His 1886 mail-order catalogue offered a variety of magnetic garments, and a complete costume contained more than 700 magnets, which provided "full and complete protection of all the vital organs of the body."

In the twentieth century, materials scientists and engineers have developed stronger and stronger permanent magnets—alnico magnets in the 1930s, ferrite (ceramic) magnets in the 1950s, and rare-earth magnets in the 1970s and 1980s. The latest rare-earth magnets, neodymium-iron-boron, are more than a hundred times more powerful than the steel magnets available in the last century to Edison, Bell, and C. J. Thacher (Livingston 1996). Both ferrite magnets and the latest "neo" magnets have had a tremendous impact on modern technology, but they have also restimulated interest in the use of permanent magnets for magnetic therapy. Most magnetic therapy products today, like most refrigerator magnets, contain inexpensive ferrite magnets, but many suppliers offer neodymium "supermagnets" in their top-of-the-line products.

MAGNETIC THERAPY TODAY

Both ferrite and rare-earth magnets, unlike earlier magnetic materials such as steels and alnicos, have great resistance to demagnetization, allowing thin disks to be magnetized. (Earlier magnets had to be long and thin to avoid being demagnetized by the internal fields produced by the poles at the ends.) This feature allows modern magnets to be mounted in a variety of thin products that can be applied to the body with the magnetic field emanating from the surface.

Some suppliers recommend applying magnetic patches directly to your aches and paints, while others recommend applying small Band-Aid-like patches to acupuncture points. Magnetic belts containing sixteen or more magnets are purported to ease back pain, and similar magnetic wraps are offered for almost any part of the body, including hands, wrists, elbows, knees, ankles, and feet (magnetic insoles are particularly popular). For headaches you can wear magnetic headbands, magnetic earrings, or magnetic necklaces. (One company marketing magnetic necklaces provides simple instructions: the necklace should be put on as soon as the headache appears and removed as soon as it goes away. Since most headaches come and go, following these instructions precisely will clearly produce persuasive evidence of the necklace's efficacy.)

Many magnetic necklaces, bracelets, and earrings are formed from silver- and gold-rich magnetic alloys and promoted as both fashionable and therapeutic. One catalog claims magnetic earrings "stimulate nerve endings that are associated with head and neck pain," and magnetic bracelets "act upon the body's energy field" and "correct energy imbalances brought by electro-magnetic contamination or atmospheric changes." Larger items include magnetic seat cushions, magnetic pillows, and magnetic mattress pads, the last claiming to produce an "energizing sleep field." One supplier offers a PCD—Prostate Comfort Device for older men. If properly placed while you sit watching television or driving your car, you will no longer have to get out of bed several times a night to relieve yourself!

To avoid trouble with the Food and Drug Administration, most   10 suppliers emphasize only "comfort" and usually specifically state "no medical claims are made." Some, however, are far less careful. One company in Kansas markets a book entitled *Curing Cancer With Supermagnets*. The authors of the book claim to have cured cancer simply by hanging a neodymium "supermagnet" around the patient's neck. The cancer discussed in the advertisement was a breast cancer, but they report that "the supermagnets influence the whole body" and "our method can cure all types of cancer."

Many magnetic therapy products have alternating arrays of north and south poles facing the patient. Some have detailed explanations of why a circular pattern of poles is optimal, while others offer poles in checkerboard or triangular patterns. Nikken, the Japan-based firm that has used a multilevel marketing scheme to expand from an annual business in the U.S. of $3 million in 1989 to $150 million today, primarily offers products with alternating poles.

One clear difference between such multipolar magnetic devices and unipolar devices (with only one pole facing the patient) is the "reach" of the magnetic field. The field from even unipolar magnets decreases very rapidly with increasing distance from the magnet, but the field from multipolar magnets decreases much more rapidly. If multipolar magnets really have any effects on the human body, they will be limited to depths of penetration of only a few millimeters. (Many refrigerator magnets are multipolar, which limits the thickness of paper they can hold to the refrigerator, but also limits the damage they can do to nearby credit and ATM cards.)

Other suppliers offer only unipolar magnets, and some emphasize the importance of having only south-seeking poles facing the body. Contrary to common scientific usage, they call south-seeking poles north poles. Since opposite poles attract, they argue that a pole that seeks south must be a north pole. (Here practitioners of magnetic therapy are perhaps more logical than mainstream science, which calls the south-seeking pole a south pole, requiring that the earth's magnetic pole in Antarctica is, by the standard scientific terminology, a north pole.) Dr. Buryl Payne, in his book *The Body Magnetic* (1988), argues that south-seeking poles calm tissue but north-seeking poles stimulate tissue, and you should therefore never expose tumors or infections to north-seeking poles. When I suggested to one practitioner that different effects from different poles seemed to violate basic rules of symmetry, he assured me that the rules were reversed in the southern hemisphere.

One of the most ardent advocates of magnetic therapy is Dr. William Philpott of Oklahoma, who publishes his own Magnetic Energy Quarterly. He is also on the board of the Bio-Electro-Magnetics Institute of Reno, Nevada, a nonprofit "research and educational organization" and an advisor to the NIH Office of Alternative Medicine. His wife happens to have a business selling "Polar Power Magnets." Dr. Ronald Lawrence of California is President of the North American Academy of Magnetic Therapy and reports that he has successfully used magnets to relieve pain in hundreds of his patients. He is associated with Magnetherapy, a Florida company that markets "Tectonic Magnets." Both Dr. Philpott and Dr. Lawrence favor unipolar magnets.

15   The efficacy of magnetic therapy (or of any other medical treatment, mainstream or alternative) does not depend on our understanding the biological mechanism. Nevertheless most promoters of magnetic therapy recognize the need for offering some plausible explanation. The mechanism most commonly offered for various therapeutic effects of magnets is improved blood circulation, despite a lack of clear evidence for such an effect. Other suggestions include alteration of nerve impulses, increased oxygen content and increased alkalinity of bodily fluids, magnetic forces on moving ions, and decreased deposits on the walls of blood vessels.

The broadest explanation was presented by Dr. Kyochi Nakagawa of Japan, who claims that many of our modern ills result from "Magnetic Field Deficiency Syndrome." Earth's magnetic field is known to have decreased about 6 percent since 1830, and indirect evidence suggests that it may have decreased as much as 30 percent over the last millennium. He argues that magnetic therapy simply provides some of the magnetic field that Earth has lost.

Magnetic therapy is also prominent in the treatment of thoroughbred racehorses. An injured racehorse represents potential loss of a substantial investment, providing considerable incentive to try "alternative medicine" to supplement mainstream veterinary treatment. Magnetic pads for a variety of leg problems, magnetic blankets, magnetic hoof pads, etc., all get ringing endorsements from many horse trainers—and even some veterinarians. One marketer of magnetic products for humans reports that he first became convinced of their effectiveness when he used them on his ailing llama! Enthusiasts argue that the placebo effect could not be effective on horses or other animals, but forget that it may influence the human who is interpreting the effect of magnetic therapy on the animal.

THE BAYLOR STUDY

These examples and the centuries-old connection between magnets and quackery, have led many to consider modern magnetic therapy as total hokum, with the many testimonials for the success of magnetic treatments explainable by placebo effects. But the Baylor study, seemingly a careful double-blind study, has surprised many.

The study was conducted by Dr. Carlos Vallbona on fifty postpolio patients at Baylor's Institute for Rehabilitation Research in Houston. Bioflex, Inc., of Corpus Christi provided both the magnets (multipolar, circular pattern) and a set of visually identical sham magnets to serve as controls. To keep the study "double-blind" neither the patients nor the staff were informed as to which devices were active magnets, and which were shams. Before and after the forty-five-minute period of magnet therapy, the patients were asked to grade their pain on a scale from 0 to 10. The twenty nine patients with active magnets reported, on average, a significant reduction of pain (from 9.6 to 4.4), while the twenty-one patients with shams reported a much smaller average reduction (from 9.5 to 8.4). This is a substantial difference, and if the double-blind study was successfully conducted, cannot be explained by a placebo effect.

For a hardened skeptic, some doubts remain. Both Dr. Vallbona   20
and his colleague, Dr. Carlton Hazlewood, had reported the successful personal use of magnets to relieve their own knee pains prior to the study, raising doubts as to their objectivity. Conscious or unconscious biases of researchers can have very subtle and unrecognized effects on the results of their studies, and a serious

difficulty of conducting any double-blind studies with magnets is the ease of distinguishing active magnets from sham magnets (although the patients were reportedly observed during the therapy period to assure that they were not surreptitiously testing their magnets). Another difficulty of any studies of pain relief is the highly subjective nature of the data.

Despite these various reasons for caution, the results of this study have altered the views of many physicians. Dr. William Jarvis, president of the National Council Against Health Fraud, had formerly dismissed magnet therapy as "essentially quackery." He now tentatively admits that it may have value for post-polio pain.

More studies will be needed before magnetic therapy will be accepted by a majority of the medical community, and some studies are already underway. Last year the NIH Office of Alternative Medicine gave a million-dollar grant to Dr. Ann Gill Taylor of the School of Nursing of the University of Virginia to study the use of magnets to relieve pain. Among other things, she will be testing the effectiveness of magnetic sleep pads in relieving pain in patients suffering from fibromyalgia, a common disease involving joint and muscle pain. While we wait for the results of these and other studies, does what we know about magnetic fields and the human body make it plausible that magnetic therapy for pain might have a physical basis beyond mind/body effects?

MAGNETIC FIELDS AND THE BODY

The electrochemical processes of the human body are extremely complex and incompletely understood, and physical effects of magnetic fields cannot be ruled out. Many thousands of papers have in fact been published on biological effects of electromagnetic fields, much of it focused on the effects of radio-frequency and microwave fields or, in recent years, on fields at power-line frequencies (fifty or sixty cycles per second). Studies of biological effects of steady magnetic fields (reviewed by Frankel and Liburdy 1996) have concentrated mostly on high fields of the level encountered in MRI magnets, typically of the order of 10,000 gauss (1 tesla). Unfortunately, research has been very limited at field levels typical of magnetic therapy products, most of which are limited to a few hundred gauss, even at the magnet surface. (Earth's field is a bit less than half a gauss.)

Viewed simply as inert material, the human body, like its primary constituent, water, is *diamagnetic*, i.e., weakly repelled by magnetic fields. In response to an applied magnetic field, the electrons in water molecules make slight adjustments in their motions, producing a net magnetic field in the opposing direction about 100,000 times smaller than the applied field. With the removal of the applied field, the electrons return to their original orbits, and the water molecules once again become nonmagnetic. (We perhaps should note that some promoters of magnetic therapy also promote "magnetized water." You can't magnetize water. Although water responds weakly to an applied field, the response disappears as soon as the field is removed.) Although the diamagnetism of water and most living things is very weak, a high-field electromagnet producing 160,000 gauss (16 tesla) at the center of the coil has recently been used to levitate not only water drops but also flowers, grasshoppers, and small frogs (Berry and Geim 1997), the "flying frogs" drawing worldwide media coverage. Since fields of that magnitude are required to balance gravitational forces, the much lower fields of magnetic-therapy devices can only produce diamagnetic forces that are thousands of times smaller than gravity. (The repulsive force will be proportional to the product of the field and the field gradient.)

Some dubious literature suggests that magnetic fields   25
attract blood, citing all the iron it contains. However, iron in the blood is very different from metallic iron, which is strongly magnetic because the individual atomic magnets are strongly coupled together by the phenomenon we call *ferromagnetism*. The remarkable properties of ferromagnetic materials are a result of the cooperative behavior of many, many magnetic atoms acting in unison. The iron in blood consists instead of isolated iron atoms within large hemoglobin molecules, located inside the red blood cells. Although each of the iron atoms is magnetic, it is not near other iron atoms, and remains magnetically independent.

The net effect of the weak *paramagnetism* of the isolated iron atoms in hemoglobin is only a slight decrease in the overall diamagnetism of blood. Blood, like water, is weakly repelled by magnetic fields, not attracted.

Although most components of the human body and other living things are weakly diamagnetic, many organisms have been shown to contain small amounts of strongly magnetic materials, usually magnetite (Fe_3O_4). The most extreme case is that of magnetotactic bacteria, originally found in mud collected from the marshes of Cape Cod. Each contains a long chain of magnetite particles that interact strongly enough with Earth's magnetic field to orient the bacteria along the field. Magnetite crystals have also been found in pigeons, honeybees, many mammals, and even in the human brain, but in proportionately much smaller amounts than in the bacteria. It seems very unlikely that there is enough magnetite within the human body to provide a possible mechanism to explain magnetic therapy. However, if magnetite particles were located at strategic places, they could locally amplify the effects of low magnetic fields and, for example, modify ion flow across cell membranes, of the type involved with electrical transmission in nerve cells.

More likely mechanisms are those based on magnetic forces on moving charged particles, possibly including ions or charged molecules in flowing blood, moving across cell membranes, moving across synapses between nerve cells, etc., or those based on more subtle effects on biochemical reactions (Frankel and Liburdy 1996). Although no physical mechanisms for magnetic therapy have been established, the possibilities are numerous and complex. Only further clinical tests, carefully controlled to account for placebo effects, can confirm or dispute the results of the Baylor study and prove or disprove the claims of magnetic therapy.

Some media reports have not sufficiently distinguished the Baylor form of magnetic therapy, based on modest static fields from permanent magnets, with a more accepted form of "magnetic therapy" based on high pulsed magnetic fields from electromagnets (Malmivuo and Plonsey 1995). Pulsed magnetic fields are very different from static magnetic fields, because, via Maxwell's equations, time-varying magnetic fields induce electric fields. Electric fields have pronounced biological effects, particularly on nerve and muscle cells, as we have known since the days of Galvani and his twitching frogs' legs. Many years ago the FDA approved the use of pulsed magnetic fields in "bone growth stimulators" for the treatment of fractures that were slow to heal, and research on "magnetic stimulation"—pulsed magnetic fields applied to the brain or other components of the nervous system—has grown rapidly in recent years. Transcranial magnetic stimulation, in which the patient receives hundreds of magnetic field pulses of 1 tesla or more, each only a millisecond in duration, has shown considerable promise as a means of treating depression. However, these forms of pulsed-field magnetic therapy are based on biological effects of induced electric fields, and are very different from the use of the static fields from permanent magnets.

CONCLUSIONS

Claims of therapeutic effects of permanent magnets should still 30
be regarded with considerable skepticism. Most of the many testimonials to the effectiveness of magnetic therapy devices can be attributed to placebo effects and to other effects accompanying their use. For example, the magnetic back braces used by many senior golfers may help ease their back pains through providing mechanical support, through localized warming, and through constant reminder to the aging athletes that they are no longer young and should not overexert their muscles. All these effects are helpful with or without magnets. One British study of pulsed-field bone-growth stimulators, which were approved decades ago by the FDA, found that they were equally successful when the devices were not activated (Barker 1984), and concluded that their effectiveness resulted from the enforced inactivity associated with their use, rather than from the pulsed magnetic fields.

The more extreme claims of magnetic therapy, such as curing cancer by hanging supermagnets around your neck, are not only nonsense but also dangerous, since they may divert patients from seeking appropriate treatment from mainstream medicine. Magnetic jewelry and most other magnetic-therapy products probably are harmless beyond a waste of money. Several years ago, a double-blind study found that magnetic necklaces produced no relief of neck or shoulder pain (Hong 1982).

The results of the Baylor study, however, raise the possibility that at least in some cases, topical application of permanent magnets may indeed be useful in pain relief, a conclusion that should be regarded as tentative until supported by further studies. Any mechanism for such an effect remains mysterious, but an effect of static magnetic fields on the complex electrochemical processes of the human body is not impossible. My own guess is that inexpensive refrigerator magnets are as likely to provide help as the more expensive magnets marketed specifically for therapy. (But since human nature leads us to expect more from more expensive items, use of refrigerator magnets will probably decrease the placebo effect!)

References

Barker, A. T. et al. 1984. Pulsed magnetic field therapy for tibial non-union. *Lancet* 994–996.

Berry, M. V. and A. K. Geim. 1997. Of flying frogs and levitrons. *Eur. J. Phys.* 18: 307–313.

Buranelli, V. 1975. *The Wizard from Vienna.* Coward, McCann & Geoghegan.

Frankel, Richard B. and Robert P. Liburdy. 1996. Biological effects of static magnetic fields (in *Handbook of Biological Effects of Electromagnetic Fields*, second edition, Charles Polk and Elliot Postow, eds. CRC Press).

Hong, C. Z. et al. 1982. Magnetic necklace: Its therapeutic effectiveness on neck and shoulder pain. *Archives of Physical Medicine and Rehabilitation* 63: 162–164.

Livingston, James D. 1996. Driving Force: *The Natural Magic of Magnets.* Harvard University Press.

Mackay, Charles. [1841] 1932. *Extraordinary Popular Delusions and the Madness of Crowds.* Reprint, L. C. Page.

Macklis, Roger M. 1993. Magnetic healing, quackery, and the debate about the health effects of electromagnetic fields. *Annals of Internal Medicine* 118(5): 376–383.

Malmivuo, Jaakko and Robert Plonsey. 1995. *Bioelectromagnetism: Principles and applications of bioelectric and biomagnetic fields.* Oxford University Press.

Payne, Buryl. 1988. *The Body Magnetic* (self-published).

Vallbona, Carlos, Carlton F. Hazlewood, and Gabor Jurida. 1997. Response of pain to static magnetic fields in postpolio patients: A double-blind pilot study. *Archives of Physical and Rehabilitation Medicine* 78(11): 1200–1203.

For Discussion and Writing

1. The author quotes Paracelsus, a sixteenth-century physician who favored the medicinal application of magnets. What did Paracelsus mean, in your view, by noting that spirit, imagination, and body work together in matters of disease and healing? How does such a view differ from simply claiming a placebo effect for any remedy?

2. Livingston provides a brief history of magnets and medicine in his essay. Since none of this actually explains how magnets heal various ailments, what does this contribute to your understanding of the issue? What might such research tell you about the differences between skeptical inquiry and mere naysaying?

3. If some companies claim that magnets can cure cancer, what sort of questions would you raise? What would you be alert to in accounts of cancer-healing magnetic therapy?
4. What was the Baylor Study? What part of its findings strike you as noteworthy? What does Livingston mean when he refers to the highly subjective nature of the data in the study? What do you make of Dr. William Jarvis' shift in position regarding magnet therapy?
5. Livingston leads his readers with a question: "Does what we know about magnetic fields and the human body make it plausible that magnetic therapy for pain might have a physical basis beyond mind/body effects?" Summarize his answer, noting its detailed points, for example, that iron in the blood differs considerably from metallic iron. Consider why such points matter.
6. Among his many interesting points, the author notes a difference between pulsed magnetic fields and the static fields of permanent magnets. How difficult do you find it to follow such distinctions? In general, characterize the intellectual demands that the author makes on you, his attentive reader.

Oxygen Is Good—Even When It's Not There

HARRIET HALL

Harriet Hall has a medical degree and writes articles in a skeptical vein that can be found online at Quackfiles.com. In noting the difference between subjective and external reality, Hall writes, "when a person experiences a result and thinks he knows the cause, that is his external reality. Science addresses the external reality accessible to all who share our material world." In the following piece, published in Skeptical Inquirer *in 2004, she argues that claims for the medical efficacy of certain oxygen-based cures are unsubstantiated, and even ludicrous. They are also quite popular. Sometimes the internal reality is more compelling to people.*

---◆---

Oxygen is not just in the air; it's on the shelves. It has been discovered by alternative medicine and is being sold in various forms in the health supplement marketplace. Back when I was an intern, we used to joke that there were four basic rules of medicine:

1. Air goes in and out.
2. Blood goes round and round.
3. Oxygen is good.
4. Bleeding always stops.

Alternative medicine has latched onto rule number three and won't let go. The rationale, apparently, is that oxygen is required to support life; therefore more oxygen should make you more healthy. It's not clear how this relates to alternative medicine's advice on anti-oxidants, but that's irrelevant.

OXYGEN IS GOOD, so we should put it in our soft drinks and breathe it at oxygen bars. Take an oxygen tank home with you—you might feel better. The oxygen vendor might feel better, too. Dr. Andrew Weil, the renowned health guru, tells patients with chronic fatigue to ask their doctors to prescribe oxygen for a home trial. Sure, why not? The money it costs will literally vanish "into thin air," but who cares? OXYGEN IS GOOD.

Ignore the fact that you could find out whether you need oxygen by testing your blood oxygen saturation with that little-clip-thingy-they-stick-on-your-finger-in-the-ER (aka pulse oximeter). Who cares if your blood is fully saturated with oxygen already? OXYGEN IS GOOD. If your oxygen saturation is a little less than 100 percent, there is no evidence that raising it will help with anything. If it is a lot less, and you do need oxygen, any competent doctor should be able to figure that out. But try an oxygen tank anyway: OXYGEN IS GOOD. Is this starting to sound like a mantra? It should. This is religious belief I am talking about, not science.

OXYGEN THERAPIES

5   Just breathing oxygen is boring: any dumb animal can do that. Why not drink it? Alternative medicine found ways to use oxygen in a liquid form. No, not liquid oxygen; that's kind of chilly (around minus 298 degrees Fahrenheit). You could buy a $1,600 home water cooler to infuse oxygen into your drinking water and call that liquid oxygen. Or you could use chemicals that release oxygen. Ozone gives off oxygen. So do hydrogen peroxide and chlorite compounds. They're corrosive chemicals, but if you mix them with liquid and drink them, they will release friendly little oxygen bubbles in your stomach and dilution will counteract the corrosive effect. Corrosion may be bad, but OXYGEN IS GOOD.

Proponents of hydrogen peroxide found it worked wonders for everything from multiple sclerosis and cancer to hemorrhoids and the common cold. They tried bathing in it, drinking it, injecting it into their veins, and pumping it up their rectums. The proponents of hydrogen peroxide never reported any adverse effects. On the other hand, the medical literature reported that hydrogen peroxide caused deaths from gas embolism, gangrene, seizures, strokes, and other complications. How could that be? Didn't those scientists know that OXYGEN IS GOOD?

Could oxygen cure cancer and AIDS? They tried ozone by enema. They tried oxygen under pressure in a hyperbaric chamber. They even put cancer patients into a coma with overdoses of insulin in the hope that it would somehow regulate oxygen delivery to the cancer cells. Scientists insisted there was no proof that these therapies worked, but they couldn't prove to the true believers that they *didn't* work. Scientists insisted that these therapies could be harmful, but how could anything as natural as oxygen possibly be harmful? OXYGEN IS GOOD.

Invention proceeded apace. Alternative "science" found a way to put "electrically activated" oxygen in water. No one knows what "activated oxygen" means, but it *sounds* impressive. OXYGEN IS GOOD, and if it's activated it ought to be even better.

Once it has been "activated" in water, you can take oxygen safely and conveniently in the form of drops. You can put a few drops under your tongue, or drink them in a glass of water, and you will feel better. Of course, the amount of oxygen in a few drops of water is many orders of magnitude less than that contained in every breath. Of course, little or no oxygen is absorbed from the stomach. But fish get their oxygen from water, and if fish can do it, we ought to be able to do it too, gills or not! OXYGEN IS GOOD. They recommend that you drink it, spray it in your nose, gargle with it, spray it on cuts, spray some on your houseplants, and spray it on vegetables, chicken, seafood, and pork to decontaminate them. You can even use it as a natural alternative to antibiotics or give it to your pets to prevent doggy breath. OXYGEN IS GOOD—for just about everything.

SELLING OXYGEN—EVEN WITHOUT OXYGEN

Several brands of activated oxygen appeared on the market, each better than all the rest. Finally, one company came up with the best idea yet. They would sell plain water with a bit of salt   10 and a trace of minerals, charge $10 an ounce for it, and *pretend* it contained activated oxygen.

The Rose Creek Company marketed oxygenated water without any oxygen in it. They said so themselves. Actually they claimed there was oxygen in it that "couldn't be detected" in the laboratory. Their excuse was that the precision equipment couldn't measure *over* 40 ppm of oxygen. I guess if they pour a whole pot of coffee into their coffee cup, the cup stays empty; and if they overinflate their tires they create a vacuum. This probably has something to do with homeopathy or an alternate reality. OXYGEN IS GOOD, even if the lab can't find it.

They called it "Vitamin O." They claimed that it would effectively prevent and treat pulmonary disease, headaches, infections, flu, colds, and even cancer. They claimed that it regulates metabolism, aids digestion, relaxes the nervous system, boosts energy, promotes sound sleep, and sharpens concentration and memory. They were selling 50,000 bottles a month until the Federal Trade Commission (FTC) spoiled the fun. A consent agreement required them to pay $375,000 for consumer redress and to stop making false statements. They were prohibited from "making any unsupported representation that the effectiveness of 'Vitamin O' is established by medical or scientific research or studies."

They changed the name of their company to R-Garden, Inc. and modified their ads, but they weren't happy. They knew that OXYGEN IS GOOD (it was definitely good for business), and they really wanted some scientific studies so they could thumb their noses at the FTC; so they hired the first scientist they could find who would stop laughing long enough to do some tests. They had to settle for an anthropologist. He reasoned that the oxygen that wasn't there should raise the blood oxygen level of people with anemia. So he decided to measure the partial pressure of oxygen and carbon dioxide in arterial blood (PaO_2 and $PaCO_2$), hypothesizing that both would rise with "Vitamin O," but not with placebo. This next bit is going to be a little technical, so you may skip the next two paragraphs if you wish.

If you are anemic, you have less hemoglobin to carry oxygen. But the blood gases, the PaO_2 and $PaCO_2$, have nothing to do with hemoglobin or anemia. They are measures of gas pressure, not of total oxygen carried by hemoglobin. So people with anemia should have a normal PaO_2. They might be able to raise their PaO_2 a little by hyperventilating, but this would lower their $PaCO_2$.

15   Anemic patients *do not* have low PaO_2 measurements. In this study, all of the anemic patients *did* have low baseline PaO_2.

The researcher didn't notice that this was abnormal. When subjects took "Vitamin O" their PaO_2 went up, but mostly not up to normal. A couple of them developed a PaO_2 of over 100 mm Hg, which is not generally thought to be possible on room air without serious hyperventilation. He didn't notice anything unusual about this. He also discovered that the $PaCO_2$ went up right along with the PaO_2. Ordinarily this would indicate hypoventilation, possibly from severe lung disease, but he wasn't alarmed. He thought it would eliminate more nasty waste matter and would probably cause "greater youthfulness, improved mobility, better circulation, sharper mental clarity, enhanced heart and lung functions, and increased physical energy." (Huh?) Of course, in several patients the CO_2 went *down* as the PaO_2 went up, but this didn't bother him. Apparently he believes, with Ralph Waldo Emerson, that a foolish consistency is the hobgoblin of little minds.

He concluded that he had definitely proved that oxygen is present in "Vitamin O." In other words, if you find unexplained abnormal blood gas values and they change in a way that wouldn't be caused by increased oxygen intake, that proves that oxygen intake was increased, which proves that the increased oxygen intake had to come from the "Vitamin O." His logic didn't work any better than his blood gas analyzers.

His subjects were all Hutterites, members of an Anabaptist sect who live communally in groups of 60–150 on collective farms, mainly in the western U.S. and Canada, and who remain aloof from outside society. He didn't explain how he persuaded them not to remain aloof from his experimental interventions. He noted that "no protocol or consent forms" were needed, since the head minister could make all the decisions for his flock and just order them to cooperate. It seems that Hutterites make even better experimental subjects than prisoners, because you have to get informed consent from prisoners. He didn't bother with any statistical analysis of his data. He didn't provide any references. He didn't expect that anyone would try to replicate his findings. As far as he was concerned, his definitive experiment had proved once and for all that there was oxygen in "Vitamin O." He broke just about every rule of scientific experimentation. After all, he wasn't searching for scientific truth, just for enough words on paper to meet the FTC's requirements.

In another study, the same researcher discovered an unbelievably high incidence of chronic fatigue syndrome among the Hutterites, and found that "Vitamin O" relieved their symptoms

better than placebo. In his report of that study he gave an intriguing definition of his experimental method:
"The three key features of this approach in assessing the efficacy of natural man-made substance [sic] were employed here: randomization, blindedness, and measurement of predetermined outcomes."

20   I don't know what a "natural man-made substance" is; I agree that some kind of "blindedness" was at work; and if the outcomes were truly "predetermined," that would explain a lot.

In essence, the company funded studies that pretended to be scientific so they could pretend to have proven that the pretend oxygen in their product is really there (and that it really works). This kind of fuzzy thinking is typical of alternative medicine advocates. They ask you to maintain your health with preventive, natural treatments that have not been proven effective, and to mistrust conventional medical treatments that have been proven effective. They exploit fears of pollution, food additives, pesticides, and side effects from pharmaceuticals. They play the science game to appease their critics, but they don't really believe in science: they believe that truth can be accessed through intuition. They seldom disprove theories or report negative results; they rarely search for alternative explanations, suggest that further studies be done for confirmation, or seek peer review. They believe in the mystical ability of the body to heal itself through communication with the vital forces of the universe. How could science understand these complex, holistic phenomena? Scientists aren't even smart enough to sell water for $10 an ounce.

Science doesn't know everything. Intuition counts for something, doesn't it? There are more ways of knowing than scientists can imagine. Anyway, isn't scientific "truth" wishy-washy? Newton contradicted Copernicus, and Einstein contradicted Newton. Paradigms are shifty. Eventually scientists will have to give up their materialistic theories and will come to understand that the Universe is just one big mind interconnected by a continuum of ineffable cosmic quantum something-or-others.

Proponents of alternative oxygen therapy will never be convinced it doesn't work. As Lewis Carroll explained in *Alice in Wonderland*, practice makes perfect:

"One can't believe impossible things."
"I daresay you haven't had much practice," said the Queen.
"When I was your age, I always did it for half-an-hour a day.

Why, sometimes I've believed as many as six impossible things before breakfast."

"Vitamin O" is still being sold. Testimonials abound. You can't argue with true believers. OXYGEN IS GOOD.

Further Reading

Barrett, Stephen. FTC Attacks "Stabilized Oxygen Claims." Online at www.quackwatch.org/04ConsumerEducation/News/vitamino.html.

FTC Charges. Online at www.ftc.gov/os/1999/9903/rosecreekcmp. html.

FTC Consent Agreement. Online at www.ftc.gov/os/2000/05/index. htm.

Hall, Harriet, 2003. A Failed Attempt to Prove That There Is Oxygen it 'Vitamin O.' *The Scientific Review of Alternative Medicine* (7)1:29–33.

Heinerman, John. Electrically-activated oxygen supplementation selectively improves energy efficiency in Hutterites demonstrating classic symptoms of chronic fatigue syndrome. Online at www.rosecreekvitamino.comchronic_fatigue.html.

Heinerman, John. Proving the existence of elemental oxygen in a liquid nutritional product ("Vitamin O") through blood gas analyses of therapy/placebo-supplemented Hutterites. Online at www.brunnerbiz.com/vitamino

Marks, Stan. Vitamin O? Online at www.brunnerbiz.com/vitamino

For Discussion and Writing

1. Hall repeats the claim OXYGEN IS GOOD. Why? How does it affect your view of her argument? Sarcasm is a rhetorical tool used by satirists and satire is aimed at specific targets. Describe the precise target here. In what circumstances is it useful?

2. Speculate about the meaning of "activated oxygen." What does the term suggest? What would motivate a seller to use such a term?

3. What does Hall refer to when she mentions that one company sold oxygenated water with no oxygen in it? How would a researcher know that oxygen was present in water if no equipment could detect that oxygen?

4. Hall admits she doesn't know what "natural man-made substance" means. Can you help her out? Why does she belittle the phrase "predetermined outcome"? What does that term suggest to you?

5. What does the reference to *Alice in Wonderland* add to the persuasive power of Hall's piece? What does Hall mean by "You can't argue with true believers"? Explain why you agree or disagree with that observation.

Wired to the Kitchen Sink: Studying Weird Claims for Fun and Profit

HARRIET HALL

A retired doctor with a family medicine practice, Harriet Hall has written often about the claims of alternative medicine. Her humorous tone belies a tough-minded view of such claims. The article that follows, published in Skeptical Inquirer *in 2003, takes on a kind of therapy based on skull manipulation.*

———————— ✦ ————————

After reading some particularly egregious nonsense, you have probably asked yourself, "How could anyone in his right mind believe that?" There is an answer to your question. In fact, the person who believes the nonsense will usually provide the answer himself if you give him half a chance. Go to the source. Read the believer's account of how he came to believe. He will probably give a clear enough description that you can see where he went wrong. It will give you an insight into human psychology. It will probably also be very entertaining. Here is an example of how it works.

I recently heard of craniosacral therapy. It is a method some osteopathic physicians use to restore health by adjusting the bones of the skull and sacrum. Anatomists can demonstrate that the skull bones are fused together in adulthood and cannot move. Other fallacies inherent in the therapy are too numerous to list: craniosacral therapy is totally implausible and has been thoroughly debunked elsewhere.

So how could anyone in his right mind believe in it? To find out, I went to the horse's mouth. My local library had a book entitled *Your Inner Physician and You: CranioSacral Therapy and SomatoEmotional Release,* by Dr. John E. Upledger, who is a major proponent of craniosacral therapy. I decided to read his account with as open a mind as I could summon, and give him a fair chance to convince me.

He describes his "eureka" moment. He was assisting a neurosurgeon by holding the dura (membrane surrounding the brain and spinal cord) steady while the surgeon removed a calcified plaque. He wasn't doing a very good job of holding still. The surgeon complained. Most of us would have thought our own muscles were at fault; however, Upledger observed that the dura was fluctuating up and down at about ten cycles per minute, overcoming his attempts to hold it still. Nobody had ever observed this before. He hypothesized that this "craniosacral rhythm" was intrinsic   5 to human health. Since the cerebrospinal fluid within the dura is in a closed space, the skull bones must move in and out to accommodate the rhythmic changes. The nervous system controls the rest of the body, so if the bones are not moving freely, nerve conduction might be abnormal and health might suffer. Perhaps he had found the basic cause of all disease.

He tried mobilizing the cranial bones through hands-on manipulation, and convinced himself he could *feel* the bones move one-sixteenth of an inch or more. Patients with autism, seizures, cerebral palsy, headaches, dyslexia, colic, asthma, and other diseases reported dramatic improvement. He found that well people treated with monthly adjustments reported more energy, felt happier, and were sick less often.

He felt he had achieved a glimpse into the "core." He states, "I'm not quite sure as yet what the core is all about, but I do know that at times the craniosacral system feels like the entrée into the deepest region of the patient's (and my own) total being, I'm not quite sure as yet what the 'total being' is all about, but it feels like the craniosacral system is where it all comes together, whatever it is."

So far, he had failed to convince me. It seems obvious that he had experienced an illusion (ideomotor activity, as experienced by Ouija boarders and water witchers). His false perception was reinforced when patients seemed to respond to treatment (perhaps from placebo effect, suggestion, hypnosis, a wish to agree with the doctor, the natural tendency of symptoms to improve with time, hands-on massage therapy, or whatever). I found his claims implausible and unbelievable.

This was bad enough, but then he really got carried away. He thought he had found a "cure-all," but apparently it wasn't enough to cure all, since he proceeded to add other treatments to his armamentarium. He discovered *tissue memory*: he found his hands "almost moving by themselves" to certain areas of the patient's body that seemed to contain some sort of memory of an old injury. He could feel heat and pulsations: under his hands these increased, then decreased until the sensations seemed to stop. At that point the patient's pain would subside. The patient sometimes felt an emotion (fear, anger) and at that time or later might remember a forgotten injury.

10   He proceeded to discover *energy cysts* (energy from an injury supposedly forms a ball deep in the tissues and stays there until released), *somatoemotional* release (touching the patient and giving permission allows old traumatic memories to surface and ventilate), and *healing energy* (which he transmits from the fingers of one hand to the other hand through the patient's body). Next he tried hypnosis. He regressed a patient to age two days, where she remembered her grandmother saying she should never have been born; insight caused her symptoms to disappear. He asked to talk to a patient's Inner Physician, who would explain the cause of the illness. One Inner Physician appeared to the patient in the form of a seagull and asked to be addressed as "Mermaid." (I am not making this up.)

He found that combinations of therapies worked even better than one at a time. Multiple hands with multiple therapists got results logarithmically faster. He tried therapy in float tanks: it worked wonders. He tried swimming with dolphins: multiple therapists surrounded the patient and were told to silently encourage the dolphins' freedom of choice, and to think that the dolphins were at least equal to them in knowledge and skill, and probably superior. (Perhaps this *was* true.) Dolphins spontaneously came up and touched the *therapist's* back to relieve the *patient's* symptoms. In one case, they reduced a leg-length discrepancy from three inches to one inch. At the same time the therapists' own skills were enhanced in "some non-conscious way."

Onward and upward, enthusiasm undaunted, he tried sound therapy for an orchestra conductor. Hearing a cello play a concert "A" tone caused back pain; "G" relieved upper and lower back pain, while "B" worked only for his upper back.

He would try anything his intuition suggested to him. He sensed that a patient had excess energy, so he *grounded the patient's big toe to a drainpipe* with copper wire, and—lo and behold—it worked! He successfully applied the same therapy to a woman with sympathetic reflex dystrophy who was in so much pain she would scream when the therapist's hand came within three inches of her body (!?). He had her husband *connect her to the kitchen sink* at home with a thirty-foot copper grounding wire so she could get around the house. (My husband says this sounds like a reasonable way to control a wife, but he may be prejudiced.)

Upledger never reports a failure. Everything seems to work for him. With that kind of reinforcement, how could he doubt? He is an intelligent and educated man and is admirable in many ways. You have to respect his creativity, imagination, and the courage to try unorthodox things in defiance of traditional medical education. New ideas should be encouraged: eventually some will lead to breakthroughs. It is obvious that he believes he has helped patients and patients believe they have been helped.

If the skull bones really could move as much as one-sixteenth   15
of an inch, it would be easy enough to measure and prove it. Unfortunately, Upledger is so convinced his treatments work that he has no motivation to prove the effect is real. He wants to keep on truckin' and to "spread the word." He doesn't pause to reflect that if his hypotheses were demonstrated to be true, it would be a major scientific discovery worthy of a Nobel Prize. He doesn't stop to think that he is subjecting his patients' money, time, health, and perhaps even their lives to unproven treatments.

Evolution has given the human mind a great ability and desire to find patterns everywhere and the motivation to seek explanations. If we can't find meaning, we will invent it. If something seems to work once, we will repeat it with the expectation that it might work again. We have a tendency to jump to conclusions because there is a survival value to deciding quickly. We rely strongly on personal testimonials, because until recently (in an evolutionary sense) that's all we had to go by. As any magician knows, our senses are prey to many kinds of illusions. Illusory perceptions allow us to accomplish things we couldn't otherwise do; for instance, our brains fill in the blind spot in our visual field. All these traits were instrumental in our developmental success as a species.

Every one of us can be fooled, so don't cast any stones. Be skeptical of weird ideas, but go to the source and listen carefully and sympathetically. Approach it as a case study of self-deception. Try to pinpoint where logic went wrong. You might learn how to better avoid making mistakes yourself, and you just might have a few laughs in the process. Just remember, you're not laughing at an individual; you're appreciating the humor in the very human failings we all share.

Further Reading

Barrett, Stephen. Massage Therapy: Riddled with Quackery. Quackwatch. Available at www.quackwatch.org/01Quackery RelatedTopics/massage.html.

Barrett, Stephen, and W.T. Javis (eds.). 1993. *The Health Robbers: A Close Look at Quackery in America.* Buffalo, New York: Prometheus Books.

Hartman, Steve, and J.M. Norton. 2002. Interexaminer Reliability and Cranial Osteopathy. *The Scientific Review of Alternative Medicine,* 6(1): 23–34.

Homola, Samuel. *Inside Chiropractic: A Patient's Guide.* Amherst, New York: Prometheus Books.

Magner, George. 1995. *The Victim's Perspective*. Amherst, New York: Prometheus Books.

Medical Economics Company, Inc. 1999. *The PDR Family Guide to Natural Medicines and Healing Therapies*. New York: Three Rivers Press.

Upledger, John. 1997. *Your Inner Physician and You: CranioSacral Therapy and SomatoEmotional Release*. Berkeley, California: North Atlantic Books.

For Discussion and Writing

1. Many pseudo therapies seem to be based on partial truths. What part of craniosacral therapy claims would you consider to be accurate? To what degree does craniosacral therapy resemble phrenology?

2. What circumstances led to Dr. Upledger's "eureka moment"? What does Upledger mean by the "core"?

3. Explain what Upledger means by "tissue memory" and discuss why such a notion might appeal or seem plausible to people. How might someone test the claim that memories are stored in the body but outside the brain? What problems can you foresee in verifying that sensations in the arms or shoulders, for example, stir up memories stored in the tissue of those body parts?

4. Assess the logic of Upledger's claims that cello music eased certain kinds of pain among patients. What are some questions that occur to you about the "finding" that grounding a patient's big toe to a drainpipe heals "excess energy"?

5. Scientists commonly speak of a placebo effect in studying patient progress under treatment. Consider a similar effect on practitioners who think they are healing patients by such treatment as "positive vibes," "energy manipulation," "healing touch," and so on. How likely is it that practitioners can fool themselves?

Homeopathy Finally Gets Some Respect

CATHERINE GUTHRIE

Homeopathy was founded by Samuel Hahnemann (1755–1843) in the nineteenth century and is popular all over the world today. It is a system of medical treatment based on the notion that like cures like. A homeopathic cure is often a "reduction," or dilution of a curative agent. As little as one molecule per million in solution might effect a cure, according to homeopathy's tenets. It's a fact that there is sometimes not even a trace of the active ingredient in the water of some homeopathic concoctions. Practitioners say that the remedy will still be effective because "the water remembers," and bears a kind of vibration or resonance that science can't detect and measure, but that works just fine nonetheless. In the article that follows, Catherine Guthrie, contributing writer to the magazine, Alternative Medicine, *reports that after years of skepticism, homeopathy is now enjoying some measure of acceptance among doctors and other healthcare workers.*

———————————— ✦ ————————————

Jesica DeHart's introduction to homeopathy came in an unexpected place—an emergency medical training class. "The instructor told us to put homeopathic remedies in our first aid kit," she says. DeHart wanted to check it out first on herself, so she took the teacher's advice and stocked up on arnica, a remedy for reducing bruising and swelling.

When she had cause to use it, she was pleasantly surprised at how well it soothed her bruises. Eventually she added other homeopathic remedies to her repertoire, including one for cramps and another for stomach upset. "Sometimes they were completely effective, other times not," she says. "But I always felt like it was worth a try."

Eight months ago, DeHart had a baby and her interest in homeopathy soared. "Having a child makes you hyper-aware of how you treat health problems, and I want a gentle option for my son," says the 30-year-old stay-at-home mom. Since Emmit was born, she's used homeopathic remedies to ease his colic and teething pain.

"Homeopathy is noninvasive," she says. "I like the idea that it's getting the body to heal itself."

Whatever homeopathy is, it's hardly new. In fact, it's 200 years old. What *is* new is that people like DeHart are fed up with the side effects, expense, and sometimes poor results of conventional drug therapy and are turning to homeopathy in record numbers. According to one report, published last year in *Annals of Internal Medicine*, the number of Americans using homeopathy sky-rocketed 500 percent in the last decade. One of the most comprehensive government surveys to date on Americans' use of complementary and alternative medicine found that more than 7.3 million people have tried it.

5

124 Catherine Guthrie

Government stats aside, everyone knows the real truth is in retail. Last year, Americans spent an estimated $425 million on homeopathic remedies, according to J.P. Borneman, the CEO of Boiron and a spokesperson for the American Association of Homeopathic Pharmacists. As the fourth generation in the business of homeopathic pharmacy, Borneman has seen business ebb and flow with Americans' love-hate relationship with Western medicine. But the real turning point for homeopathy, he says, came in the 1990s when remedies made the leap from health food stores to chain behemoths like Target, Kmart, and Walgreens.

Still, add up all the statistics, sales numbers, and anecdotal stories, and the fact remains that no one has yet proved how homeopathy works—a fact that emboldens skeptics and causes consternation among practitioners.

"I use it in my clinic, but every time I do, I roll my eyes," says David Katz, associate clinical professor of public health at the Yale-Griffin Prevention Research Center. "I wish I knew if and how it works. Maybe the whole thing is a placebo effect."

Katz's use of the "p-word" touches on the biggest criticism of homeopathy—that the practice is nothing but a placebo. In the United States, the National Council Against Health Fraud, a nonprofit watchdog agency, calls homeopathy a cult and practitioners quacks. In France last September, the Académie de Medecine, the country's most respected medical authority, denounced homeopathy as mumbo jumbo. That blow was especially low considering the French are the world's largest consumers; roughly 70 percent of France's population uses homeopathy, and French physicians routinely prescribe it.

10   But the cries that it's only a placebo are weakening. Perhaps the best thing to happen to homeopathy in recent years is the research showing it to be much more than that.

The good press started back in 1997 when the well-respected medical journal *The Lancet* published a meta-analysis of placebo-controlled studies on homeopathy. In 89 studies rigorously designed to evaluate its ability to treat and prevent various illnesses, the odds consistently showed homeopathy to be more effective than a placebo.

More recently, Wayne B. Jonas, a physician and director of the Samueli Institute for Information Biology, in Alexandria, Virginia, assembled an even more comprehensive overview of homeopathy studies, published in the *Annals of Internal Medicine*. The paper took into account four different meta-analyses and found homeopathy to be effective in treating allergies, childhood diarrhea, postoperative trauma, and influenza. "The weight of the current evidence right now falls slightly in favor of homeopathy," says Jonas.

BOTTOM LINE: IT WORKS

Homeopathic physician Corey Weinstein hasn't let the discussions about how homeopathy works get in his way. Each year, hundreds of patients flow through his office in San Francisco. Weinstein has practiced homeopathy for 30 years and prescribes homeopathic remedies for everything from colds to cancer. "I've never seen an illness or condition that homeopathy hasn't helped," he says.

While he doesn't hold any romanticized notions that homeopathy is a cure-all, he does think it's too valuable to dismiss. "The idea that for homeopathy to be good science we have to understand how it works is absurd," he says. "If that were the case for everything allopathic medicine offers, we never would have okayed the use of aspirin."

LIKE CURES LIKE

Developed in the late 18th century by the German physician   15
Samuel Christian Hahnemann, homeopathy is based on the "law of similars." After noticing that a common remedy for malaria, cinchona, produced malaria-like symptoms in people, Hahnemann came up with the idea that "like cures like."

The premise is that illness can be treated with small doses of a substance—animal, vegetable, and/or mineral—that mimics the malady's symptoms. The last thing you'd think to give a stressed-out person, for example, is caffeine, yet that's the primary ingredient in a common homeopathic remedy for promoting relaxation. According to Hahnemann's theory, homeopathy jump-starts the body's own healing process by introducing tiny amounts of the right substances.

But just how tiny is tiny? That's the question that makes most conventional practitioners shake their heads in disbelief. The end result is so tiny, they say, as to be virtually nonexistent. To reduce the toxicity of his remedies, Hahnemann diluted substances in alcohol and water several times over. In between each dilution, he shook the mixture. Later, he described the diluting and shaking process as essential to bringing forth a substance's "vital essence."

And in fact, modern-day makers of homeopathic remedies hold the time-honored process sacred. The label on a bottle of a homeopathic remedy says how many times it has been diluted. Homeopaths acknowledge that most remedies are so diluted that laboratory tests cannot locate a single molecule of the original substance.

And that's the stumbling block for many scientists in considering homeopathy as a medical treatment. "It's very hard for a Western brain to accept the fact that you are treating more and more effectively as you use less and less," says Katz. "But we seem to be standing on the brink of being able to explore the mechanism behind it."

20   One possible explanation is that the remedies leave an electronic fingerprint on the water in which they are diluted, which is then used in the actual remedy. Konrad Kail, a scientist at the Southwest College Research Institute in Tempe, Arizona, who's doing research on homeopathy, says the mark may be too subtle to register on regular lab equipment but still big enough to affect the body, working on an electronic rather than a biochemical level.

"Normally, we think of biochemical reactions as a lock and key," he says. When the key fits into the lock a reaction occurs. "I believe you can get the same effect with an electronic signal." (Think of a car's keyless entry.)

Jonas, author of *Healing with Homeopathy: The Complete Guide*, is also trying to decipher the riddle of homeopathy. Scientists in his lab recently discovered that in a vial of water there are interactions between the water and the glass; when you shake the vial, the silica comes off the glass and produces various chemical subspecies, some of which may be biologically active. "That kind of chemistry could be producing some of the effect we're seeing in homeopathy," he says.

Another theory centers on the importance of the practitioner/ patient relationship. Corey Weinstein's initial appointment with a patient, for instance, can easily last an hour and a half. The goal is to ascertain what remedy, out of the thousands available, might best address the person's complaint.

Could it be that patients simply feel better once a health care provider listens raptly to their woes? Jonas thinks it's a real possibility, but that doesn't detract from homeopathy's power, he says. "If that turns out to be a major reason for the effects of homeopathy, it's still a huge contribution to medicine."

25   Needless to say, this idea is unpopular among homeopaths, who don't appreciate being seen as glorified therapists doling out sugar pills. Still, Jonas is a homeopath and a scientist who likes to weigh all the possibilities. "Only in the last 25 years have we

begun to understand the power of expectation," he says. "I think this is one of the theories of homeopathy that has some viability and needs to be explored."

In fact, Jonas is working on a new study that he hopes will ferret out whether it's the remedies or the practitioner's attentiveness that stimulate homeopathic healing. His results won't be available until next year.

In the meantime, the caring-practitioner theory still leaves an inexplicable gap in the equation. What about people whose symptoms improve with over-the-counter homeopathic remedies? When Sheri McGregor injured her tailbone a few years ago, the pain was debilitating. The San Diego resident swallowed over-the-counter pain relievers, to no avail.

Finally, she tried hypericum, a homeopathic remedy for treating nerve injuries. Following the label's instructions, she dissolved several tablets under her tongue every 15 minutes. Within two hours, the pain was gone. By the end of the day, she'd stopped using the remedy, and never experienced another twinge from her troublesome tailbone. "It was spectacular," she says. "It turned me on to homeopathy for life."

For Discussion and Writing

1. Guthrie acknowledges that "most [homeopathic] remedies are so diluted that laboratory tests cannot locate a single molecule of the original substance." What do you make of her metaphor that the remedies leave an electronic fingerprint in the water? What other metaphors do supporters of the treatment use in this article?

2. What explanations can you make for the great increase in homeopathic patients in recent years? What are some conclusions you might reach from the fact that Americans spent $425 million on such remedies in 2005?

3. What does the author say about self-treatment? How would you compare various "products" to ensure that you get a good one? What stumbling block to tests on products can you foresee?

4. The author asks, "could it be that patients simply feel better once a health-care provider listens raptly to their woes." What do you think of her answer and that of Dr. Jonas? How can homeopaths counter the claim that the placebo effect does all the work in their medicine?

5. Under what circumstances might you go to a homeopath? What questions would you ask the practitioner? If you know people who have tried homeopathy, try to find out about their experiences both with this treatment and with more conventional medicine and discuss your findings.

Alternative Medicine: Research and Writing Possibilities

1. Alternative medicine practitioners often make sensible-sounding claims about the body and about the power of their particular therapy. Their language warrants scrutiny. Visit a couple of web sites devoted to cranial sacral therapy, sometimes called CST, and zero in on particular remarks. For example, one CST web site offers a page by Sher Smith, R.N., R.P.P., R.C.S.T., that says, "The cranial bones are lined on the inside by membranes. When there are blocks or tension in the body, the membranes are pulled out of position. The membranes then pull on the bones of the skull, which cause them to move out of alignment." What does Smith mean by "blocks"? Can these be detected directly? How much tension, exactly, pulls the membranes out of alignment? What sort of tension? Doesn't practically everyone have "tension" in their lives? Can we connect anything precise to the alleged movement of cranial bones? Analyze the language, raise questions from a skeptical standpoint, and propose tests to measure these claims.

2. Research some claims for the healing powers of magnets. How do they work? What is the mechanism? What sort of tests have been done to validate merchant claims? You might start by visiting the site of a successful company, Nikken, and reading some of the testimonials. Consider the language here. "She felt unbelievably better" after using the *Palmag*, says one person, who goes on to refer to the patient's "testimony." What connotations does that term suggest to you? Compare the "testimony" and claims for magnets with more specific claims that might be made about more conventional treatments, for example, "after a course of injections with a steroid-based drug, swelling around the patient's joint was visibly reduced." Here, for example, is a quote found at http://www.ncbi.nlm.nih.gov/entrez/query.fcgi?cmd=Retrieve&db=Pub Med&list_uids=7892010&dopt=Abstract. It refers to a course of treatment involving injections of cortisone for a specific malady. "Ninety-two percent of the cysts healed or healed with residuals according to the Neer classification. Additional osteosynthesis was done in pathological fractures of the femoral neck. The results are achieved with little morbidity, and low cost which justifies continuation of this treatment protocol." How does this language differ from claims for magnet therapy? What do the differences suggest to you?

3. What is the placebo effect? What is its possible role in the use of some products like those offered by aromatherapists? Isn't it possible that using essence of lavender in a warm bath will help reduce "stress levels"? What's wrong with that? Write a paper that argues for the curative uses

of aromas. Try to set limits to your claims. That is, notice the difference between saying something general, like "sage-scented incense can help relax you," and "sage-scented incense can offset ulcer-causing stress and may also lower your blood pressure, thus reducing the risk of stroke."

4. Skeptics often dismiss the efficacy of chiropractors or acupuncturists because their claims can't be verified precisely. That's often the case with reports of pain relief. "I feel ten times better" endorses the medical practice, but hardly in a measurable way. In the past, some insurance companies refused to cover acupuncture because its methods were hard to evaluate. An organization called American Acupuncture (ACP), which supports this alternative medicine, lists three objections often raised to the practice: It uses non-scientific language; it hasn't been tested in traditional double-blind studies; and there is a lack of scientific explanation for how it works. Look into acupuncture. Find a reasonably concise account of how it works. Contact a practitioner and ask about her practice, training, and so on. Argue for or against including acupuncture in a list of covered benefits.

5. Parody, which is an unflattering imitation of style, is sometimes a useful way to study things. Read some issues of journals devoted to aromatherapy, iridology, or another non-traditional medical practice. Study their language, their actual claims, the links they offer to other therapies, and so on. Read some ads in their pages and notice the credentials of various practitioners. Then write up a mock issue of an all new alternative practice. Make a masthead, introduce a half-dozen or so articles with short descriptions in a table of contents, and make some ads for products. You might even make up an interview with a shaman/barista who has "received instruction" from ancients while visiting the ruins at Machu Picchu. You want to have fun, but stay very close to your models in the actual realm of alternative healing. If you do well, a casual viewer might not be able to pick out your fake from a group of actual practices.

CHAPTER 4

Psychics and the Paranormal

Glendower: I can call spirits from the vasty deep.
Hotspur: Why, so can I, or so can any man;
But will they come when you do call for them?
                                          —SHAKESPEARE, 1 HENRY IV

The first principle is that you must not fool yourself and you are the easiest person to fool.
                                          —RICHARD P. FEYNMAN

Recently, my little mountain community was host to a "Psychic Fair," and our local high school grounds, of all places, were chosen as the venue. The irony was at least as interesting as the displays—there were a couple dozen—which offered visitors all sorts of healing techniques, psychically charged baubles, aura readings, and general information about that world beyond our senses. In preparing this introduction, I Googled psychic fairs and found events scheduled all over California. I'm certain other states host such fairs as well.

You may wonder what sort of "providers" you can find at a psychic fair. If you attended the Carlsbad gala, you would have met Belinda Bentley, among others, whom the event web site describes as "Direct Psychic, Tarot Reader, Soul Mate Reader, Medium, Reiki & Heart Healer." Tarot reading is common at these fairs. "Direct psychics" are a bit less common, and I found only one "direct intuitive," a person named Susan Norgren, who also does "readings on a cellular level." For me, the most interesting participants were Naz Koda and Patrice Amore Carington, both of whom specialize in "Angel Therapy." Ms. Carington considers herself a "certified angel therapist." I wondered how one gets certified in so arcane a practice, and found the answer in her biographical sketch:

> After 30 years of studying communication, relationships, emotional well-being, human potential and spirituality, [Patrice Carington] confirmed what she had known at three years old. She is a Certified Angel Therapy Practitioner and works closely with the Angel of Adoration (Archangel Chamuel).

It would seem that Ms. Carington is self-certified. Credentials, to be fair, usually belong to a world that is more formal than that of psychic fairs, and they hardly amount in any context to a guarantee of performance. Most of the featured mediums etc. plainly state that they are natural or born psychics, mediums, or angel therapists. One doesn't go to school to learn some things, although there are training centers like the Elysium Psychic School, run by "the TV medium Craig Hamilton-Parker." Training is online. This site claims the school "may even change your life," and at the very least offers the opportunity to meet "spiritual and interesting people."

Many people who may regard psychics and mediums warily will, however, eagerly follow revelations about Bible codes or crop circles or classic ghost stories. There may be a common thread among mediums and these other things: at the very least, they all provide some relief from everyday cares. For some people, they promise contact with extraordinary events, maybe even a key to life's meaning. Like the astronomer in Samuel Johnson's wonderful little tale "Rasselas," some paranormal enthusiasts are completely convinced of the reality of their subject. Johnson's astronomer came to believe that he controlled the world's climate, and some believers just know they are in touch with creatures from other worlds, that they can pick up "vibes" from crop circles, or that the spirit from a person dead for a thousand years is guiding their minds and sending a message that can save the world. Most people fantasize about such things, maybe because we can easily imagine a world that is better, safer, and more interesting than the one we live in. How easy is it to slip from fantasy to obsession to belief? Given our culture's preoccupation with the unusual and the unworldly, I would say it's remarkable that more people aren't deluded. Certainly television caters to our hunger for the paranormal. As is noted elsewhere in this book, there are many TV shows devoted to mediums and psychics. But some reputedly down-to-earth people and organizations also feed interest in these things. According to Donald Regan, President Ronald Reagan's former chief-of-staff, Nancy Reagan actually consulted an astrologer for the best times to set the president's various meetings. The astrologer, Joan Quigley, claimed to "have a direct line to the president." Joe Nickell has written a startling account of the White House connection to astrology for *Skeptical Inquirer*, noting the claims of two astrologers linked to the Reagans. Nickell's brief article also mentions Tamara Rand, who claimed to have predicted the assassination attempt on Reagan. Rand was supposed to have made the claim on TV months before the event, but an "AP reporter discovered the [TV] video was a fake, filed the day *after* the assassination attempt." Still, a sitting American president's belief in astrology goes a long way in supporting that pseudoscience is in our culture. When police departments consult psychics for help in solving crimes, another powerful boost is given to unfounded beliefs. It also seems that debunking fraud and delusion have less impact on belief than skeptics would like, and proof that seers have gotten things wrong doesn't appear too often in the papers.

The essays in this section amount to a small sampling of a vast body of writing about the mysterious, the supernatural, and the generally weird. Martin Gardner reflects on the history and sad demise of the Heaven's Gate cult, while David E. Thomas casts a cold eye on the phenomenon of the Bible code. He explains how the code is alleged to work, then applies the methods to books that no one would consider sacred or remarkable. In an excerpt from his book, *The Demon-Haunted World*, Carl Sagan discusses the origins and development of crop circle tales, proving among other things that true believers won't let the facts stand in their way. Gary P. Posner examines the claims of success made by Noreen Renier, a "psychic detective" who has been credited with some investigative successes. Finally, Sonya Fitzpatrick, who appears in print and on TV as the "Pet Psychic," gives an account of her "communications" with a depressed and somewhat gossipy pet turtle. As you read these essays, bear in mind that questioning claims is not cynicism, it's rational behavior.

Heaven's Gate: The UFO Cult of Bo and Peep

MARTIN GARDNER

The short-lived Heaven's Gate cult focused the nation's attention on cults when most of its members committed mass suicide in 1997. Cult members believed in the imminent destruction of earth, and believed they would escape this end by rising up to meet a spacecraft hidden in the wake of the very real comet Hale-Bopp. All the members killed themselves in an attempt to rise to that spacecraft. Martin Gardner, author of the following article, has written many books, among them The Annotated Alice; Mathematics, Magic, and Mystery; *and* Did Adam and Eve Have Navels?, *from which the Heaven's Gate essay is taken.*

◆

For there are some eunuchs, which are so born from their mother's womb; and there are some eunuchs, which were made eunuchs of men, and there be eunuchs which have made themselves eunuchs for the kingdom of heaven's sake. He that is able to receive it, let him receive it.

—JESUS, MATTHEW 19:12

The nation's shocked reaction to the suicide in March 1997 of thirty-eight happy brainwashed innocents and their demented leader, at Rancho Santa Fe, California, has been twofold. The event has reawakened public awareness of the enormous power of charismatic gurus over the minds of cult followers, and it has focused attention on the extent to which the myth of alien spacecraft has become the dominant delusion of our times. A recent *Newsweek* poll revealed that almost half of Americans believe UFOs are for real and that our government knows it. As if a secret this monumental could be kept by our political leaders for more than a few hours!

Rumors about space aliens and their snatching of humans show no signs of abating. Harvard psychiatrist John Mack has published a book about the abductions of his patients. The rumors are magnified mightily by endless other books, lurid movies, and shameless radio and television shows. Ed Dames, who runs Psi Tech, a psychic research center in Beverly Hills, California, was the first to proclaim that his "remote viewers" had spotted a massive spacecraft trailing Comet Hale-Bopp.

Dames's claim was "confirmed" by three psychics at the Farsight Institute in Atlanta, headed by Courtney Brown, Dames's former pupil. Brown teaches political science at Emory University. He is as embarrassing to Emory as Mack is to Harvard. The previous chapter reviews Brown's *Cosmic Voyage*, a crazy book telling how aliens are being shuttled to Earth to live under a mountain near Santa Fe, New Mexico.

Who was most responsible for the Rancho Santa Fe horrors? They were two neurotic, self-deluded occultists: Marshall Herff Applewhite and his platonic companion Bonnie Lu Trousdale Nettles. Their story reads like bad science fiction.

5   Born in Spur, Texas, in 1931, the son of a Presbyterian minister, Applewhite graduated as a philosophy major at Austin (Texas) College in 1952. He had brief stays in seminary school and in the Army Signal Corps. But he was gifted with good looks and a fine baritone voice, and his chosen career was in singing and music. He received a master's degree in music from the University of Colorado, starring in numerous operas produced in Houston and in Boulder while pursuing his degree. Throughout his musical career, he held a number of teaching positions and conducted numerous church choirs.

For several years in the sixties, Applewhite taught music at St. Thomas University, a small Catholic school in Houston. The university fired him in 1970 over an affair with a male student. Struggling to control his homosexual impulses, depressed, and hearing voices, he checked into a psychiatric hospital in 1971. He told his sister he had suffered a heart attack and had a near-death experience.

It was in this hospital that Applewhite's life took its fateful turn. His registered nurse, Bonnie Nettles[1] (she was forty-four, he forty), was a former Baptist, then deep into occultism, theosophy, astrology, and reincarnation. Somehow she managed to convince Applewhite that they were aliens from a higher level of reality who had known each other in previous earthly incarnations. In the coming months and years, they would develop their bizarre religion, believing they had been sent to Earth to warn humanity

---

[1]Some sources say that Applewhite met Nettles when he was visiting a friend in the hospital. Nettles's daughter says they met at a drama school. (See *New York Times*, April 28, 1997.)

that our civilization was about to collapse as foretold in Revelation, to be replaced by a new one after the battle of Armageddon and the destruction of Lucifer. They believed that Lucifer (a cut or two below Satan), aided by his "Luciferians," had long controlled our planet. It is, in fact, Lucifer's demons who have been piloting those spaceships that are abducting humans.

How can one escape the coming holocaust? Not by being "raptured," as Protestant fundamentalists teach, but by being beamed up to spacecraft operated by benign superbeings and taken to the gates of heaven. (Judging by the recent tragedy at Rancho Santa Fe, if you are male, the best way to make this journey is to cut off your testicles, then kill yourself!)

Shortly after their meeting, and fired with the divine mandate to rescue as many humans as possible from the destruction of our world as we know it, Applewhite and Nettles embarked on their mission, Nettles abandoning a husband and four children in the process. (Applewhite, a father of two, was already divorced.) The pair quickly became inseparable in a strange bond that psychiatrists call the "insanity of two." It develops when two neurotic persons live together and reinforce each other's delusions.

Indeed, Applewhite and Nettles began calling themselves The   10 Two. They came to believe they were the "two witnesses" described in Chapter 11 of Revelation. Verse 7 predicts that when the two witnesses "finish their testimony" they will be murdered. After three and a half days, God will resurrect them. A voice from heaven will say, "Come up hither," and their enemies will see them taken to heaven by a "cloud."

"I'm not saying we are Jesus," Nettles wrote to her daughter. "It's nothing as beautiful but it is almost as big. . . . We have found out, baby, we have this mission before coming into this life. . . . It's in the Bible in Revelation." The Two taught that on six occasions God had sent souls to earth to uplift humanity: (1) Adam. (2) Enoch, who was Adam reincarnated in a new vehicle. (3) Moses. (4) Elijah. (5) Jesus. (6) Bo and Peep.

The Two's first move was to open an occult bookstore in Houston. After it failed in 1973, they took to the road to gather converts. A group was started in Los Angeles called Guinea Pig. Applewhite was Guinea, Nettles was Pig. Soon they were calling their movement HIM (Human Individual Metamorphosis). Later it became TOA (Total Overcomers Anonymous). Because they considered themselves shepherds to a flock of sheep, Applewhite took the name of Bo, and Nettles became Peep. Over the years they liked to give themselves other whimsical names such as

Him and Her, Winnie and Pooh, Tweedle and Dee, Chip and Dale, Nincom and Poop, Tiddly and Wink. Eventually they settled on the musical notes Do and Ti.

In a 1972 interview in the *Houston Post*, Nettles said her astrological work was assisted by Brother Francis, a nineteenth-century monk. "He stands beside me," she said, "when I interpret the charts." Both Do and Ti constantly channeled voices from superbeings who lived on the Evolutionary Level Above Human, or Next Level (the Kingdom of Heaven).

It all sounds so childish and insane, yet those who attended early cult meetings, mostly on college campuses, have testified to the pair's persuasive rhetoric. Early converts were mainly young hippies, drifters, and New Agers, disenchanted with other cults, eager to be told what to believe and do.

15   In 1975 about twenty followers were recruited in the seaside village of Waldport, Oregon, then taken to eastern Colorado, where they expected to board a flying saucer and be carried to the Next Level. It was a vague region ruled by the great EGB (Energy God Being). When the spacecraft failed to appear, it was such a blow to Bo and Peep that they plunged underground for seventeen years.

There was a period when The Two preached that the "Demonstration" foretold in Revelation 11 would occur. As I said earlier, this would be their assassination, followed by their resurrection and journey to the Heavenly Kingdom in a spacecraft that the Bible called a cloud. "The chances it won't happen," Applewhite told a *New York Times* reporter in 1976, "are about as great as that a rain will wash all the red dirt out of Oklahoma." The interview got him fired as choir director of St. Mark's Episcopal Church in Houston.

Never sexual lovers, the peculiar pair surfaced in the mid-seventies as leaders of about fifty followers who wandered with them here and there. They camped out or lived in motels with funds donated by wealthy recruits or obtained from odd jobs and occasional begging. For several years they hunkered down in a camp near Laramie, Wyoming. HIM was now a full-blown cult with members strictly regulated by what they called the Process. Recruits assumed new names. Sex, alcohol, tobacco, and pot were taboo. Ti, whom Do always considered his superior, died of cancer in 1985 after losing an eye to the disease. Until his suicide, Do said he was in constant communication with Ti, who had reached the Next Level.

Precise details about the cult's nomadic history remain obscure. Do convinced his sheep that they, too, were aliens from the Next Level, now incarnated in a body they called the soul's container, vehicle, instrument, or vessel. When the time was right, they would all be teleported to one of the spaceships operated by angels.

Time reported (August 27, 1979) that cult members were then wearing hoods and gloves, obeying "thousands" of rules, studying the Bible intensely, and undergoing periods in which they communicated with each other only by writing. It's not easy to believe, but the cult received so much media attention in the late seventies that a TV series called *The Mysterious Two* was planned. A pilot actually aired in 1982 featuring John Forsythe and Pricilla Pointer as The Two.

After the Internet became widely available to the public, the cult intensified its recruiting by way of a website called Heaven's Gate. A few followers had developed sufficient skills not only to go online, but also to run a service called Higher Source that designed websites for customers.   20

In 1996 the cult rented a sprawling Spanish-style villa, with pool and tennis court, in Rancho Santa Fe, a few miles north of San Diego. The rent was $7,000 a month. Members began the day with prayers at 3 A.M., ate only two meals a day, had their hair cropped short, and wore baggy clothes to make themselves look genderless and unsexy. Their lives were more regulated than the lives of soldiers. Guns were stored just in case government forces attacked them as they had the Branch Davidians in Waco. Meticulous plans were drawn for a mass suicide as soon as the higher beings gave them a "marker" in the heavens. The marker, Do decided, was the giant spacecraft that psychics had convinced him (perhaps verified by the voice of Ti) was following Comet Hale-Bopp. A lunar eclipse on March 23, 1997, may have strengthened the sign.

Haunting videotapes were made on which the smiling and happy sheep said how joyfully they were looking forward to escaping from their vehicles and from a doomed planet. "We are happily prepared to leave 'this world' and go with Ti's crew," they posted on their website. Evidently they believed their beloved Ti was on the Hale-Bopp spacecraft!

As everyone now knows, eighteen men and twenty-one women put themselves to sleep with phenobarbital mixed into pudding or applesauce and washed down with vodka. Plastic bags were tied over their heads so they would suffocate in their sleep. Faces and upper bodies of the "monks," as they called themselves, were neatly covered with a square of purple cloth. All thirty-nine were dressed alike—black shirts, black pants, and black Nike running shoes. The last two to die were women with bags on their heads but unshrouded by a purple covering.

The most perplexing aspect of these ritualized deaths was the neatly packed travel bags beside their bunks, and a $5 bill and some quarters in each of their pockets. Did they expect the super-beings to take the bags along with their souls? And what use did they suppose the money would have when they reached the spaceship?

25   The odor of rotting "vehicles" was so strong that the first police at the scene on March 26 suspected poison gas.

To me the saddest aspect of this insane event was the firm belief, expressed on the incredible videotapes, that cult members were killing themselves of their own free will. Nothing could have been more false. Although Do always told his robots they were free to go at any time—and hundreds had done just that—so powerful was his control over the minds of those who stayed that they believed anything he said, obeyed every order. Autopsies showed that Do and seven of his followers had been surgically castrated.[2]

Do said he was dying of cancer. Yet his autopsy showed no sign of cancer or any other fatal illness. The wild-eyed expression on his face, reproduced on the covers of both *Time* and *Newsweek*, was not a look of illness. It was a look of madness.

Media reports have made fun of the belief that our bodies are mere containers and that in our next life we will be given glorious new bodies. This, of course, is exactly what St. Paul taught, and what conservative Christians, Jews, Muslims, and most Eastern faiths believe. Similar mixtures of New Testament doctrine with New Age nonsense is what makes so many recent cults appealing to converts with Christian backgrounds. Members of Heaven's Gate firmly believed that Jesus was an extraterrestrial sent to Earth like Do and Ti to collect as many souls as possible and lead them upward to acquire new containers. When Jesus finished his work, he went back to heaven in a UFO.

---

[2]Earlier cults have recommended castration to curb male sexual passions. The most famous intentional castration in the history of Christendom was the self-castration of Origen, the greatest of the church fathers next to Augustine. Unable to curb his lust for young women pupils, Origen sliced off his testicles. He was sorry later that he'd done it. Do may have felt a kinship with Origen, who believed in a plurality of inhabited worlds, the pre-existence of human souls, and the ultimate salvation of all sinners, including the devil.

The great adventist movements in America—Seventh-day Adventism, the Jehovah's Witnesses, and Mormonism—are flourishing today as never before despite the long delay in Jesus' Second Coming. None of the major adventist faiths recommend suicide, but there may be more suicides by other weird little cults that surely will be capturing the minds of lonely, gullible souls.

So pervasive is the worldwide belief in alien UFOs that a   30 London company recently offered to insure anyone against abduction, impregnation, or attack by aliens. About four thousand people, mostly in England and the United States, bought policies. In October 1996, Heaven's Gate paid $1,000 for a policy covering up to fifty members for $1 million each. After their mass suicides, the London firm decided to abandon its insurance against space aliens.

Some insight into the sort of people who were followers of Bo and Peep can be gained from a sad story distributed by the Associated Press in early April 1997. Lorraine Webster, age seventy-eight, now living in Rollo, Missouri, abandoned her husband in 1978 to help found Heaven's Gate. She left the cult only because of a health problem. Her daughter was among those who died at Rancho Santa Fe.

Was Lorraine Webster disturbed by the suicides? Not in the least. Like all cult members, she doesn't like to call her cult a cult. It was a "movement." Do, she told the reporter, was a "kind and wonderful man." She misses her daughter but admires her for acting "like an angel." Ti frequently talks to Ms. Webster. She recently appeared at Webster's window in the form of a "chirping bird."

At the fifth annual Gulf Breeze (Florida) UFO Conference, March 21–23, 1997, Courtney Brown announced that his psychics' most recent remote viewing of Comet Hale-Bopp showed that the spacecraft was no longer there. It had moved, he said, to a spot behind the sun. Evidently this news failed to reach Do and his sheep. However, if Do was in touch with Ti on the ship, he probably would have taken her word over Brown's.

The *Village Voice*, covering the cult in its December 1, 1975, issue, included a prophetic passage: "The whole operation has lost that silvery crazy glitter. Now it seems black, dark, and a little ugly. It has the smell of ordinary death."

References

"UFO Cult Mystery Turns Evil." Victoria Hodgetts, in *Village Voice*, December 1, 1975, pp. 12–13.
"Looking For the Next World." James S. Phelan, in *New York Times Magazine*, February 29, 1976, pp. 12–13, 58–64.

UFO Missionaries Extraordinary. Edited by Hayden Hewes and Brad Steiger. Pocket Books, 1976.

"Flying Saucery in the Wilderness." *Time*, August 27, 1979, p. 58.

How and When Heaven's Gate May Be Entered. Published by the cult on the Internet, 1995, 200 pages.

Cover story in *Newsweek*, April 7, 1997.

Cover story in *Time*, April 7, 1997.

Cover story in *People*, April 14, 1997.

Numerous reports in *New York Times*, *Washington Post*, *Los Angeles Times*, and other newspapers during the weeks following the discovery of the suicides on March 26, 1997.

"The Faithful Among Us." Howard Chua-Eoan, in *Time*, April 14, 1997.

"De-Programming Heaven's Gate." *New Yorker*, April 14, 1997.

"Eyes on Glory: Pied Pipers of Heaven's Gate." Barry Bearak, in *New York Times*, national edition, April 28, 1997.

"Heaven Couldn't Wait." John Taylor, in *Esquire*, June 1997.

"UFO Mythology: Escape to Oblivion." Paul Kurtz, in *Skeptical Inquirer*, July/August 1997.

Heaven's Gate Cult Suicide in San Diego. New York Post staff. Harper Paperbacks, 1997.

For Discussion and Writing

1. What are some of the tales and delusions that Gardner links to the Heaven's Gate cult? Gardner is suggesting that this cult pieced its beliefs together from many such sources. Discuss that suggestion, considering especially the possibility that people might construct beliefs out of distinct notions and ideas.

2. The author supplies a brief biography of the cult's founders. Which details seem most significant to you? What does Gardner mean by "madness of two"?

3. What role did biblical texts play in the cult's beliefs? Perhaps you would not take a person seriously who claimed to be the successor to Jesus. In your view, why do some people come to believe such a person? Under what circumstances would you become susceptible to such claims?

4. Discuss the role of journalists and media outlets in reporting on the cult before and after its demise. What impact would skeptical coverage have on believers? Who might be influenced by such coverage?

5. At the end of his essay, Gardner refers back to a 1975 article about the cult, which remarked that the cult had a smell of death about it. What do you think that could have meant? What was there in Heaven's Gate that, in your view, could be associated with death? Discuss some of the ways that philosophy and religion concern themselves with death.

Hidden Messages and the Bible Code

DAVID E. THOMAS

A few years ago, Michael Drosnin's The Bible Code *was a bestseller, and hordes of readers were convinced that the Hebrew Bible contains a secret code that predicted many events occurring long after the texts were written, as well as events that haven't yet come to pass. David E. Thomas takes a look at Drosnin's claims and evidence, and also finds "hidden" messages in secular books. Thomas has written many articles on UFOs, Roswell lore, and bible codes. He is the president of New Mexicans for Science and Reason, and the following article offers alternative explanations for the spectacular messages Drosnin and others find in the Bible.*

———————— ✦ ————————

BIBLE CODE: THE BOOK

A book entitled *The Bible Code* came out in June 1997 and occupied the bestseller lists for months. It is written by journalist Michael Drosnin, who claims that the Hebrew Bible contains a very complex code that reveals events that took place thousands of years after the Bible was written. Drosnin contends that some foretold events later happened exactly as predicted.

The book has been reviewed widely and has prompted articles in *Newsweek* and *Time*. Drosnin has also been making the rounds of the talk-show circuit, including the *Oprah Winfrey Show* in June 1997. *Time* said that Warner has reportedly bought the movie rights (Van Biema 1997).

Drosnin's technique is heavily based on that of Eliyahu Rips of Hebrew University in Israel, who published an article entitled "Equidistant Letter Sequences in the Book of Genesis" in the journal *Statistical Science* (Witztum Rips, and Rosenburg 1994). Like Rips, Drosnin arranges the 304,805 Hebrew letters of the Bible into a large array. Spaces and punctuation marks are omitted, and words are run together one after another. A computer looks for matches to selected names or words by stepping to every *n*th letter in the array. One can go forward or backward; and for each value of "step distance," *n*, there are *n* different starting letters. Drosnin's match for "Yitzhak Rabin" had a step value n equal to 4,772.

Both Rips and Drosnin work with the original Hebrew characters, which are said to have been given by God to Moses one character at a time, with no spaces or punctuation, just as they appear in "the code." The code is considered to exist only in the Hebrew Bible and not in translations or any other books. The code concept, however, can be easily demonstrated with English characters. Consider the following verse from the King James Version (KJV) of the Book of Genesis:

> 31:28 And hast not suffered me to kiss my sons and my daughters? thou hast now done foolishly in so doing.

If you start at the R in "daughters," and skip over three letters to the O in "thou," and three more to the S in "hast," and so on, the hidden message "Roswell" is revealed! This message has a step value of 4, as shown in figure 1.

When Drosnin finds a name or word match for a given step value n, he then rearranges the letters into a huge matrix (which he calls a "crossowrd puzzle"). The matrix is n letters wide, and inside this puzzle, the letters for the "hidden message" line up together vertically. (Sometimes, a slightly different procedure is used to make the hidden word run diagonally, every other row, and so forth.) The analyst or the computer can then look for more keyword-related "hits" around the given hidden word. Secondary matches can be picked off vertically, horizontally, or diagonally. Drosnin found the word "Dallas" (connected with keywords "President Kennedy") in one of his puzzles by starting at a D, and then picking the next letters by moving one space over to the right and three spaces down several times.

An example of such a matrix for the "Roswell" mention in KJV Genesis appears in figure 2. The letters of "Roswell" now appear vertically at the center of the puzzle. The actual matrix of unique letters is only four characters wide here (dashed box), but I took the liberty of showing extra letters for context. A companion hidden message—"UFO"—is indicated within circle symbols. This "UFO"

G H T E R S T H O U H A S T N O W D O N E F O O L I S H L Y I N S

Figure 1 "Roswell" hidden in KJV Genesis 31:28.

Figure 2   Matrix or "crossword puzzle" for "Roswell/UFO" hidden in KJV Genesis.

is itself a hidden message with a step value of 12. Drosnin accepts any such messages, even words running *horizontally* (i.e., the actual words of the Bible strung together). If either "Roswell" or "UFO" had been found encoded in the Hebrew Bible, Drosnin would not have hesitated to use words from the direct text as a "match" (for example, the words "thou hast now done foolishly").

The unusual pairing of "Roswell" and "UFO" is shown in linear form in figure 3. This match is as stunning as any described in Drosnin's book—yet none claim that the Bible code would have translated gracefully over to the KJV Genesis.

Drosnin claims mathematical proof that "no human could have encoded the Bible in this way" (Drosnin 1997, 50–51). He says, "I do not know if it is God," but adds that the code proves "we are not alone."

HIDDEN MESSAGES

Some believe that these "messages" in the Hebrew Bible are not just coincidence—they were put there deliberately by God. But if someone finds a hidden message in a book, a song played backwards,

T E R̲ S T H O̲ U̲ H A S̲ T N O W̲ D O N E̲ F̲ O O L̲ I S H L̲ Y I N S O̲ D O

Figure 3   "Roswell" and "UFO" hidden in KJV Genesis 31:28.

funny-looking Martian mesas, or some other object or thing, does that prove someone *else* put the message there *intentionally*? Or might the message exist only in the eyes of the beholder (and in those of his or her followers)? Does perception of meaning prove the message was deliberately created?

10   Most of the data cited in favor of the purported intelligent alien construction of the "Face on Mars" is based on mathematical relationships among various Martian structures and locations. For example, author Richard Hoagland finds the "Cydonian" ratio (the "face" lies on the Cydonia plains region of Mars), e/π, in the tangent of the face's latitude of 40.868 degrees north, in the ratios of angles of the D&M Pyramid, and in numerous other places (Hoagland 1992). Does that mean the "face" and "city" on Mars were "designed" for the express purpose of spreading that very message? Hoagland emphatically says, "Yes!" My inner skeptic says, "Not so fast!"

In my research into such phenomena, I have found numerous instances of Hoagland's Martian ratios on objects we know were not designed or built by aliens, such as the U.S. Capitol rotunda (figure 4). Does that prove that Martians built this structure? Or is this phenomenon related mainly to the determination and skill of the person looking for a special message? *Any* special message?

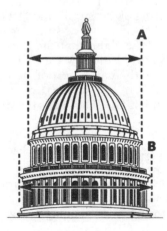

Figure 4 The "Martian" ratio $e/\pi \simeq A/B$, hidden in the Capitol rotunda (precise measurements of A and B yield $A/B \simeq 0.863$, while $e/\pi \simeq 2.71828/3.14159 \simeq 0.865$, an error of less than one half of one percent).

There are dozens of books about Nostradamus. In one (Hewitt and Lorie 1991), the authors find hidden predictions by scrambling the seer's quatrains (in French, no less), and then decoding according to an extremely complicated and mysterious formula. The back cover prominently displays one such unscrambled prediction: "1992—George Bush re-elected." (Wrong.) The authors should have known that it's much safer to find hidden predictions of events that have already happened.

Some critics of Drosnin say the journalist is just "data mining." Mathematician Brendan McKay of Australian National University and his colleagues searched Hebrew texts besides the Bible. They found fifty-nine words related to Chanukah in the Hebrew translation of *War and Peace*. But McKay doesn't think someone engineered this remarkable feat for his or anyone's benefit. Since then, McKay has responded to the following challenge Drosnin made in *Newsweek*. "When my critics find a message about the assassination of a prime minister encrypted in *Moby Dick* I'll believe them" (Begley 1997). McKay found assassination "predictions" in *Moby Dick* for Indira Gandhi, Rene Moawad, Leon Trotsky, Rev. M. L. King, and Robert F. Kennedy (see http://cs.anu.edu.au/~bdm/dilugim/moby.html). Eliyahu Rips himself has denied Drosnin's implication that they worked together, and has said, "I do not support the book as it is or the conclusions it derives" (Van Biema 1997).

HIDDEN NAMES IN KJV GENESIS AND *EDWARDS V. AGUILLARD*

I have very recently carried out a study on finding hidden names in both the KJV Genesis and the U.S. Supreme Court's 1987 ruling on *Edwards v. Aguillard* (a well-known ruling on creationism, hereafter referred to as simply *Edwards*). I used the same set of rules for both the KJV Genesis (about 150,000 characters) and *Edwards* (about 100,000 characters). I loaded a list of preselected names and let the computer search for each one in turn, for equidistant letter sequences with step distances from 2 to 1,000, and for every possible starting letter. I searched forward only.

One would expect that special biblical messages hidden in the Hebrew Bible would simply not make it into the King James Version, much less into *Edwards*. And since the Hebrew alphabet doesn't include vowels, it should be much harder to find matches in the English texts, because an additional character match is requried for each vowel.

Drosnin's control was the Hebrew text of *War and Peace*. Drosnin claims that when they searched for words (such as "comet," "Jupiter," etc.) in the Bible, they often found them there, but *not* in *War and Peace*.

I picked a set of names carefully. The list contained five names of four letters, five of five letters, five of six letters, five of seven letters, and five of either eight or nine letters. I was more whimsical in my choice of subjects and chose talk show hosts, scientists, and just plain folks as well as political or historical figures. I found *thousands* of hidden occurrences of these names in both Genesis and *Edwards*. The results appear in table 1.

It is striking that tens of thousands of hidden occurrences were found for the twenty-five names submitted, for both Genesis and *Edwards*. More matches were found in the former, but it does have 50,000 more letters to work with. Another important observation is immediately apparent in table 1—short names like "Leno" or "Reed" were found much more frequently than long names like "Gingrich" or "Matsumura." ("Matsumura" is, of course, Molleen Matsumura of the National Center for Science Education, in Berkeley, and "Romero" is Albuquerque boxer Danny Romero.) "Martin Gardner" was found hidden in *Edwards,* much as Gardner anticipated could happen in his discussion of gematria and the work of Rips and his colleagues (Gardner 1997).

The results are clear and compelling, and certainly not surprising. It is much easier to find short names than long names. There might be thousands of occurrences of the four-letter name "Rich," for example. But matching "Gingrich" is much harder, since few or none of the thousands of instances of "Rich" will be preceded by "Ging" at exactly the right step locations. But there are 2,554 hidden occurrences of "Newt" in KJV Genesis, so one could *imagine* that the Speaker of the House is certainly mentioned copiously.

20   There is, of course, another factor in the success of hidden word searches. Simply put, some letters are more common than others. Figure 5a and 5b give the relative frequencies for the letters in Genesis and *Edwards*.

The charts show that certain letters (such as A, D, E, H, I, N, O, R, S, and T) appear more often than others. Obviously, words made with these "hot" letters (such as "Reed," "Deer," "Stalin," or "Hitler") have a better chance of being found than words containing any "cool" letters like J or Q. "Rosie" had 202 Genesis matches, more than the 49 for "Oprah"—but "Oprah" contains a cool P. (I also searched for "Harpo," which is just "Oprah" backwards, and found 62 hits.)

Table 1 Counts of hidden words found in KJV Genesis and *Edwards v. Aguillard*, at steps of 1,000 or less, forward only.

Length	Name	Genesis	Edwards
4 Letters	Deer	7440	3255
	Dole	2692	1349
	Leno	3353	2836
	Newt	2554	1026
	Reed	7340	3326
5 Letters	Gould	5	4
	Oprah	49	31
	Regis	51	71
	Rosie	202	341
	Sagan	107	62
6 Letters	Asimov	1	0
	Darwin	3	1
	Hitler	18	13
	Romero	6	1
	Stalin	15	10
7 Letters	Clinton	0	0
	Frazier	0	0
	Gardner	0	1
	Hillary	0	0
	Kennedy	0	0
8 or 9 Letters	Einstein	0	0
	Gingrich	0	0
	Churchill	0	0
	Letterman	0	0
	Matsumura	0	0
	Sum	**23836**	**12327**

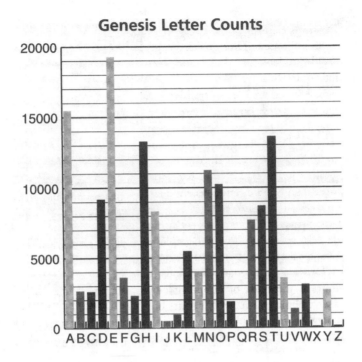

Figure 5a Frequencies of letters of the alphabet in KJV Genesis.

When I performed a separate search for "Roswell" in KJV Genesis, I only found one hidden match for this seven-letter word. But I found 5,812 matches for "UFO," 187 for "disk," five for "MOGUL," 4,798 for "NYU," two for "weather," 1,552 for "gear," seventy-seven for "crash," four for "dummy," 295 for "alien," and two for "saucer." I couldn't find "Roswell" in *Edwards* at steps of 1,000 or less, but I did find most of the others, and in similar numbers.

HOW UNUSUAL ARE PAIRED MESSAGES?

Drosnin and others sometimes admit that finding isolated hidden names or messages can be the product of random chance. But they claim that finding *linked* pairs or triples of names or words is so improbable that doing so proves the supernatural, divine, or alien origin of the "message." In Drosnin's words,

Edwards v. Aguillard Letter Counts

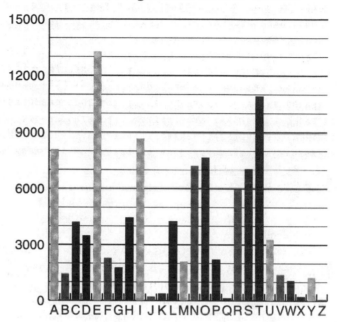

Figure 5b Frequencies of letters of the alphabet in *Edwards v. Aguillard*.

Consistently, the Bible code brings together interlocking words that reveal related information. With Bill Clinton, President. With the Moon landing, spaceship and Apollo 11. With Hitler, Nazi. With Kennedy, Dallas.

In experiment after experiment, the crossword puzzles were found only in the Bible. Not in *War and Peace*, not in any other book, and not in ten million computer-generated test cases. (Drosnin 1997, 26)

Perhaps there was a bug in Drosnin's computer program. Or perhaps he didn't really want to find hidden message pairs outside of the Hebrew Bible. All I know is that I was able to easily produce complex hidden messages in all the texts I worked with.

I developed a computer program that takes various words already located as hidden codes (such as "Hitler" and "Nazi") and

25

```
COMEAFLOODTODESTROYALLFLESHANDTHEBOWSHALLBEINTHECLOUDANDIW
NANHEWASUNCOVEREDWITHINHISTENTANDHAMTHEFATHEROFCANAANSAWT
INTHETENTSOFSHEMANDCANAANSHALLBEHISSERVANTANDNOAHLIVEDAFTE
INTHEIRNATIONSANDTHESONSOFHAMCUSHANDMIZRAIMANDPHUTANDCANAA
UDIMANDANAMIMANDLEHABIMANDNAPHTUHIMANDPATHRUSIMANDCASLUHIM
IESANDINTHEIRNATIONSUNTOSHEMALSOTHEFATHEROFALLTHECHILDRENO
ONSOFJOKTANANDTHEIRDWELLINGWASFROMMESHAASTHOUGOESTUNTOSEPH
FORSTONEANDSLIMEHADTHEYFORMORTERANDTHEYSAIDGOTOLETUSBUILDU
UPONTHEFACEOFALLTHEEARTHANDTHEYLEFTOFFTOBUILDTHECITYTHEREF
LIVEDTHIRTYYEARSANDBEGATEBERANDSALAHLIVEDAFTERHEBEGATEBERF
DAFTERHEBEGATNAHORTWOHUNDREDYEARSANDBEGATSONSANDDAUGHTERSA
```

Figure 6a Step matrix for Genesis, "Hitler/Nazi," step = 500.

plays them against each other to find the best-linked pairs. The
starting letters and equidistant steps provide all the necessary
information, provided one learns how to manipulate it.

I then used this approach to develop the puzzles shown in
figures 6a (Genesis, step = 500) and 6b (*Edwards*, step = 157),
both with direct coded linkages of "Hitler" and "Nazi." These
puzzles are striking counterexamples of Drosnin's claims.

```
UISIANADEPARTMENTOFEDUCATIONTHESCHOOLSUPERINTENDENTSIN
EDINTHESTATUTEABOUTPERCENTOFLOUISIANASSUPERINTENDENTSS
INTENDENTSINTERPRETEDCREATIONSCIENCEASDEFINEDBYTHEACTT
CHINGTHEVIEWTHATTHEUNIVERSEWASMADEBYACREATORIDATETHECO
GTHEINTENTOFTHELEGISLATURECONTEMPORANEOUSTOTHEPASSAGEO
THATFOUNDSTATESTATUTESTOBEUNCONSTITUTIONALHAVEBEENDISP
ONNORJOINSCONCURRINGIWRITESEPARATELYTONOTECERTAINASPEC
RETIONACCORDEDSTATEANDLOCALSCHOOLOFFICIALSINTHESELECTI
ERMINEWHETHERAPARTICULARSTATEACTIONVIOLATESTHEESTABLIS
INVOLVINGTHESENSITIVERELATIONSHIPBETWEENGOVERNMENTANDR
ARLEGISLATIVEPURPOSELEMONVKURTZMANSUPRAATSEECOMMITTEEF
THEESTABLISHMENTCLAUSEIATHESTARTINGPOINTINEVERYCASEINV
NCEDTREATMENTFORCREATIONSCIENCEANDEVOLUTIONSCIENCEACTA
TREATMENTTOCREATIONSCIENCEANDTOEVOLUTIONSCIENCEBALANCE
```

Figure 6b Step matrix for *Edwards v. Aguillard*, "Hitler/Nazi," step = 157.

```
W I T H Q U I C K S H O R T S W A Y I N G S T E P S H E
E S S A T D O W N O N A S O F A N E A R T H E S I L V
H E R S E L F A N D T O A L L A R O U N D H E R I H A V
R B A G A N D A D D R E S S I N G A L L P R E S E N T M
C K O N M E S H E A D D E D T U R N I N G T O H E R H O
P T I O N A N D J U S T S E E H O W B A D L Y I A M D R
W A I S T E D L A C E T R I M M E D D A I N T Y G R A Y
R E A S T S O Y E Z T R A N Q U I L L E L I S E Y O U W
N N A P A V L O V N A Y O U K N O W S A I D T H E P R I
T U R N I N G T O A G E N E R A L M Y H U S B A N D I S
L M E W H A T T H I S W R E T C H E D W A R I S F O R S
I T I N G F O R A N A N S W E R S H E T U R N E D T O S
E L I G H T F U L W O M A N T H I S L I T T L E P R I N
T H E N E X T A R R I V A L S W A S A S T O U T H E A V
A C L E S T H E L I G H T C O L O R E D B R E E C H E S
R O W N D R E S S C O A T T H I S S T O U T Y O U N G M
L K N O W N G R A N D E E O F C A T H E R I N E S T I M
```

Figure 7 *War and Peace*, "Hitler/Nazi," puzzle step = 69, "Hitler" step = 3, "Nazi" step = 207.

In response to Drosnin's challenge, I decided to look for "Hitler" and "Nazi" linked in Tolstoy's *War and Peace* as well. I found an English translation of the epic novel on the Internet, and downloaded the first twenty-four chapters of Book 1, giving me about 167,000 characters. By the time I got to steps of just 750, I already had found more than half a dozen excellent puzzle linkages of "Hitler" and "Nazi." The best appears in figure 7: this entire puzzle text spans just five paragraphs of Chapter 2 of Book 1 of Tolstoy's novel.

Drosnin uses many methods to improve the odds of "impossible-by-chance" linkages. For one, he uses horizontal words taken directly from the original text. For example, when Drosnin found "Clinton" linked to "president," the word "president" was just the Hebrew word for "chief," taken from its actual context in the original Bible. Secondly, Drosnin found some hidden dates referring to the Hebrew calendar; for example, Gulf War activity on January 18,

1991, was found in the words "3rd Shevat." But, he found other dates referring to the Gregorian calendar, such as that of the Oklahoma City bombing, which was linked in the Bible by the hidden date "Day 19," and interpreted as a reference to both April 19, 1995, the date of the bombing, and April 19, 1993 (Waco). And finally, Drosnin takes full advantage of the eccentricities of the Hebrew language, in which words can be condensed and letters occasionally dropped.

My study generated several other examples that are just as spectacular, and just as unlikely (if not more so), than most of Drosnin's matches. Now, Drosnin and his colleagues would probably say that the "Roswell/UFO" connection in KJV Genesis was just a lucky break and couldn't happen again. But I found 5,812 hidden "UFO's" in Genesis, and dozens of these happen to be flying right around and *through* the hidden word "Roswell." As the puzzle step is changed, linked matches appear and disappear with astonishing frequency. Three such examples appear in figure 8, for steps of 88,

```
T H E E A W A Y W I T H M I R T H A N D W I T H S O N G S W I T
A U G H T E R S T H O U H A S T N O W D O N E F O O L I S H L Y
R F A T H E R S P A K E U N T O M E Y E S T E R N I G H T S A Y
N O W T H O U G H T H O U W O U L D E S T N E E D S B E G O N E
A S T T H O U S T O L E N M Y G O D S A N D J A C O B A N S W E
```

Figure 8a Step matrix for Genesis, "Roswell/UFO," step = 88.

```
A L L T H E R I C H E S W H I C H G O D H A T H T A K E N F R O
R E T H R E N W I T H H I M A N D P U R S U E D A F T E R H I M
E R S T H O U H A S T N O W D O N E F O O L I S H L Y I N S O D
E R V A N T S T E N T S B U T H E F O U N D T H E M N O T T H E
E N T Y Y E A R S H A V E I B E E N W I T H T H E E T H Y E W E
```

Figure 8b *S*tep matrix for Genesis, "Roswell/UFO/UFO," step = 589.

```
K A N D S A I D U N T O T H E M I S E E Y O U R F A T H E R
L T H A T L A B A N D O E T H U N T O T H E E I A M T H E G
O L D H I M N O T T H A T H E F L E D S O H E F L E D W I T
G H T E R S T H O U H A S T N O W D O N E F O O L I S H L Y
H E D A L L T H E T E N T B U T F O U N D T H E M N O T A N
```

Figure 8c Step matrix for Genesis, "Roswell/UFO/IFO," step = 753.

589,and 753. Hoagland claims multiple discoveries of the same hidden message are indicative of "redundancy" used by the code-maker to assure us the message is real (Hoagland 1992). But all that is really happening here is that codes can be engineered— *made* to happen. You just have to know how to harvest the field of possibilities.

Figure 9 is another striking linkage I found in KJV Genesis, 42:18 through 45:21. Here, the name "Regis" appears at a step distance of 808, but also at a step of 810, which makes a nice "X" pattern if the puzzle step is 809. (Perhaps someone should notify Regis Philbin and agents Mulder and Scully.)   30

If you work at any given puzzle for a while, large numbers of unexpected names and words invariably turn up. Consider the puzzle of figure 10. This text is a *contiguous* rendition of Genesis 41:38–46. This particular puzzle is easy for the reader to verify manually, since it has a relatively small step of 40. The puzzle itself is 41 characters wide, so the rightmost column is a repetition of the leftmost. I used the computer to find several diagonal messages here: "Deer," "Regis," "Nazi," "Leno," "Dole." Many vertical messages were simple enough to be found just by poring over the puzzle: for example, "Oprah," "here," "Leia," "Hale," "sent," "nude," "pure," "hate," "data," "Roe," "Reed," "Meg," "hood," "pins (snip)," "Deion," and "lone." "Newt" is in there too, but at an off-beat step that makes for a jilted arrangement. And then, there are all those horizontal words too!

I suspect that with diligence, one could find enough matches to make almost all of the characters in the puzzle parts of hidden words. The puzzle below is rife with additional hidden surprises.

```
U S A L I T T L E F O O D A N D J U D A H S P A K
E R E D S U R E L Y N O W W E H A D R E T U R N E
N D T H E M E N W E R E A F R A I D B E C A U S E
R A N D T H E Y M A D E R E A D Y T H E P R E S E
E E G Y P T I A N S M I G H T N O T E A T B R E A
B Y I N D E E D H E D I V I N E T H Y E H A V E D
R O U N D A N D J O S E P H S A I D U N T O T H E
E S A I D U N T O M Y L O R D T H E L A D C A N N
A N T S S H A L L B R I N G D O W N T H E G R A Y
```

Figure 9 Step matrix for Genesis, first "Regis" at step = 808, second "Regis" at step = 810 (puzzle step = 809).

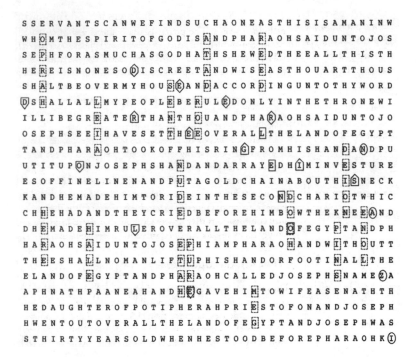

Figure 10 Genesis 41:38–46, multiple matches, step = 40.

Rips himself appears in "spirit" read backwards. "Pour," "Alan," and "sash" run vertically. And diagonal messages of varying complexity lurk everywhere. Can you find the "apes" swinging between "data" and "Reed"? "Love" intersecting with "nude"? How about "Ares," "reel," "deft," "lion," "dogs," "pony," "hard," "diet," "trace," "card," "Poe," and "wart"? They are all in there—and more.

There are dozens of linked messages in the puzzle. But how are we to know which words are linked by the secretive author? Is the "real" message "Nazi sent pure hate here," or is it "Deion pins nude Oprah?" All of these hits are authentic, encoded names that have lurked inside the text of the King James Version of Genesis for hundreds of years. But the whimsical combinations they appear in show that these surprises are simply lucky breaks, and not authentic messages from above.

WHAT ARE THE ODDS, REALLY?

Drosnin and his colleagues say that getting linked matches by coincidence is statistically impossible and cite the odds against such coincidences as more than 3,000 to 1 (and sometimes *much* more). Using numbers like these, the Bible code promoters try to convince their readers that the existence of God is now proven statistically *beyond the shadow of a doubt*, simply because they can find linked pairs like "Clinton" and "chief" in the same general area of the Bible.

But their core conclusions are based on severely flawed probability arguments. Drosnin's formulation of the improbability of the occurrence of linked pairs is implicitly based on the assumption that you have only one opportunity to get the match. But, with the help of the computer, Drosnin gets to take advantage of *billions* of opportunities.

Let's look at Drosnin's approach with a lottery analogy. The probability of winning a lottery with a single ticket is very small, and Drosnin says the probability of getting an improbable match (such as "Clinton" and "president") is also very small. But what happens if you buy more than one ticket?

In the New Mexico "Daily Millions" lottery, the odds of winning the $1 million jackpot with just one ticket are about ten million to one against. With two tickets, the odds plummet, to about five million to one. If you buy one million tickets, your odds drop to only about ten to one against. And if you invest $10 million in tickets, the odds become approximately two to one in your favor! Most people can't afford to buy millions of tickets. Those who *do* have that kind of money usually don't dump it on the lottery, because you almost always end up losing.

But in Drosnin's game, you don't have to win more than you lose. You don't even have to break even. All you need for success is to win *every once in a while*. And, you can have what amounts to millions of "free lottery tickets" simply by running a computer program, or poring over crossword-puzzle printouts. Drosnin routinely tests *billions* of letter sequences for matches to selected words or names, and goes to steps of many thousands. By using steps lower than 1,000 only, I limited myself to using only about 3 percent of the potential of Genesis or *Edwards*. Brendan McKay (in personal communication) showed me how to find hidden words much more efficiently, and a search of KJV Genesis at all possible steps for my list of twenty-five names came up with over one million additional matches. These include six hits for "Clinton," fifteen for "Gardner," three for "Hillary" and "Einstein," and two for "Kennedy."

35

CONCLUSION

The promoters of hidden-message claims say, "How could such amazing coincidences be the product of random chance?" I think the real question should be, "How could such coincidences *not* be the inevitable product of a huge sequence of trials on a large, essentially *random* database?"

40   Once I learned how to navigate in puzzle-space, finding "incredible" predictions became a routine affair. I found "comet," "Hale," and "Bopp" linked in KJV Genesis, along with "forty" and "died," which could be interpreted as an obvious reference to Heaven's Gate. I found "Trinity," "Los Alamos," "atom," and "bomb" encoded together in *Edwards*, in a section containing references to "security," "test," and "anti-fascist." And I found "Hitler" linked to "Nazi" dozens of times in several books. When I set out to engineer a "hidden code" link of "code" and "bogus" in KJV Genesis, I was able to produce sixty closely linked pairs. And every single one of these pairs could fit inside a reasonably sized puzzle.

      The source of the mysterious "Bible code" has been revealed—its *homo sapiens*.

      Now somebody go tell Oprah.

References

Begley, Sharon. 1997. Seek and ye shall find. *Newsweek*, June 9, pp. 66–67.

Drosnin, Michael. 1997. *The Bible Code*. New York: Simon and Schuster.

Gardner, Martin. 1997. Farrakhan, Cabala, Baha'i, and 19. *Skeptical Inquirer* 21 (2): 16–18, 57.

Hewitt, V. J., and Peter Lorie. 1991. *Nostradamus: The End of the Millennium*. New York: Simon and Schuster.

Hoagland, Richard C., 1992. *The Monuments of Mars: A City on the Edge of Forever*. Berkeley, Calif.: North Atlantic Books.

Van Biema, David. 1997. Deciphering God's plan. *Time*, June 9, p. 56.

Witztum, Doron, Eliyahu Rips, and Yoav Rosenburg. 1994. Equidistant letter sequences in the Book of Genesis. *Statistical Science* 9(3).

For Discussion and Writing

1. What is a step value in the Bible code? Explain how it works.
2. Suppose that such a code actually lay hidden in a text. How would it be of use to someone who could "read" it? That is, suppose you were able to see "Roswell" and "Butkus" next to each other in a section of Deuteronomy. What would that tell you?

3. Thomas asks "Does perception of meaning prove the message was deliberately created?" What is he asking? Think this over, and then explain your answer to his question.
4. Thomas reports that one skeptical investigator "found" a prediction of Robert Kennedy's assassination in *Moby Dick*. Explain how this might be possible. If you picked a book at random and found such a message in it, what would you conclude?
5. Try to imagine this code from a believer's point of view. What assumptions do you make about prophecy, God, encoding, and so on? What is most appealing and convincing to a believer in this context?
6. The author uses the step-system on a number of texts. What do his findings demonstrate? Why is it impossible to disprove the claim that the Bible contains such a code? Is this a problem in logic? In psychology?

The First Crop Circles—Mystery Solved

CARL SAGAN

Carl Sagan was an astronomer, a professor, and a writer who influenced public views enormously. He won a Pulitzer prize for his book The Dragons of Eden, *which was one of his more than 20 books. With his wife, Ann Druyan, he was co-producing a major motion picture from Warner Brothers based on his novel,* Contact. *It was released after his death. The following excerpt is from his book,* The Demon Haunted World: Science as a Candle in the Dark. *Sagan reveals here the humble origins of crop circles, while at the same time making a plea for rational thought.*

———————————— ✦ ————————————

How modest our expectations are about "aliens," and how shoddy the standards of evidence that many of us are willing to accept, can be found in the saga of the crop circles. Originating in Great Britain and spreading throughout the world was something surpassing strange.

Farmers or passersby would discover circles (and, in later years, much more complex pictograms) impressed upon fields of wheat, oats, barley, and rapeseed. Beginning with simple circles in the middle 1970s, the phenomenon progressed year by year, until by the late 1980s and early 1990s the countryside, especially in southern England, was graced by immense geometrical figures, some the size of football fields, imprinted on cereal grain before the harvest—circles tangent to circles, or connected by axes, parallel lines drooping off, "insectoids." Some of the patterns showed a central circle surrounded by four symmetrically-placed smaller circles—clearly, it was concluded, caused by a flying saucer and its four landing pods.

A hoax? Impossible, almost everyone said. There were hundreds of cases. It was done sometimes in only an hour or two in the dead of night, and on *such* a large scale. No footprints of pranksters leading towards or away from the pictograms could be found. And besides, what possible motive could there be for a hoax?

Many less conventional conjectures were offered. People with some scientific training examined sites, spun arguments, instituted whole journals devoted to the subject. Were the figures caused by strange whirlwinds called "columnar vortices," or even stranger ones called "ring vortices"? What about ball lightning? Japanese investigators tried to simulate, in the laboratory and on a small scale, the plasma physics they thought was working its way on far-off Wiltshire.

5   But especially as the crop figures became more complex, meteorological or electrical explanations became more strained. Plainly, it was due to UFOs, the aliens communicating to us in a geometrical language. Or perhaps it was the devil, or the long-suffering Earth complaining about the depredations visited upon it by the hand of Man. New Age tourists came in droves. All-night vigils were undertaken by enthusiasts equipped with audio recorders and infrared vision scopes. Print and electronic media from all over the world tracked the intrepid cerealogists. Best-selling books on extraterrestrial crop distorters were purchased by a breathless and admiring public. True, no saucer was actually seen settling down on the wheat, no geometrical figure was filmed in the course of being generated. But dowsers authenticated their alien origin, and channelers made contact with the entities responsible. "Orgone energy" was detected within the circles.

Questions were asked in Parliament. The royal family called in for special consultation Lord Solly Zuckerman, former principal scientific adviser to the Ministry of Defence. Ghosts were said to be involved; also, the Knights Templar of Malta and other secret societies. Satanists were implicated. The Defence Ministry was covering the matter up. A few inept and inelegant circles were judged attempts by the military to throw the public off the track. The tabloid press had a field day. The *Daily Mirror* hired a farmer and his son to make five circles in hope of tempting a rival tabloid, the *Daily Express*, into reporting the story. The *Express* was, in this case at least, not taken in.

"Cerealogical" organizations grew and splintered. Competing groups sent each other intimidating doggerel. Accusations were made of incompetence or worse. The number of crop "circles" rose into the thousands. The phenomenon spread to the United States, Canada, Bulgaria, Hungary, Japan, the Netherlands. The pictograms—espccially the more complex of them—begaii to be quoted increasingly in arguments for alien visitation. Strained connections were drawn to the "Face" on Mars. One scientist of my acquaintance wrote to me that extremely sophisticated mathematics was hidden in these figures; they could only be the result of a superior intelligence. In fact, one matter on which almost all of the contending cerealogists agreed is that the later crop figures were much too complex and elegant to be due to mere human intervention, much less to some ragged and irresponsible hoaxers. Extraterrestrial intelligence was apparent at a glance . . .

In 1991, Doug Bower and Dave Chorley, two blokes from Southampton, announced they had been making crop figures for 15 years. They dreamed it up over stout one evening in their regular pub, The Percy Hobbes. They had been amused by UFO reports and thought it might be fun to spoof the UFO gullibles. At first they flattened the wheat with the heavy steel bar that Bower used as a security device on the back door of his picture framing ship. Later on they used planks and ropes. Their first efforts took only a few minutes. But, being inveterate pranksters as well as serious artists, the challenge began to grow on them. Gradually, they designed and executed more and more demanding figures.

At first no one seemed to notice. There were no media reports. Their artforms were neglected by the tribe of UFOlogists. They were on the verge of abandoning crop circles to move on to some other, more emotionally rewarding hoax.

Suddenly crop circles caught on. UFOlogists fell for it hook,   10 line, and sinker. Bower and Chorley were delighted—especially when scientists and others began to announce their considered judgment that no merely human intelligence could be responsible.

Carefully they planned each nocturnal excursion—sometimes following meticulous diagrams they had prepared in watercolors. They closely tracked their interpreters. When a local meteorologist deduced a kind of whirlwind because all of the crops were deflected downward in a clockwise circle, they confounded him by making a new figure with an exterior ring flattened counterclockwise.

Soon other crop figures appeared in southern England and elsewhere. Copycat hoaxsters had appeared. Bower and Chorley carved out a responsive message in wheat: "WEARENOTALONE." Even this some took to be a genuine extraterrestrial message (although it would have been better had it read "YOUARENOTALONE"). Doug and Dave began signing their artworks with two Ds; even this was attributed to a mysterious alien purpose. Bower's nocturnal disappearances aroused the suspicions of his wife Ilene. Only with great difficulty—Ilene accompanying Dave and Doug one night, and then joining the credulous in admiring their handiwork next day—was she convinced that his absences were, in this sense, innocent.

Eventually Bower and Chorley tired of the increasingly elaborate prank. While in excellent physical condition, they were both in their sixties now and a little old for nocturnal commando operations in the fields of unknown and often unsympathetic farmers. They may have been annoyed at the fame and fortune accrued by those who merely photographed their art and announced aliens to be the artists. And they became worried that if they delayed much longer, no statement of theirs would be believed.

So they confessed. They demonstrated to reporters how they made even the most elaborate insectoid patterns. You might think that never again would it be argued that a sustained hoax over many years is impossible, and never again would we hear that no one could possibly be motivated to deceive the gullible into thinking that aliens exist. But the media paid brief attention. Cerealogists urged them to go easy; after all, they were depriving many of the pleasure of imagining wondrous happenings.

15   Since then, other crop circle hoaxers have kept at it, but mostly in a more desultory and less inspired manner. As always, the confession of the hoax is greatly overshadowed by the sustained initial excitement. Many have heard of the pictograms in cereal grains and their alleged UFO connection, but draw a blank when the names of Bower and Chorley or the very idea that the whole business may be a hoax are raised. An informative exposé by the journalist Jim Schnabel (*Round in Circles*; Penguin Books, 1994)—from which much of my account is taken—is in print. Schnabel joined the cerealogists early and in the end made a few successful pictograms himself. (He prefers a garden roller to a wooden plank, and found that simply

stomping grain with one's feet does an acceptable job.) But Schnabel's work, which one reviewer called "the funniest book I've read in ages," had only modest success. Demons sell; hoaxers are boring and in bad taste.

The tenets of skepticism do not require an advanced degree to master, as most successful used car buyers demonstrate. The whole idea of a democratic application of skepticism is that everyone should have the essential tools to effectively and constructively evaluate claims to knowledge. All science asks is to employ the same levels of skepticism we use in buying a used car on in judging the quality of analgesics or beer from their television commercial.

But the tools of skepticism are generally unavailable to the citizens of our society. They're hardly ever mentioned in the schools, even in the presentation of science, its most ardent practitioner, although skepticism repeatedly sprouts spontaneously out of the disappointments of everyday life. Our politics, economics, advertising, and religions (New Age and Old) are awash in credulity. Those who have something to sell, those who wish to influence public opinion, those in power, a skeptic might suggest, have a vested interest in discouraging skepticism.

For Discussion and Writing

1. What is meant by the general term "crop circle"? Describe some of the features of a crop circle.
2. What is Occam's razor, and how might it apply to the phenomena of strange figures in fields of grain?
3. In their early days, crop circles were not always linked to aliens. Discuss the process by which such a link could take hold of the popular imagination. What other explanations have been offered for the origins of the phenomena? Who were some of the "explainers"?
4. Sagan says that one of his scientist acquaintances claimed he found sophisticated mathematics encrypted in the cereal designs. Compare this "find" to Bible code "hits." What do you see?
5. Two friends confessed to making the original circles, and then showed how they did it. Why, in your view, did the confession *not* dissuade further belief in the mysterious designs? Does debunking have no real effect on rational people?
6. What does Sagan mean by the term "the democratic application of skepticism"? He claims that our culture is "awash in credulity." What evidence can you mention in support of this claim?

A Not-So-Psychic Detective? A Case Study of Noreen Renier's Latest and Greatest "Success" Story

GARY P. POSNER

Gary Posner, a medical doctor, has written numerous articles deal-ing with the paranormal. His publications include contributions to the anthology, Skeptical Odysseys: Personal Accounts by the World's Leading Paranormal Inquirers, *and a chapter in* The Skeptical Encyclopedia of Pseudoscience. *He is a regular contribu-tor to* Skeptic Magazine, *and to the* Skeptical Inquirer *as well. Humor often finds its way into his sharp analyses. He once wrote that "a well-done spirit-medium performance is rare," bringing a playful tone to a serious critique of James Van Praagh's conversa-tions with the dead. In the following article, Posner evaluates the psychic performance of Noreen Renier, a woman who claims she has mysterious powers of perception.*

◆

On April 3, 1996, the skeletal remains of seventy-six-year-old Norman Lewis, missing for two years, were recovered from the murky waters of a limestone quarry in the tiny Florida town of Williston, located just southwest of Gainesville. The April 5 Associated Press story, as headlined in the *St. Petersburg* (Florida) *Times*, revealed: "Psychic tip leads to missing man's body." Although she was not present during the search or recovery, the "tipster" was Florida "psychic detective" Noreen Renier, who boasts a successful history of assisting in hundreds of police investigations into unsolved homicides and missing-person cases.

Before specializing as a "psychic detective," Renier, age 60, was credited with having predicted the 1981 assassination attempt on President Ronald Reagan, and the assassination of Egyptian President Anwar Sadat later that year. Through the years, she has appeared on numerous national television programs including the *Joan Rivers Show*, *Geraldo*, *Sightings*, and even the CBS news-magazine *48 Hours*. In the classic textbook *Practical Homicide Investigation*, used by the FBI and many other police academies, the author identifies Renier as "a psychic and recognized authority on the phenomena of extrasensory perception."

According to press accounts, on March 24, 1994, after telling his girlfriend that he would be right back, the elderly Mr. Lewis drove off from home, leaving behind his wallet and respiratory inhaler, and (along with his truck) was never seen or heard from again. In its April 11, 1994, edition, the *Ocala* (Florida) *Star-Banner* quoted Williston Police Chief Olin Slaughter as observing, "It's like he fell off the edge of the earth."

After spending more than a year following-up on "hundreds" of leads and conducting numerous land and aerial searches, all to no avail, the Williston police, and the Lewises, decided to enlist the aid of a psychic. Investigator Brian Hewitt suggested Noreen Renier, having previously been impressed by a performance of hers. The Lewis family reportedly provided the $650 fee for her services (the police department was said not to have had sufficient funds).

On July 17, 1995, three weeks after Hewitt's initial phone call to   5
her, Renier performed her "psychic" reading, at her home. Clutching one of Mr. Lewis' possessions, she tuned into his vibrations and provided a number of specific clues intended to help lead the police to his body. The *Williston Pioneer* (on April 4 and June 27, 1996) quoted Chief Slaughter as saying that Renier indicated Lewis had traveled "*east* from his home to an area where there is . . . water in something like a pit." (Emphasis added.) The *Chiefland* (Florida) *Citizen* (April 11, 1996) quotes Slaughter: "She could see he was surrounded by metal. . . . She could see a cliff wall, and loose bricks, a railroad track, and a bridge." The numbers "45" and "21" were also said to have been offered as helpful clues.

A subsequent look by the police into several bodies of water proved as fruitless as the earlier searches. But because of Renier's reading, the police called in a team of Navy divers from Jacksonville to search one particular limestone quarry among many scattered throughout the area. Although about eight months elapsed before the team could arrive, on April 3, 1996, with the assistance of a $70,000 detection device, the divers did indeed locate the missing truck containing Lewis' remains, submerged in twenty feet of murky water.

When the Williston police announced that the case had been solved largely as a result of Renier's psychic clues, the story quite naturally captured the attention of the media. In addition to regional newspapers and television, the Associated Press and national radio icon Paul Harvey reported upon it, and the TV show

Sightings devoted a segment to it in November 1996. The "Williston Case" quickly became the pinnacle of Renier's storied career.

ENTER THE SKEPTIC

My involvement in the Williston case began in May 1996 when I received a telephone call from a researcher for Towers Productions, which was producing a series called *The Unexplained* for the A&E Network. Their program on "Psychic Detectives" (which first aired in January 1997) would feature several individuals, including Renier, and would specifically cover Williston. My participation was requested to insure a balanced presentation.

Two months later, the police and I were interviewed for the show (in Williston), as was Renier the following day (at her Orlando home). By then, I had accumulated a number of newspaper articles and maps and had come to an unexpected and provocative conclusion: Norman Lewis' remains appeared to have been found *not* because the police had the Navy divers search the body of water *best* fitting Renier's psychic clues, but because they had the Navy search the *wrong* watery pit!

10   Scanning my roadmap of Williston, I immediately noticed its most striking feature—a blue body of water nearly in the heart of town, less than one mile east of Mr. Lewis' home. This limestone quarry, when approached from the west, is located adjacent to the intersection of U.S. 41 and State Route 121. Flipping that map over I saw that the map on the opposite side reveals that U.S. 41 is also known in Williston as State Route 45. If Lewis had indeed traveled *east* from his home to a watery pit, as Chief Slaughter indicated Renier had seen in her psychic vision, he would have encountered such a quarry just beyond the junction of State Routes 45 and 121. Renier's two numerical clues were reportedly "45" and "21"—had she offered "45" and "*121*," someone might have cynically accused her of having researched the case and consulted a map!

The U.S. Geological Survey's "Williston Quadrangle" map, which I purchased at a Tampa map store, shows this clearly marked "Quarry" area in more detail. Of note is the Seaboard Coast Line's north/south railroad track 3/4 of a mile east of the quarry's eastern circumference, with a branch directed westward into the heart of the quarry area. One of Renier's clues was "railroad track."

As I told the Towers producer, I cannot be certain if Renier's clues were the result of "psychic" power or some other, purely natural, process. But, I added, forget about "psychic" power for a moment and just employ "ordinary" detective-style reasoning and common sense. Consider that the intensive ground and aerial searches had turned up nothing. If Mr. Lewis and his truck were somewhere within the potential reach of the Williston police, where could they possibly be? In the middle of a densely wooded area? In an abandoned building? (Either, perhaps, if only a body was missing. But a truck?) Only one possibility even comes to mind—submerged in a body of water.

Chief Slaughter, it seems, had the right idea all along, even if he was not consciously aware of it. It did indeed appear "like [Lewis] fell off the edge of the earth"—and into a bottomless, or at least very deep, watery pit. A quick glance at the Williston roadmap revealed an obvious potential site, as confirmed by the U.S.G.S. map.

One minor problem: The logical site, the one that Renier's "psychic" clues seem tailored to—the limestone quarry less than a mile east of Lewis' home, at the junction of State Routes 45 and 121, serviced by a railroad track—was *not* where Lewis' truck and remains were ultimately found! Rather, they were located in a different limestone pit, one nearly due *north* of Lewis' home and more than twice as far away! The recovery site, known as the Whitehurst pit, is also located adjacent to State Route 45, but not Route 121.

Renier's "21" clue, in fact, played no beneficial role whatsoever in assisting in the location of Lewis' body. Yet, this clue has been hailed by the police as perhaps her most eerily precise of all. Why? Because, *after* Lewis' body had been recovered, it was announced that he had been found "2.1" miles from his home—even though, as the crow flies, the distance appears to measure only about 1.6 miles on the U.S.G.S. map.

Nor was her "railroad track" clue of any value in deciding which of these two quarries to have the Navy divers search. Although the U.S.G.S. map clearly shows an "abandoned" track traversing the Whitehurst quarry east/west, the police did not become aware of the buried track until a portion of it was unearthed after the divers had already been called in.

Nor did her "bridge" clue offer any assistance in targeting this particular pit, or in helping narrow down the search area within the 30-acre Whitehurst quarry. But, as WTVT-TV 13 (Tampa) reported on April 19, 1996, "Another clue that amazed [Chief] Slaughter was that the psychic saw a bridge nearby. Turned out [after the fact] that he'd passed it countless times and never saw it—on the access road to the quarry—an old, wooden truck scale that smacks for all the world of a bridge, if you take the time to stare at it."

And as for her apparently precise State Route "45" clue, read on.

"HITS" AND MISSES

In July 1996, a skeptical Tampa attorney made a Florida Public Records Act request of the Williston police department to provide him with a copy of its entire file on this case, which he then forwarded to me. Investigator Hewitt responded by sending copies of all the paperwork, which included two items of immediate interest: a May 12, 1995, report (supplemented on June 15) filed by Hewitt, and the "clues" jotted down by Hewitt from Renier's July 17, 1995, "psychic" reading.

20   In his two-page May 12/June 15 report (I have corrected a few spelling errors), Hewitt notes that a

> handyman . . . had recently told [a client] that [Lewis] had told him that if [Lewis] were not able to take care of himself because of illness, he would find a river or pit rather than the [retired] sailors home. . . . Four days before his disappearance, [Lewis] told [the handyman] that if his health were failing, he would never be cared for by relatives or submit to the sailors home, that there were too many pits and canals. . . . [The handyman later] arrived at the police station . . . and he related [to Hewitt] the last conversation he had with Norman Lewis . . . indicating it [actually] took place approx. three weeks before his disappearance. He stated Norman seemed agitated and dissatisfied with . . . his life [including having] problems at the house with his girlfriend, relating she did not make him feel needed. . . . Told [handyman] not to get old, and made some reference to knowing every rock pit in the county! . . .

This "smoking gun" document had been previously unknown to me and to the A&E producer. But it was now apparent that as a result of his failing health and other personal problems (an early newspaper article had also described him as "despondent" over financial matters), Lewis had threatened to commit suicide in a "river" or a "rock pit." Further, word of this had begun to spread through his tiny community and had become known to the police *two months prior to their session with Renier.* Might Renier have actually learned of this, in advance, *from the police?*

The Tampa attorney had also specifically requested any video/audio tapes of Renier's reading. After inquiring as to why only written records were released, Hewitt advised him that an audiotape did in fact exist and would be provided. As for a video-tape, Hewitt wrote: "As I have advised you in several telephone conversations, the only [video] tape contained in the requested file . . . is of the recovery, which you indicated you did not want."

When even the promised audiotape failed to arrive, the attorney threatened a lawsuit "if a copy of the [audio] tape is not presented to us within seven (7) days." Hewitt finally responded by delivering what he termed "a copy of the field audio tape [which] contains portions of the session with Noreen Renier." To my dismay, upon playing the tape, it was evident that there was a cut/edit after nearly every sentence spoken by Renier (and often in mid-sentence or mid-word). Further, the entire tape runs for a mere *five minutes and forty-three seconds*. Yet, it does contain some "clues" worth discussing:

- "A lot of rocks. . . . Swallowed up [down there in the water] but there's hardness higher up. . . . We have a lot of things that go straight down. No one really knows what's down there because it's so hazardous and dangerous and people don't go down there. . . . There's a railroad track that goes through there." [Did she know about the suicide threat? Or consult maps, as I did?]
- "Let me have a starting place. . . . We want to get you in the quadrant from 9 to 12 . . . into that pie-shaped area." And from Hewitt's handwritten notes from Renier's reading: "Where do you want me to start? At his house . . . " [Starting from Lewis' house, his body was found in the 12:00 to 3:00 quadrant, not "9 to 12."]
- "Speedometer is zero in front of the house. . . . Maybe 4, maybe 5. If it's 45 miles, if it's 4.5 miles. I want to go to my left. I want to go to 9. . . . I feel 45, 45 degrees. You know how they have that little baby circle up there? [i.e., a degree symbol]. . . . Looking for H and 45." [This is the "45" clue being credited as a "hit" because Lewis was found near State Route 45!]
- "Must be still somehow in the vehicle. I feel the metal very, very strongly." [Renier had been told in advance that Lewis' truck was also missing.]
- "We're not too far from an old bridge. Either it's been decayed or it's broken or it's not used. . . . It's called the old bridge or is an old bridge." [The old truck scale was nearby, although it was certainly not known as "the old bridge."]

- "One point, or one-one point two. I see two-two-I [the letter "I"]. I believe a very strong H, 'Ha'-sounding or an H in it." And from Hewitt's notes: "221 . . . 22 . . . 21 . . . 21 . . . H . . . EML . . . E . . . 11.2" [Renier was credited with an eerily accurate "hit" because Lewis was supposedly found 2.1 miles from his home! But what about "45 miles" and "4.5 miles"?]

Among the pages in the police file is a map of Williston with a 90 degree (L-shaped) area from 11:00 to 2:00 (not "9 to 12") drawn on it and labeled "Noreen's quadrant." The point of convergence of the two lines is correctly marked "Norman's House," and the quadrant includes the northern Whitehurst pit where the body was found (at about 1:00) but not the eastern pit that her clues appear to more closely fit (at about 3:30–4:00).

25   In stark contrast to A&E's balanced coverage of the case on *The Unexplained*, the Sci-Fi Channel's *Sightings* coverage included no skeptical input. The *Sightings* narrator asks, but is not able to answer, the question: "Why did Norman disappear?" No mention is made of Investigator Hewitt's report, filed two months prior to Renier's "psychic" reading, regarding Lewis' "rock pit" suicide plan. But in fairness to *Sightings*, the police had also withheld this crucial information from the A&E producer.

In Renier's re-created reading for the *Sightings* cameras, with her eyes closed, feigning a trance-like state, she strays from her original reading so as to now specifically associate the number "21" with miles: "Numbers—21. I feel miles." On the edited audiotape, there is no mention of "21" in any context (although, as shown earlier, "21" does appear in Hewitt's notes in the midst of a stream of numbers/letters with no particular regard to mileage), and the only numbers associated with "miles" are "45" and "4.5." Nor is there a "21" clue on the edited *video*tape (yes, it did finally materialize—see below).

The "45 miles" clue is especially puzzling, as Renier has been credited with correctly determining that Lewis would be found a short distance from his home. From her *Sightings* re-creation: "I'm driving for a short distance, and then something happens, and I see him in the air, going downward." And from the edited videotape of her original reading:

Norman's house is here [gesturing to the right with her right arm]. Here's the road [gesturing straight ahead with her left arm]. We go this way [pointing straight ahead with her left hand]. . . . But we don't go very far that way, we're going to veer off here [pointing left with her left hand] . . . towards the river. And for some reason the river is down below [as if describing Lewis' arrival at the pit/quarry's sheer cliff].

This passage on the videotape appears to be a second "smoking gun," this time with regard to the particular body of water to which Renier's directions actually lead. As I earlier indicated, Renier's clues (as I understood them even before receiving this video) seemed to lead *not* to the Whitehurst pit (located north of Lewis' home) where the body was ultimately found, but rather to another rock pit much closer to, and nearly due east of, his home.

During my two visits to Williston, I viewed the former Lewis residence, located on N.W. 7th Blvd. With the home on the right side of the street, proceeding straight ahead (as per Renier's "psychic" vision) leads *southeasterly* for approximately one-third mile, at which time the road curves left to a *due east* bearing, until N.W. 7th Blvd. ends at its intersection with U.S. 41, approximately one-half mile from the Lewis home. Another quarter-mile or so due east, dead ahead (no pun intended), is the massive "eastern" rock quarry, the most prominent feature on the Williston roadmap.

Summarizing Renier's role in this case, the *Sightings* narrator says, "Investigator Hewitt put all of Renier's clues together, used some gut instinct of his own, and came up with one word— 'Quarry.'" But we now know that Hewitt had actually learned *two months earlier* of Lewis' plans for ending his life in a quarry. And in the edited video of Renier's actual reading, she refers to the body of water not as a "pit" or "quarry," but as a "river" (although she appears puzzled as to why it goes "down" such a sheer cliff). The word "quarry" is heard once on the videotape, *not* after Hewitt has a chance to digest all of Renier's clues and apply his "gut instinct," but in the midst of the session, by an unidentified male questioner present with Hewitt in Renier's living room: "Now look at that quarry. As you're looking at it and looking at it from the entrance there . . . "

Following Renier's reading, did the police zero-in on one quarry to which Noreen's directions pointed? Hewitt says on *Sightings* that he "walked around probably 30 quarries" before deciding that the Whitehurst pit most closely matched the totality of Renier's clues. Perhaps that was his reason for having the Navy divers scour that one pit, which did result in Lewis' body and truck being recovered. But his initial rationale for concentrating on the Whitehurst pit was described this way in his report filed six days after Renier's reading: " . . . the Whitehurst pits are an obvious first

30

impression . . . being the closest and the most accessible from the Lewis residence." (Although the "eastern" pit was fenced off by this time, it had been easily accessible when Lewis disappeared, and it is half as far from Lewis' home as is Whitehurst.)

As for this "eastern" pit, a person with some inside knowledge of the police investigation (who allowed me to tape our conversation but requests anonymity) told me that this had been the "prime target for the investigation" immediately following Renier's reading. "They didn't think there was a [railroad] track [at Whitehurst]."

At the conclusion of the *Sightings* report, the narrator explained how Renier's "22" clue (remember that stream of numbers?) had also been remarkably accurate: When Lewis' body was recovered, "the calendar date on Norman's diving watch was stopped on the number 22." For the record, he had disappeared and presumably committed suicide on the 24th of March, 1994. As a clue to the location of Mr. Lewis' missing body, "22" was utterly useless.

THE VIDEOTAPE'S CURIOUS ARRIVAL

The ultimate arrival of the edited videotape came as a complete surprise. When the *audio*tape turned out to have been heavily and crudely edited, the attorney wrote back to Hewitt requesting "a complete copy of the audiotape." Hewitt's reply explained that the tape "is the only audio tape I have regarding Noreen Renier's session [and] was expressly made [from a more lengthy original] for field use with regard to the location of Mr. Lewis." Most curiously, the letter continued: "You are requesting additional material. . . . We are under no obligation to provide you with any material without prepayment. Therefore, with your payment of [an additional $14.00] . . . I will forward to you the only remaining tape I have regarding this case."

35   The attorney assumed that the "only remaining tape" was a video of the recovery of the truck and body, as Hewitt had previously indicated. Nonetheless, he decided to fork over the $14.00. Incredibly, a month later, he received from Hewitt the videotape which, despite having been edited down to about 14 minutes, still contained the "smoking gun" segment.

In a letter accompanying the videotape. Hewitt informed the attorney that he had "filed for mediation with the State Attorney General's office . . . to assure you [that] we are in full compliance under the Florida Public Records Act." Through the mediator, the attorney then posed several questions, including these: "Why did the police department initially deny having a videotape and thereafter send us one?" "One map . . . depicts an area labeled 'Noreen's quadrant.' Who drew this quardrant on the map?" [see earlier discussion]. "What is the personal relationship, if any, between Detective Hewitt and Noreen Renier?"

This third question was prompted by two peculiar circumstances—the apparent initial withholding of information by Hewitt, and a stunning move by Renier: After living in Orlando for more than 20 years, she has now packed her bags and relocated to Williston!

Another question relates to an undated police report, filed by Hewitt, which does not appear to comport with Renier's reading, at least as excerpted on the tapes. Writes Hewitt, "She picked out [Levy County Road] 501 on local map which I provided, indicating it was the road Lewis had traveled after leaving his residence, in a *northerly* direction." (Emphasis added.) CR 501 is the northern extension of Lewis' street, but according to the video's "smoking gun" segment, Renier actually indicated that he headed *south*.

But the answers to these questions have not been forthcoming. The mediator has written back informing the attorney that the Public Records Act does not compel Hewitt to respond. And the City Attorney for the town of Williston has sternly weighed in: "[Y]ou have [already] received all public records in possession of the City relating to [this] investigation."

AFTER-THE-FACT REASONING

Two final questions, fundamental to the very nature of "psychic" phenomena, require consideration. In my chapter on Renier for the book *Psychic Sleuths* (edited by Joe Nickell, Prometheus Books, 1994), I showed at the time how Renier (like the rest of the psychics profiled in the book) had yet to convincingly demonstrate genuine "psychic" power under proper observing conditions. Has Renier now become the first psychic to successfully do so? Or might her "success" in the Williston case be explainable in more mundane terms, perhaps as the result of a combination of factors such as advance research, common sense/intuition, feeding back information gleaned from the police themselves, and "retrofitting"—interpreting ambiguous clues, after the fact, as having been remarkably accurate and valuable "hits"?

40

To those who believe in "psychic" power and other supernatural phenomena, the answers to these two questions no doubt remain "crystal ball" clear. And they remain equally clear, though through quite another prism, to those skeptics of the paranormal who demand extraordinary proof of such extraordinary claims.

For Discussion and Writing

1. Describe Renier's "psychic reading" method. What does she "tune into"? Discuss the nature of Renier's clues. How much room do they leave for interpretation? What could the clue "surrounded by metal" suggest other than a car? In the original "session," how were the numbers "45" and "21" presented?
2. Posner notes that a USGS map of the Williston area shows a railroad track just east of the quarry where police found the missing man's body. What is Posner's point?
3. Why does Posner refer to Brian Hewitt's May 12/June 15 report as a "smoking gun"? What, if anything, links this report to Renier?
4. Renier mentioned the number "22" in her initial reading of events linked to the disappearance of Norman Lewis. The narrator of the television show "Sightings" mentions that Mr. Lewis' watch had stopped on the date "22." Discuss the limits of assigning significance to this parallel. How does Posner treat it?
5. Posner mentions that Renier moved to Williston after the investigation. He asks what relation might exist between Renier and Hewitt, who lived in Williston. What difference would a personal relation between the psychic and the detective make to you?

The Turtle Jean Lafitte: Adventures of a Pet Psychic

SONYA FITZPATRICK

Sonya Fitzpatrick's book, The Pet Psychic: What the Animals Tell Me *was published in 2003. Her work with animals forms the basis of a television show aired on the Animal Planet television network, and Discovery.com features an ad for her services as an "animal communicator." The excerpt that follows recounts her encounter with and treatment of an unhappy turtle, Jean Lafitte.*

◆

My friend Pat's son Carter had been greatly disappointed to discover he couldn't fit his new "pirate turtle" out with a brass earring and peg-leg, but nonetheless, Jean Lafitte had turned out to be a most satisfactory pet. Pat's family had owned the turtle for almost two years, and in that time, his shell had grown from less than two inches to more than six inches across.

During the first cold snap of 1993, Jean Lafitte quit eating. This was puzzling because he'd always had quite an appetite. Pat phoned the vet and he told her that when turtles get cold, they often go off their food. He advised her to move the aquarium away from the window where it might be drafty to a more secluded spot inside the house. She moved it to her dining room, which has no exterior windows.

But the move didn't help. Jean Lafitte still wouldn't eat. Within a few days, he started to drift aimlessly in his tank, spewing mucus from both nostrils. Pat's son was terribly upset and she felt panicked, wondering what to do to restore the turtle to good health. It had now been seven days since it had eaten anything.

That morning, I'd made arrangements to meet Pat, but she was distracted and worried about the turtle, and she couldn't concentrate.

I immediately picked up on Pat's distress and asked her what   5
was wrong. She told me, and I offered to speak to the turtle and find out what was wrong, an offer which astounded her. Pat had no idea what I was talking about. Though we had been friends for more than a year, I had never mentioned my ability to communicate with animals to her.

Briefly, I described my telepathic gift. Though Pat was quite skeptical, she felt so desperate she would have tried anything to save the turtle.

I asked Pat for the turtle's name. When she told me, "Jean Lafitte," I couldn't help but reply, "That's quite a posh name for a turtle."

"He's quite a posh turtle," Pat responded, still not sure of the value of this experiment.

I closed my eyes and within moments, I was able to tell Pat that the turtle was quite unhappy about its tank being moved from its accustomed spot in her son's bedroom window. He wanted it moved back immediately. Pat was amazed because she had only just moved the tank a few days before and hadn't mentioned it to me.

The turtle told me he was dying. He told me he was very sad   10
because he loved Pat's family and did not want to leave them.

Then he started to give me a laundry list of the things that were wrong in his habitat, all things that had contributed, along with the cold weather, to his illness.

Speaking in a small, tinny voice, he told me he had out-grown his aquarium tank, and that it didn't have any stones on the bottom where he could get proper traction to walk and dive. He sent me a picture of his feet slipping on the bottom of the tank. He also informed me his water needed to be much deeper so he could swim, and filtrated to stay fresher and cleaner. "As long as I was a small turtle, this tank was fine, but now I am too big for it and have no room to swim and the water gets dirty too quickly," the turtle told me. Finally, Jean Lafitte asked for a larger rock for basking and diving, a green plant and a small fish for a companion.

Pat quickly drove to the nearest pet store to rescue the turtle, though she was still feeling quite unconvinced of the wisdom of what she was doing. I have quite a sense of humor, and I think Pat wondered if she hadn't become the unwitting victim of an elaborate prank. To encourage her as she left, I emphasized again that speed was necessary as the turtle was near death.

While Pat was in the store, she made the mistake of telling the pet store owner she was buying the goldfish for her turtle. He looked at her like she was crazy and told her, "Lady, you can't put a goldfish into a tank with a turtle. He'll eat it."

"Oh, no," Pat assured him. "My turtle told me he just wants the fish for a friend."

15   "Your turtle told you what?" the man said, looking at Pat even more strangely.

Pat turned her head as if she hadn't heard him and hurried out of the store with her $79.53 worth of turtle goods, thinking it was all an act of futility, that it was too late and the turtle was going to die anyway, and she'd be stuck with an elaborate turtle habitat and no bread or milk for her children for the rest of the week.

Pat set up the new aquarium in her son's bedroom window and moved the turtle into his new home. For the next three days, she hovered over Jean Lafitte, watching closely for some sign of improvement. There was none, but at least he didn't get any sicker; he was still alive.

On the fourth day, the turtle ate two sticks of turtle food and Pat noticed his nose was no longer running. She and her children celebrated this obvious turn for the better and called to inform me of the good news.

Jean Lafitte continued to improve. By the seventh day, he was swan-diving off his new basking rock and marching around his tank like some lord of the deep, fully recovered. Pat called and thanked me profusely, still not quite sure what she was thanking me for, but knowing that somehow, I was at least partly responsible for saving the turtle's life. She didn't understand it, but to her credit, she accepted it. That was Pat's introduction to the world of animal communication.

Unfortunately, the goldfish had become a bit more relaxed   20
too, losing that look of sheer terror he'd assumed when he first realized he was confined in a ten-gallon tank with a turtle. One evening when Pat came home, she went to greet Jean Lafitte and noticed there was no goldfish in the tank. She looked everywhere, but there simply weren't that many places for a goldfish to hide in the tank. In a panic, she called me and I immediately connected to Jean Lafitte, asking him where the goldfish was.

"I've eaten him," he replied. "I knew I would never get the fish if I'd told you I was going to eat him."

I chastised him for misrepresenting the real reason he wanted the fish. To this day, I haven't forgiven myself for my role in the hapless goldfish's death. He really deceived me, that turtle. I didn't realize he was so crafty. He told me he wanted a friend, when all he wanted was a filet!

For her part, Pat thinks that perhaps there were some nutrients, minerals or vitamins in that fish that Jean Lafitte needed to complete his recovery. At any rate, she hasn't given him any more fish to munch upon, and he continues to be a very happy, healthy turtle. As often happens with animals I help, John Lafitte has turned into a regular gossip and now keeps me informed of all the goings-on in Pat's house, especially noticing when she fails to wash up the dishes. Pat just wishes he would quit telling me when she hasn't done the laundry.

SEVEN SIMPLE STEPS TO COMMUNICATING WITH YOUR PET

1. Begin with a calm and tranquil mind and seek out a calm and tranquil atmosphere for you and your animal.
2. Say your animal's name telepathically to get its attention.
3. Visualize your animal as you say its name.
4. Send a picture of its physical body. Direct this to it, along with its name.

5. Ask if there is anything your pet would like you to do for it. Imagine your animal is sending an answer back to you and accept whatever you receive in your imagination.
6. Always acknowledge the answer, whatever you receive back from your animal.
7. Continue to ask it other questions, and remember to trust your imagination for what you are receiving back from your animal.

For Discussion and Writing

1. The author notes that she first picked up on the turtle's unhappiness about having been moved. She is in her client's home. Offer a prosaic explanation for her awareness that the turtle tank had been moved.
2. As you read what the turtle "says" to the pet psychic, what sort of questions arise for you? What do you find most remarkable? What sort of voice does Jean Lafitte have? Why does he sometimes just "send a picture" to the author? Why does the turtle keep in touch with the pet psychic? What does he share with her?
3. How would you test the claims of a pet psychic? How would you test Fitzpatrick's powers? You might, for the sake of inquiry, pose as a pet psychic for your classmates. You don't have to visit anyone's home, and a confederate who vouches for your claims would be useful, too. Report some communication from your partner's cat or ferret. How can anyone test you?
4. Study the "Seven Simple Steps to Communicating with Your Pet." If you can, try them out. If you follow step 2, how many times did you have to say your cat's name "telepathically" to get its attention? Why does the author advise a reader to "trust your imagination for what you are receiving"? To what degree does auto suggestion seem to be at work?
5. Find out a little about serious attempts to communicate with other species. Try to determine what distinguishes human language from animal language. What sort of barriers do you see in efforts to "talk" to animals?

Psychics and the Paranormal: Research and Writing Possibilities

1. The yellow pages of my little town's phonebook lists six telephone numbers for psychics. In the city where I work, there are many more Tarot readers, palm readers, psychics, and mediums. One ad presents Terri, who gives "Crossing Over Style Readings," and who multitasks as a "psychic, grief counselor, horse whisperer, energy healer and life coach." Another ad offers the services of a "psychic love specialist" who "reunites lovers

immediately." This specialist mentions "infidelity-anxiety disorders" and "depression" without actually claiming to treat these. Write a narrative that begins by surveying such ads critically, and then if possible actually speak with or even visit one of these psychics. Get a session if you can afford it. Take careful notes of all that is said and all that occurs so that your narrative has the strength and appeal of appropriate details.

2. Browse the Internet for materials about Bigfoot. See if you can find video excerpts to examine. Audio clips were available as of this writing, and although their content was unclear, the site authors claimed that they were the cries of mysterious creatures. Next, go to some skeptical sources like *Skeptical Inquirer* and *Skeptic* for articles critical of Bigfoot sightings One online site that may prove helpful is at http://skepdic.com/bigfoot.html. What questions and concerns do the skeptics raise? Are these answered or dealt with through evidence presented by believers? If the evidence isn't compelling, why do such stories persist? Who gains from them? What fears or wishes lie behind Bigfoot and other crypto zoology tales?

3. Research some "psychic predictions" for recent years. Sort out specific claims such as "a democrat will win the White House in 2004," from more general ones such as "a new disease will appear in South America this year causing great chaos." If at all possible, contact via email some of the "seers" who were wrong and ask what went wrong. This may strain your skills in fact but try to ask in a way that doesn't put your prophet on the defensive. Write a paper that evaluates the "batting record" of several of these people.

4. Look into the history of the Heaven's Gate cult, most of whose members died by mass suicide in 1997. Who were they? What did they believe? What evidence persuaded them to follow their two leaders? One of their members once told an audience in Montana that "we feel like the usefulness of this planet has reached its peak. We feel this is the end of this planet, but don't know if we'll depart before this end or after." (http://www.cnn.com/US/9703/28/cult.members/index.html, March 06) Believers connected, with disastrous effects, their cult's "departure and the appearance of the Hale-Bopp comet." Expand your research to include several other cults whose members committed mass suicide. Analyze these accounts for similarities, raising such questions as: What do they have in common? What are their leaders like? What sorts of promises are held out for believers? What sort of demands are made on them?

5. Crop circles first appeared in Great Britain in the 1970s. They caused quite a stir, leading to a new category of experts: cerealogists. These folk saw in the designs evidence of a higher and very subtle intelligence communicating through design features. Then, as you've read, two guys confessed in 1991 that they had begun the whole thing after downing their favorite form of cereal, barley mixed with hops—beer, that is. Did

their confession put an end to the mystery of crop circles? Not at all. Public interest is easier to ignite than douse. Explore the literature of crop circles on web sites but also in such texts as *Vital Signs: A Complete Guide to the Crop Circle Mystery*. Study photographic evidence, tests, testimony, and speculation. Write an essay that scrutinizes the believers' position. No easy outs allowed: it's just one's opinion; there's proof either way; or some such dodge. You might keep in mind the bottom line: no aliens have ever been caught composing in the fields. It would also be wise to recall that those who make extraordinary claims are obliged to give substantial proofs.

CHAPTER 5

Science and Pseudoscience

I maintain there is much more wonder in science than in pseudoscience. And in addition, to whatever measure this term has any meaning, science has the additional virtue, and it is not an inconsiderable one, of being true.

— CARL SAGAN

The whole history of science has been the gradual realization that events do not happen in an arbitrary manner, but that they reflect a certain underlying order, which may or may not be divinely inspired.

— STEPHEN HAWKING

What is science? It seems useful to ask this at the outset of a chapter focused mainly on pseudoscience. You won't be surprised to find that most simple definitions of science are met with debate among scientists. There is no single method of inquiry that defines science, no universal creed that gets recited on special occasions, no badge or credential that guarantees authenticity in research. Still, we expect something definite in this matter. After all, science is supposed to come up with facts and knowledge about the physical world. Science produces things, gets results, solves mysteries and problems, and generally advances civilization along its way from low to high technologies. Science is at work behind medicine, communication, and travel, explaining to us our own genetic structure, creating machines that let us talk to each other, fabricating vessels that sail through the atmosphere, and past it—surely we can define the thing behind all these wonders. It must be a way of advancing what is known. Maybe it can be described as a method of asking questions about facts that are always being gathered, a way of arriving at certainty about the physical nature of the universe, and so on.

In its root sense, the word "science" signifies "knowing." Its many branches share a pursuit of knowing, the building up of bodies of knowledge. Science serves the human urge to inquire and the human need to understand. It also serves to disprove— to find out error and discard it. If the facts don't support a geocentric view of the solar system, then that view is dropped in favor of one more agreeable to new data. If medical science identifies a bacteria as the cause of influenza, fine. Make vaccine. If the vaccine fails, it's back to seeking out the cause. If it turns out to be viral, then medicine must advance with that knowledge. It is communal in its work, skeptical by disposition, and persistent. If these descriptions sound like they come from human nature it's because they do. Science is a human activity, organized and with a very extensive memory system stretching over centuries. However, it is human nonetheless, and subject to all the faults that term suggests. Sure, science shares things with old time religion, like humility (in the face of ignorance), awe in the consciousness of the vast universe, and an urge toward community and sharing. At times it even displays a doctrinal impulse that identifies heresy and tries to punish the heretics. Nothing so complex as the behavior and knowledge we label with the term *science* can be free of all taint of imperfection. Despite its shortcomings, it isn't the same as pseudoscience.

And what is that? Is it just error? Mistakes or falsity not yet recognized as such? No. Pseudoscience isn't merely error. It's defined more by bad faith, loose methods, and low standards. Consider the case of "polywater." According to the National Academic Press web site,

> [i]n 1966 the Soviet scientist Boris Vladimirovich Derjaguin lectured in England on a new form of water that he claimed had been discovered by another Soviet scientist, N. N. Fedyakin. Formed by heating water and letting it condense in quartz capillaries, this "anomalous water," as it was originally called, had a density higher than normal water, a viscosity 15 times that of normal water, a boiling point higher than 100 degrees Centigrade, and a freezing point lower than zero degrees. (http://www.nap. edu/readingroom/books/obas/contents/values.html)

Researchers even warned that "if polywater escaped from the laboratory, it could autocatalytically polymerize all of the world's water," which must remind some readers of Kurt Vonnegut's wonderful novel *Cat's Cradle* and its amazing substance "Ice Nine." However, skeptical researchers tested samples of polywater and noticed that they were contaminated. As the NAP site notes,

> [g]radually, the scientists who had described the properties of polywater admitted that it did not exist. They had been misled by poorly controlled experiments and problems with experimental procedures. As the problems were resolved and experiments gained better controls, evidence for the existence of polywater disappeared.

The polywater claims thus turned out to be "pseudo" or fake science, and they didn't stand up under the sharp scrutiny of real scientists. It is often the case that fads and "discoveries" originate in our society among non-scientists. Tales of impending planetary alignments that will doom the earth come from excitable people schooled in astrology more than in astronomy. Miracle machines that produce more energy than they consume are "invented" in home garages. Americans in particular like the tale of an independent inventor who beats the system and the odds, and maybe gets around some laws of physics, too. Take the case of a recent "miracle cure" for cancer. The Associated Press recently reported that Dan Raber, a "pastor-turned-healer," got into trouble with the FDA after he began marketing an herbal paste containing bloodroot as a topical treatment for cancer. He claimed he cured himself of cancer with the paste. According to the AP story, Raber "said his father's paste is being singled out because it's an old remedy that can't be patented and therefore wouldn't generate large profits for the medical establishment or giant pharmaceutical companies." Readers may sympathize with the little guy here who tries to help folks out, while fighting off the giant medical establishment and the monstrous pharmaceutical companies out to protect their turf. The story's luster fades a bit when you read on and discover that a number of women who took the cure for breast cancer allegedly suffered mutilation and intense pain. (Reported on Netscape, 22 Sept. 2005, http://channels. netscape.com/news/story.jsp?idq=/ff/story/0001/20050829/ 2002016426.htm&ewp=ewp_news_0905anti_cancer)

Once again, we face questions about scientific literacy in the general public. As Paul Recer reports, "[f]ew Americans understand the scientific process and many believe in mysterious psychic powers and may be quick to accept phony science reports, according to a national survey." (Paul Recer Study: Science Literacy Poor in US Associated Press, posted: 10:37 am ET 01 May 2002) The survey noted that "the belief in 'pseudoscience' is common in America." Do you think our solar system is heliocentric? Can you give some reasons for that belief? Is the earth flat? Can you explain how you know it isn't? Apparently, science teachers across the country are not very confident that we can answer such basic questions. We are ripe for silliness and worse, on a grand scale.

The readings in this section present both the failings of science education and the foothold that false science has among us. If you are among the minority who do have a sound basic education, you are to be congratulated, and encouraged to do your small part to spread science literacy. The readings begin with Robert Park's "Only Mushrooms Grow in the Dark," a chapter from his book *Voodoo Science*. Park considers the role of secrecy in the spread of nonsense about Roswell and UFOs, secret x-ray weapons, and sniffer planes that find oil fields from the air. Philip C. Plait debunks the "astronomy" of people who predicted a doomsday planetary alignment and explains the bad science behind the belief in "The Disaster That Wasn't: The Great Planetary Alignment of 2000." In "My Favorite Pseudoscience," Eugenie Scott explains her quarrel with creationism while at the same time laying out the traits that make science scientific. In "Dr. Down's Syndrome," Stephen Jay Gould examines the role of a pseudoscientific theory of racial hierarchy in the diagnosis of an all too real genetic disorder. Finally, Elizabeth Loftus considers the phenomenon of therapy based on recovered memories and finds striking parallels between it and sixteenth-century panic over witches in "Remembering Dangerously."

Only Mushrooms Grow in the Dark
ROBERT PARK

Robert Park, professor of physics and former chair of the Department of Physics at the University of Maryland, has written many science articles for the Washington Post, *op-ed pieces for the* New York Times, *and the popular book* Voodoo Science, *from which the following is taken. Park subtitles that book "The Road* from Foolishness to Fraud," *and its chapters cover such things as failed perpetual energy machines, unfounded fears of power lines, and junk science in the courts. The following essay links foolish beliefs to a tendency toward secrecy by government officials.*

———————————— ✦ ————————————

THE ROSWELL INCIDENT

In 1994 Secretary of the Air Force Sheila Widnall agreed to issue an unprecedented blanket order relieving anyone with information about an alleged 1947 UFO incident near Roswell, New Mexico, from any obligation to keep the information secret. A no-nonsense physicist and aeronautical engineer on leave from MIT, Secretary Widnall thought the air force had more important business than chasing down UFO stories, but Representative Steven Schiff of New Mexico was insisting on an all-out search for records and witnesses. Schiff wanted to reassure the public that there was no government cover-up. I did not expect anyone to come forward with new information, but I recalled with some chagrin my own "Roswell incident."

As a young air force lieutenant in the summer of 1954, I had been sent on temporary assignment to Walker Air Force Base in Roswell to oversee the installation of a new radar system. I was returning to the base after a weekend visit with my family in South Texas. It was after midnight, and I was driving on a totally deserted stretch of highway in one of the most desolate regions of West Texas. It was a moonless night but very clear, and I could make out a range of ragged hills off to my left, silhouetted against the background of stars. Suddenly the entire countryside was illuminated by a dazzling blue-green light streaking across the sky just above the horizon. It flashed on and off as it passed behind the hills—and vanished without a sound. It was all over in perhaps two seconds. It came at a time when reports of UFO sightings were in the news almost daily. Most of the reported sightings were not nearly so spectacular as the event I had just witnessed, but I was pretty sure I knew what this one was.

The pale blue-green color is characteristic of the light emitted by frozen free-hydroxide radicals as they warm up. A free radical is a fragment of a molecule; the hydroxide, or OH, radical is a water molecule that is missing one of its hydrogen atoms. Free radicals are highly reactive, anxious to reconnect with their missing parts, and do not ordinarily stick around very long. However, if molecules are broken up by radiation at very low temperatures, the fragments can be frozen in place and unable to recombine. As soon as the severed parts of the molecule are warmed up, they react with other fragments to form stable molecules. The law of conservation of energy, once again, tells us what to expect: the energy it took to break the chemical bonds in the first place will be liberated when the fragments recombine. The liberated energy appears as blue-green fluorescence. An ice meteoroid, traveling through the cold depths of space for eons, will gradually accumulate more and more free radicals as a result of cosmic ray bombardment. I must have been fortunate enough to see an ice meteorite as it plunged into the upper atmosphere. The meteorite must have evaporated without a trace before reaching the ground.

As I continued down the highway and crossed into New Mexico, I was feeling rather smug. The UFO hysteria that was sweeping the country, I told myself, was for people who don't understand science. It was then that I saw the flying saucer. It was again off to my left between the highway and the distant hills, racing along just above the range land. It appeared to be a shiny metallic disk viewed on edge—thicker in the center—and it was traveling at almost the same speed I was. Was it following me? I stepped hard on the gas pedal of the Oldsmobile—and the saucer accelerated. I slammed on the brakes—and it stopped. Then I could see that it was only my headlights, reflecting off a single phone line strung parallel to the highway. Suddenly, it no longer looked like a flying saucer at all.

5   It was humbling. My cerebral cortex may have sneered at stories of flying saucers, but the part of my brain in which those stories were stored had been activated by the powerful impression of the ice meteorite. The belief engine did the rest. I was primed to see a flying saucer—and my brain filled in the details. Whenever I become impatient with UFO believers, as I often do, I try to remember that night in New Mexico when, for a few seconds, I believed in flying saucers.

ABDUCTED

Who has not seen in the dusk an animal that turns into a bush as you grow closer? But something more than the mind playing tricks with patterns of light is needed to explain why hundreds, by some accounts thousands, of people claim to have been abducted by aliens, taken aboard a spaceship, and subjected to some sort of physical examination, usually focusing on their erogenous zones. The examination is frequently followed by the aliens inserting a tiny implant into the abductee's body. Often the memory of these abductions has a dreamlike quality, and the subjects are able to recall the details only under hypnosis.

For these people, space aliens are a serious reality, but it's not clear how much science can help. Indeed, scientists themselves are not immune to such beliefs. In 1992 a five-day conference was held at MIT to assess the similarities among various alien abduction accounts. The conference was organized by John Mack, a professor of psychiatry at Harvard, and David Pritchard, a prizewinning MIT physicist. Mack had been treating patients who believed they had been abducted. His treatment consisted of assuring them that they were not suffering from hallucinations—they really had been abducted.

Pritchard, an experimentalist, was more concerned with examining any physical evidence, particularly the tiny implants many abductees reported. The best candidate seemed to be an implant that abductee Richard Price said had been inserted mid-shaft in his penis. The implant was clearly visible, amber in color, the size of a grain of rice. Under a microscope, what appeared to be wires could be seen protruding from the device. What wonders of alien technology might be revealed by this tiny device? In an atmosphere of high expectations, the "implant" was removed and examined by sophisticated analytical techniques. It was not from Andromeda. It was of distinctly terrestrial origin: human tissue that had accreted fibers of cotton from Price's underwear.

It is hardly surprising that there are similarities in the accounts of the abductees; they've all been exposed to the same images and stories in the popular media. In my local bookstore, there are three times as many books about UFOs as there are about all of science. Aliens stare at us from the covers of magazines and appear in television commercials. They are the subject of hundreds of movies and television series—even "documentaries," if you want to call them that.

As time goes by, there is a growing uniformity in the descriptions of aliens. A six-year-old child can now sketch what an alien looks like. We are, in fact, witnessing a sort of alien evolution. The mutations are created by moviemakers and science fiction novelists. The selection mechanism is public approval. The aliens subtly evolve to satisfy public expectations, resulting in a sort of   10 composite alien. In effect, the public is voting on what aliens should look like. The same holds true for UFOs.

If you attempt to trace the process back to a common ancestor, the trail seems inevitably to lead back to the strange events near Roswell, New Mexico, in the summer of 1947.

PROJECT MOGUL

On June 14, 1947, William Brazel, the foreman of the Foster Ranch, seventy-five miles northwest of Roswell, spotted a large area of wreckage about seven miles from the ranch house. The debris consisted of neoprene strips, tape, metal foil, cardboard, and sticks. He didn't bother to examine it very closely at the time, but a few weeks later he heard about the first reports of flying saucers and wondered if what he had seen might be related. He went back with his wife and gathered up some of the pieces. The next day, he drove to the little town of Corona to sell wool, and while he was there he "whispered kinda confidential like" to the Lincoln County sheriff, George Wilcox, that he might have found pieces of one of these "flying discs" people were talking about. The sheriff reported it to the army air base in Roswell. The army sent an intelligence officer, Major Jesse Marcel, to check it out. Marcel thought the debris looked something like pieces of a weather balloon or a radar reflector. All of it together fit easily into the trunk of his car.

It might have ended there, but the Public Information Office at Roswell Army Air Field issued a garbled account to the press the next day saying the army had "gained possession of a flying disc through the cooperation of a local rancher and the sheriff's office." The army quickly issued a correction describing the debris as a standard radar target. It was too late. The Roswell incident had been launched. With the passage of years, the retraction of that original press release would come to look more and more like a cover-up.

When I was sent to Roswell a few years later to install the new radar, Roswell Army Air Field had been renamed Walker Air Force Base. It was home to a force of B-36 long-range bombers. The Soviet Union had the bomb, and a rapid buildup of our strategic forces was underway. The bachelor officers' quarters on base were filled up when I arrived, so I took a room in town, in a large boardinghouse on a pleasant street lined with cottonwoods. The other residents of the boardinghouse, all Roswell natives, were much older. It was almost like a family, but they went out of their way to make me feel at home, chiding me good-naturedly about all the "secret stuff" going on at Walker. One balmy July evening on the front porch, the conversation turned to flying saucer stories. They knew about the wreckage found on the Foster Ranch in 1947—it had all been in the *Roswell Daily Record*. Not a single person believed the government explanations about weather balloons or radar targets; everyone seemed to agree the debris must have been from a secret government project, or maybe some sort of experimental Russian aircraft. I do not recall anyone suggesting it was from outer space.

It was not until 1978, thirty years after William Brazel spotted wreckage on his ranch, that alien bodies first showed up in accounts of the "crash." The story of Major Marcel loading sticks, cardboard, and metal foil into the trunk of his car had grown over the years into a major military operation to recover an entire alien spaceship that was secretly transported to Wright-Patterson Air Force Base in Ohio. Even as the number of people who might recall events thirty years earlier dwindled, incredible new details began to be added by second- and third-hand sources: there was not one crash but two or three; the aliens were small with large heads and suction cups on their fingers; one alien survived for a time but was kept hidden by the government; and on and on.

Like a giant vacuum, the story had sucked in accounts of unrelated plane crashes and high-altitude parachute experiments using anthropomorphic dummies, even though in some cases these events took place years later and miles away. Various UFO "investigators" managed to stitch together fragments of these accounts to create the myth of an encounter with extraterrestrials—an encounter covered up by the government. The truth, according to believers, was too frightening to share with the public.

If the pieces didn't fit, they were trimmed until they did. If they couldn't be made to fit, they were left out. To fill the huge gaps that remained, the faithful speculated. In time, the distinction between fact and speculation faded. A string of profitable books was generated, and then a string of skeptical responses by aerospace writer Philip Klass. It is an axiom in the publishing business, however, that pseudoscience will always sell more books than the real science that debunks it.

Roswell was a gold mine. The unverified accounts were shamelessly exploited for their entertainment value on television programs that represented themselves as documentaries, such as NBC's *Unsolved Mysteries* with host Robert Stack, and even more serious news programs, such as CBS's *48 Hours* with Dan Rather, not to mention talk shows, including CNN's *Larry King Live*.

20   The bottom was reached by Fox TV, which in 1995 showed grainy black-and-white film of what was purported to be a government autopsy of one of the aliens. The film was immediately denounced by experts as an obvious hoax, but it scored high ratings with the viewing public. The experts, people shrugged, were probably paid off or threatened by the government. Fox continued showing the film over and over.

When the ratings for *Alien Autopsy* finally began to slip after three years, Fox announced that it had hired its own experts to examine the film. Using high-tech "NASA-type video enhancements," they revealed the shocking truth: the film was a fake. Was Fox chagrined at having been duped? Not at all. Fox boasted of having exposed "one of the biggest hoaxes of all time." A highly promoted special was aired that described how the autopsy film had been faked. Fox had managed to make a profit from the Roswell incident coming and going.

Meanwhile, however, to the astonishment of believers and skeptics alike, the search of air force records for information about the Roswell incident uncovered a still-secret government program from the 1940s called Project Mogul. There really was a cover-up—but not of an alien spaceship.

In the summer of 1947, the Soviet Union had not yet detonated its first atomic bomb, but it was clearly only a matter of time. It was imperative that the United States know about it when it happened. A variety of approaches to detect that first Soviet nuclear test was being explored. Project Mogul was an attempt to use low-frequency acoustic microphones placed at high altitude to actually "hear" the explosion. The interface between the troposphere and the stratosphere creates an acoustic "duct" that can propagate sound waves globally. Acoustic sensors to pick up the explosion, radar tracking reflectors, and other equipment was sent aloft on trains of weather balloons as long as six hundred feet.

The balloon trains were launched from Alamagordo, New Mexico, about a hundred miles west of Roswell. One of the surviving scientists from Project Mogul, Charles B. Moore, a retired physics professor, recalls that Flight #4, launched on June 4, 1947, was tracked to within seventeen miles of the spot where William Brazel spotted the wreckage ten days later. At that point, contact was lost. The debris found on the Foster Ranch closely matched the materials used in the balloon trains. The air force now concludes that it was, beyond any reasonable doubt, the crash of Flight #4 that set off the bizarre set of events known as the Roswell incident. Had Project Mogul not been highly secret, unknown even to the military authorities in Roswell, the entire episode might have ended in July 1947.

From today's perspective, it is difficult to understand why   25
Project Mogul was secret at all. It was abandoned even before the Soviets tested their first atomic bomb, pushed aside by more promising detection technologies. There was nothing in Project Mogul that could have provided the Soviets with anything but amusement, and yet it was a tightly kept secret for nearly half a century; even its code name was secret. It would still be secret if it had not been for the investigation initiated by Representative Schiff. Secrecy, it seems, is simply a part of the military culture, and it has produced a mountain of secret materials.

No one really knows the size of the classified mountain, but in spite of periodic efforts at reform, there are more classified documents today than there were at the height of the cold war. The direct cost of maintaining them is estimated by the government to be about $2.6 billion per year, but the true cost in terms of the erosion of public trust is immeasurable. In a desperate attempt to bring the system under control, President Clinton issued an executive order in 1995 that will automatically declassify documents more than twenty-five years old—estimated at well over a billion pages—beginning in the year 2000.

If there is any mystery still surrounding the Roswell incident, it is why uncovering Project Mogul in 1994 failed to put an end to the UFO myth. There appear to be several reasons, all related to the fact that the truth came out almost half a century too late. Rather than weakening the UFO myth, Project Mogul was pounced on by believers as proof that everything the government had said before was a lie, and there was no reason to believe this was not just another lie. Government denials are by now greeted with derision.

But if it was Project Mogul that started the UFO myth, it was another secret government program that kept it going. It was common during the cold war to create cover stories to protect secret operations, including flights of the U-2 spy plane over the Soviet Union. Initially, the U-2s were unpainted; that is, their skin was shiny, metallic aluminum, which strongly reflected sunlight. Particularly in the morning and evening hours, when the surface below was dark, the U-2s would pick up the Sun's rays, becoming very visible. The CIA estimates that over half of all UFO reports from the late 1950s through the 1960s were secret reconnaissance flights by U-2 spy planes. To allay public concern while maintaining the secrecy of the U-2 missions, the air force concocted far-fetched explanations in terms of natural phenomena. Keeping secrets, we learn early in life, leads directly to telling lies.

The U.S. Air Force collected every scrap of information dealing with the Roswell incident into a massive report in hopes of bringing the story to an end. The enormous task of locating and sifting through old files and tracking down surviving witnesses had actually started even before Representative Schiff's call for full disclosure. Responding to Freedom of Information Act requests from self-appointed UFO investigators had become a heavy burden on the air force headquarters staff at the Pentagon, and they were eager to get ahead of the Roswell incident. Release of *The Roswell Report: Case Closed* drew the largest attendance on record for a Pentagon press conference.

30   Although the people involved insist it was not planned that way, the air force report was completed just in time for the fiftieth anniversary of William Brazel's discovery of the Project Mogul wreckage. Thousands of UFO enthusiasts descended on Roswell, now a popular tourist destination, in July 1997 for a golden anniversary celebration. They bought alien dolls and commemorative T-shirts and snatched up every book they could find on UFOs and aliens. The only book that sold poorly was the massive air force report. Who, after all, could take the government seriously? Fox TV continued to show its alien autopsy film to appreciative audiences. Recent polls indicate that the number of people who believe there is a UFO presence that is being covered up by the government is still growing.

Nevertheless, it is eary to read too much significance into reports of widespread public belief in UFOs and alien visits to Earth. Carl Sagan saw in the space-alien myth the modern equivalent of the demons that haunted medieval society, and for a susceptible few they are a frightening reality. But for most people these do not seem to be deeply held beliefs. UFOs and aliens are a way to add a touch of excitement and mystery to uneventful lives. They're also a way for people to thumb their noses at the government.

The real cost of the Roswell incident must be measured in terms of the loss of public trust. In the name of national security, every government in this troubled world feels compelled to grant itself the authority to hold official secrets. Those in power quickly learn to love secrecy. It enables the government to control what the public hears: bad news is squelched, good news is leaked. In the long run, however, episodes like Roswell leave the government almost powerless to reassure its citizens in the face of far-fetched conspiracy theories and pseudoscientific hogwash.

The release of *The Roswell Report: Case Closed* on June 24, 1997, came just three months after the bodies of thirty-nine members of a UFO cult called Heaven's Gate were found in San Diego. They had committed mass suicide in the belief that a giant UFO following the Hale-Bopp comet would pick them up and carry them to the "next level." Behind the curtain of official secrecy, however, far more dangerous deceptions have gone undetected.

THE SNIFFER PLANE

In 1976 a Belgian count persuaded the government of France to conduct trials of a secret device that purportedly used the echo from a newly discovered particle to map mineral deposits from the air. In its initial tests, flying over areas that had already been mapped by conventional geologic techniques, *l'avion renifleur*, or "the sniffer plane," was spectacularly successful in picking out oil fields. Realizing that such an invention could alter the course of history, French president Valery Giscard d'Estaing ordered tight government secrecy to maintain France's lead in this new technology.

Over the next three years France invested some $200 million in the idea, but by 1979 government officials were growing nervous. In spite of its demonstrated ability to spot known oil fields, *l'avion renifleur* had yet to uncover any new petroleum reserves. And so far, no government official had even had a close look at the device, having been warned of dangerous levels of radiation. Eventually, the government appointed a prominent nuclear physicist, Jules Horowitz, to investigate.

It didn't take long for Professor Horowitz to devise a simple demonstration. Could these mysterious particles be used to image a metal object through an opaque screen? Yes, of course, he was assured; all that would be necessary would be to "tune" the instrument to the object before it was placed behind the screen. Horowitz chose a simple metal ruler to be the object. He placed the ruler in front of the screen for the tune-up. He then moved it behind the screen, but as he did so, he surreptitiously bent the ruler into an L shape. The device produced a splendid image—but

35

it was of an unbent ruler. Count de Villegas and his associates promptly disappeared. When the device on board *l'avion renifleur* was dismantled, it turned out to be nothing more than a clever video recorder that stored the images of existing geologic surveys.

Tight government secrecy had permitted the deception to go unchallenged for three years. Now that *l'avion renifleur* was exposed as a fake, the original justification for secrecy no longer existed. Ironically, the lid was screwed down even more tightly. The French government now relied on secrecy to avoid embarrassment. It was no longer mere economic dominance at stake; it had become a matter of political survival. Politicians can survive sex scandals or fiscal mismanagement, but they cannot survive being laughed at.

In May of 1981, however, the conservative Giscard was defeated in a runoff election by his liberal nemesis, François Mitterand. It was another two years before the Mitterand government stumbled on the cover-up. Mitterand immediately revoked the secrecy order, gleefully revealing the episode in its entirety, thus dooming any plans of Giscard's to again seek the presidency.

What we cannot know, of course, is how many similar episodes in all countries have never been exposed. Only the censor knows for certain what is hidden. As the story of Project Mogul demonstrated, secret programs can escape public exposure for decades.

For Discussion and Writing

1. What is Park's point, in the opening account of his 1954 trip to Roswell, about his "belief engine"? Think of one time in your life when your "belief engine" may have taken over from your sensory data.
2. The Roswell legend of today actually has a kernel of fact. What is the undisputed part of the tale? Briefly retell it. Why do you think the government waited 47 years to declassify the alleged UFO incident? To what degree has this 47-year blackout contributed to unscientific accounts of the Roswell event?
3. What was Fox Network's contribution to the public understanding of Roswell events?
4. Who was Charles B. Moore, what was Project Mogul, and how was this linked to the Roswell event? Why, according to Park, was government secrecy unnecessary in this matter?
5. What was the sniffer plane? How did secrecy contribute to the fiasco? Characterize professor Horowitz's test of the secret particles' power to see through earth. What was the effect of his test results on the French government's policy of secrecy ?

The Disaster That Wasn't: The Great Planetary Alignment of 2000

PHILIP C. PLAIT

Philip C. Plait works in the Department of Physics and Astronomy at Sonoma State. A columnist for Astronomy.com, he also maintains a very popular web site called badastronomy.com. There you might find articles on the moon landing "hoax," the poor record of astrologers, or a killer cloud of space matters being reported by "the twinkies at Yahoo news." He has also written a book entitled, Bad Astronomy, *from which this excerpt is taken. The following essay examines the prediction, circa 2000, that the earth would be destroyed by an imminent and extraordinary alignment of planets. If you are reading this, relax. We survived.*

------------------ ✦ ------------------

On May 5, 2000, the Earth was not destroyed.

Perhaps you missed this, since you were busy living, eating, going to work, brushing your teeth, etc. However, in the months before May 5, 2000, a lot of people actually thought the Earth would be destroyed. Instead of the usual culprits of nuclear war, environmental disaster, or the Y2K bug, this particular brand of global destruction was to have been wrought by the universe itself, or, at least, our small part of it.

On that date, at 8:08 Greenwich Mean Time, an "alignment of the planets" was supposed to have caused the Final Reckoning. This Grand Alignment—also called the "Grand Conjunction" by the prophesiers of doom to make it sound more mysterious and somehow more *millennial*—would throw all manner of forces out of balance, causing huge earthquakes, a possible shift in the Earth's poles, death, destruction, higher taxes, and so forth. Some even thought it would cause the total annihilation of the Earth itself. The tool of this disaster was to have been the combined gravity of the planets in the solar system.

These people, obviously, were wrong. Some of them were honest and simply mistaken, others were quacks and didn't know any better, and still others were frauds trying to make money off the misinformed. Nonetheless, they were all wrong, plain and simple.

5   Of course, there's a long and not-so-noble history of misinter-
preting signs from the sky. Long before studying the skies was a
true science, there was astrology. Astrology is the belief that—
contrary to every single thing we know about physics, astronomy,
and logic—somehow the stars and planets control our lives. The
reason astrology came about is not so hard to understand.
People's lives can seem to be out of their control. Capricious
weather, luck, and happenstance seem to influence our lives
more than we can ourselves. It's human nature to be curious
about the causes of such things, but it's also human nature to
pervert that curiosity into blame. We blame the gods, the stars,
the shaman, the politicians, everyone but ourselves or simple bad
luck. It's natural to try to deny our own involvement and wish for
some supernatural causation.
         There *is* some connection between what happens in the sky
and what happens down here on Earth. Agriculture depends on
weather, and weather depends on the Sun. Agriculture also
depends on the seasons, and these can be predicted by watching
the skies. In winter, the Sun is lower in the sky during the day and
it is not up as long. Certain constellations are up when it's cold, and
others when it gets hot. The sky and the Earth seem irrevocably
connected. Finding patterns in the sky that seem to have spiritual
puppet strings tied to us here on Earth was perhaps inevitable.
         Eventually, everything in the sky, from comets to eclipses, was
assumed to portend coming events. It may be easy to laugh off
such superstitions as the folly of simple people from ancient times.
However, even today, firmly into the twenty-first century, we still
deal with ancient superstitions that we simply cannot seem to cast
off. Just a few months into the new century we had to deal with yet
another instance of the shadow of our primitive need to blame the
skies. The May 2000 planetary-alignment-disaster-that-wasn't
spawned a whole cottage industry of gloom and doom, but, like all
signs from the sky throughout history, it turned out to be just
another false alarm. As with most superstitions, the rational
process of the scientific method came to the rescue. To find out
how, let's take a look at what an "alignment" really is.
         All the planets in the solar system, including the Earth, orbit
the Sun. They move at different speeds, depending on how far
they are from the Sun. Tiny Mercury, only 58 million kilometers
from the Sun, screams around it in just 88 days. The Earth,
almost three times as far, takes one full year—which is, after all,
how we define the year. Jupiter takes 12 years, Saturn 29, and distant, frigid Pluto 250 years.

All the major planets in the solar system formed from a rotating disk of gas and dust centered on the Sun. Now, nearly 5 billion years later, we still see all those planets orbiting the Sun in the same plane. Since we are also in that plane, we see it edge-on. From our vantage point, it looks like all the planets travel through the sky nearly in a line, since a plane seen edge-on looks like a line.

Since all the planets move across the sky at different rates,   10 they are constantly playing a kind of Nascar racing game. Like the hands of a clock only meeting every hour, the swifter planets can appear to "catch up" to and eventually pass the slower-moving ones. The Earth is the third planet out from the Sun, so we move in our orbit faster than Mars, Jupiter, and the rest of the outer planets. You might think, then, that they would appear to pass each other in the sky all the time.

However, the planets' orbits don't all exist perfectly in the same plane. They're all tilted a little, so that planets don't all fall exactly along a line in the sky. Sometimes a planet is a little above the plane, and sometimes a little below. It's extraordinarily rare for them to actually pass *directly* in front of each other. Usually they approach the same area of the sky, getting perhaps to within the width of the full Moon, then separate again. Often they never even get that close to each other, passing many degrees apart. For this reason, surprisingly, it's actually rather rare for more than two planets to be near each other in the sky at the same time.

Every so often, though, it does happen that the cosmic clock aligns a bit better than usual, and some of the major planets will appear to be in the same section of the sky. In 1962, for example, the Sun, the Moon, and all the planets except Uranus, Neptune, and Pluto appeared to be within 16 degrees of each other, which is roughly the amount of sky you can cover with your outstretched hand. Not only that, but there was also a solar eclipse, making this a truly spectacular event. The Moon and the Sun were as close as they could possibly be, since the Moon was directly in front of the Sun. In the year 1186, there was an even tighter alignment, and these planets could be contained with a circle just 11 degrees across.

On May 5, 2000, at 8:08 A.M. Greenwich Time, the planets Mercury, Venus, Mars, Jupiter, and Saturn were in very roughly the same section of the sky. Even the new Moon slid into this picture at that time, making this a very pretty family portrait indeed, although it was a bit of a dysfunctional family. This particular alignment wasn't a very good one, and even if it had been, the Sun was between us and the planets like an unwelcome relative standing in front of the TV set during the football playoffs.

The fact that this wasn't a particularly grand alignment is easy to show. The planets involved were within about 25 degrees of each other. That's half again as far as the 1962 alignment, and more than twice as bad as the one in 1186. Both of these years, it should be noted, are ones in which the Earth was *not* destroyed. As a matter of fact, there have been no fewer than 13 comparable alignments in the past millennium, and in none of them was there any effect on the Earth.

15   Still, this hardly even slowed the doomsayers down. The combined gravity of the planets, they claimed, was still enough to destroy the Earth. Since we're still here, we know that wasn't true. Still, it pays to look at this a little more carefully.

The force of gravity is overwhelming in our daily lives. It keeps us stuck to the Earth unless we use tremendously powerful rockets to overcome it. Gravity is what holds the Moon in orbit around the Earth, and the Earth around the Sun. It makes parts of us sag as we get older, and even manages to keep the highest vertical leap of the greatest basketball players in the world under a measly meter.

But gravity is also mysterious. We cannot see it, touch it, or taste it, and we know that the math involved in predicting it can be complicated. So it's easy—and all too human, I'm afraid—to assign all sorts of powers to gravity without really understanding it. In a way, understanding the effects of gravity is like a prize fight: science and its retinue of observations, facts, and math versus our superstitions, emotions, and the human power to jump to conclusions without much evidence. Which side will win the day?

Let's take a quick look at what we know about gravity: for one thing, it gets stronger with mass. The more massive an object is, the stronger its gravity. From a kilometer away, a mountain has more of a gravitational effect on you than, say, a Volkswagen.

However, we also know that gravity gets weaker very quickly with distance. That Volkswagen may be a lot smaller than the mountain, but its gravity will actually overwhelm the gravity of the mountain if the car is close and the mountain far away.

20   It's all relative. Indeed, the planets are massive. Jupiter tips the scales at over 300 times the Earth's mass. *But it's far away.* Very far. At its absolute closest, Jupiter is about 600 million kilometers (400 million miles) away. Even though it outweighs the Moon by a factor of 25,000, it is nearly 1,600 times farther away. When you actually do the math, you find that the effect of Jupiter's gravity on the Earth is only about 1 percent of the Moon's!

Despite the old saying, size doesn't matter; distance does.

If you add up the gravity of *all* the planets, even assuming they are as close to the Earth as possible, you still don't get much. The Earth's tiny little Moon exerts 50 times more gravitational force on us than all the planets combined. The Moon is small, but it's close, so its gravity wins.

And that's true only if the planets are lined up as close to the Earth as they can get. As it happens, on May 5, 2000, the planets were on the *far* side of the Sun, meaning that you need to add the diameter of the Earth's orbit—another 300 million kilometers (185 million miles)—to their distances. When you do, the combined might of the planets is easily overwhelmed by the gravity of a person sitting next to you in that Volkswagen. Sorry, doomsayers, but round 1 of this fight goes to science.

Usually at this point I am challenged by some people who say that it isn't the gravity of the planets that can cause damage, it's the *tides*. Tides are related to gravity. They are caused by the *change* in gravity over distance. The Moon causes tides on the Earth because at any moment one side of the Earth is nearer the Moon than the other. The side nearer the Moon therefore feels a slightly higher gravitational force from the Moon. This acts to stretch the Earth a tiny amount. We see this effect as a raising and a lowering of the sea level twice a day, which is what most people normally think of as tides.

Earthquakes are caused by the movement of huge tectonic   25
plates that make up the Earth's crust. They rub against each other, usually smoothly. However, sometimes they stick a bit, letting pressure build up. When enough pressure builds up, the plates slip suddenly, causing an earthquake. Since tides can stretch an object, it's reasonable to ask whether tides can trigger earthquakes. Are we still doomed?

Happily, no. When doomsayers bring up tides, they are shooting themselves in the foot. The force of tides fades even faster with distance than gravity. If the force of gravity on Earth is piddly for the planets, then tides are even weaker. Comparing the Moon, again, to all the combined might of the planets, we find that the Moon has *20,000 times* the tidal force of all the other planets in the solar system, even at their closest approach to the Earth. Remember, in May 2000 the planets were *as far away as they possibly could be*. The tidal force was so small that even the finest scientific instruments on the planet were not able to measure it. Round 2 of the fight goes to science as well.

Math and science show pretty definitively that the gravity and tides of the planets are too small to have any effect on the Earth.

However, it would be foolhardy to assume that emotions are swayed by logic. In one sense, the side of science is lucky: since the planets were all on the far side of the Sun, we had to look past the Sun to see them. That means they were only up during the day, when they are practically invisible. It would not have helped the situation if people could actually look up at night and see the planets approaching each other, even if it were a pretty weak grouping.

Still, even armed with hard numbers, it's always an uphill fight to battle the doomsayers. There were a lot of people out there trying to make money by scaring people about the alignment. Certainly some of these folks were honest, if misguided. Richard Noone wrote a book about the alignment, *5/5/2000 Ice: The Ultimate Disaster*, where he claims that the Earth's axis would tilt due to the combined pull of the planets, plunging the Earth into an ice age. Noone was sincere, and felt he had done the research to back up his claims. The problem is, his research involved almost no astronomy at all. He related *Bible* prophesies, Nostradamus, and even the shape of the Great Pyramid in Egypt to a disaster in the year 2000, and figured the planets must have something to do with it. Yet, in his meandering book precious little space is devoted to the planets, and nowhere—nowhere!— does he talk about the actual measurable effects of the planets.

I am almost willing to give Noone the benefit of the doubt and assume he really was concerned about global catastrophe. But I wonder: if he really felt that the Earth would be destroyed on May 5, 2000, why not give away his book for free so that people could be warned? I can't imagine he thought the royalties he got on the book would be worth much on May 6.

Noone wasn't even the first. In the 1980s astronomer John Gribbin and his coauthor Stephen Plagemann wrote an infamous book entitled *The Jupiter Effect*, which claimed—again, without the benefit of any math—that the gravity of the planets would affect the Sun, causing more solar activity, causing a change in the Earth's rotation, causing massive earthquakes. This tissue-thin string of suppositions led them to predict very matter-of-factly that Los Angeles would be destroyed in 1982. The book was a runaway best seller.

When, in fact, L.A. was *not* destroyed as predicted, Gribbin and Plagemann wrote *another* book called *Beyond the Jupiter Effect*, making excuses about why things didn't work out quite as they had predicted, and of course they never simply admitted they were wrong. You may not be surprised to find out that this second book was another best seller. It's *possible*, barely, that the first book was a simple mistake and they honestly believed what they preached. The motivation for the second book perhaps isn't as clear.

If Noone and Gribbin were simply misguided, during the May 2000 alignment the "Survival Center" company was far more deliberate. Peddling disaster nonsenese, this company had a web site promoting Noone's book as well as equipment to help you survive the oncoming onslaught. On their web site (http://www.zyz.com/survivalcenter/echange.html), they reported,

> Some scientists have already reported a distinct increased wobble to the earth as it begins to respond to the gravitational pull of the alignment . . . predictions [of the results of the alignment] range from a few earthquakes to major earth crust movement (slippage), polar ice cap movement, sea levels rising 100 to 300 feet or more, huge tidal waves, high winds 500 to 2000 miles per hour, earthquakes so massive that Richter 13 or more could be possible, both coasts of USA under water, magnetic shift and much more.

In 1998, I e-mailed them with this question: "May I ask, who are the people making these predictions? I would appreciate being able to contact them so that I may present my arguments on this issue." They replied, basically informing me that I had my sources and they had theirs. They wouldn't tell me who their sources or what their credentials were. I'm not surprised; backed up by hard science, no one can truthfully claim that the planets can have any sudden and catastrophic effect on the Earth. I would have serious doubts about the Survival Center's expertise in this matter anyway, even if they *had* revealed their sources. My opinion in situations such as these is, "Beware the science of someone trying to sell you something."

Of course, I'm trying to sell you something as well. But in my case, I'm peddling skepticism. You can go and find this stuff out for yourself if you try hard enough. The math isn't hard, and the conclusions are, well, *conclusive*.

My only real complaint about this whole alignment business— besides the vultures preying on people's fears—is that we weren't able to see it. The Sun was in the way, completely overwhelming the relatively feeble light from the planets and our Moon. So, not only were we denied the excitement of impending disaster, but also we couldn't even take a picture of it to show our grandkids! And we'll have to wait until September of 2040 for the next good alignment. At least that one *will* be visible at night.

For Discussion and Writing

1. To what degree, in your view, was fear about the "grand conjunction" fueled by its timing, coming just at the millennium?
2. Plait suggests that it is easy to "laugh off" superstitions from ancient times, but that in fact we still deal with such superstitions today. Why are our current superstitions less ridiculous than ancient ones? What are some of our current superstitions about the stars and planets?
3. Plait explains that all the planets in our system exist in nearly the same plane. Seen from earth, the planets seem to travel in a line. The planets, at times, thus seem fairly well-aligned and close together. Why does this optical effect matter in the prophesies of imminent doom? Compared to other "great alignments" how unusual was the 2000 configuration?
4. Gravity, the author points out, gets stronger with mass. Planets are certainly massive, and in alignment their combined effect might spell disaster. Right? Why not?
5. Plait explains how the moon's mass affects our tides. How does he link this to his debunking of the "grand conjunction"? What do you understand about the link between the moon and our tides?
6. Plait asks why Richard Noone, the author of a book predicting the end of the world, didn't simply give his book away. After all, what good would money be if Noone was right? Plait also derides merchants who marketed survival gear to people expecting planetary chaos. What do you think of Plait's tone here. If it seems sarcastic or comical, in what ways is that persuasive? What do you think of satire and sarcasm as tools of persuasion?

My Favorite Pseudoscience
EUGENIE SCOTT

Among Eugenie Scott's many honors are the James Randi Award from the Skeptic Society, the Distinguished Alumna Award from the University of Missouri College of Arts and Sciences, and the Bruce Alberts Award from the American Society for Cell Biology. She is a former college professor who still speaks on campuses across the country on matters related to science education. She is the author of a text entitled Evolution vs. Creationism: An Introduction *that deals with the ongoing argument between science and religion in American education. In the following article, which appeared in* Skeptical Odysseys *(2001), Scott relates how she came to be fascinated with "creation science," which she characterizes as a pseudoscience. Her argument with creationists leads to a discussion of the nature of science and how it differs from pseudosciences. The former, she argues, attempts to explain the natural world in terms of natural processes. The explanations of science, she notes, are tentative, "and may change with new data or new theory."*

◆

Paul Kurtz's letter inviting me to contribute to this volume suggested that I describe "my own personal involvement" in the skeptical movement. My introduction to skepticism was a fascination with a particular pseudoscience, "creation science." From the day I first heard this phrase, I was hooked.

In 1971, I was a graduate student in physical anthropology at the University of Missouri. One day, my professor, Jim Gavan, handed me a stack of small, brightly colored, slick paper pamphlets from the Institute for Creation Research. "Here," he said, "take a look at these. It's called 'creation science.'"

Wow. Here I was studying to be a scientist, and here were people calling themselves scientists, but we sure weren't seeing the world the same way. They were looking at the same data: the same fossils, the same stratigraphy, the same biological principles, and so on. But from these data, creationists were concluding that all living things had appeared in their present form, at one time, a few thousand years ago. I was concluding that living things had branched off from common ancestors over scarcely imaginable stretches of time. They were concluding that the entire planet had been covered by water, and that all the present-day geological features of Earth had been determined by this flood and its aftermath. I couldn't see any evidence for this at all, and much evidence against it. Why were we coming up with such different conclusions? The data weren't all that different, but the philosophy of science and the approach to problem solving sure were.

I began collecting creation science literature as an academic enterprise: an interesting problem in the philosophy of science and critical thinking. Due to the pressures of graduate school and my first teaching job, I wasn't able to pursue it especially deeply, but students would occasionally bring up the topic. I would tell them that even if proponents of creation science claimed they were doing science, one cannot claim that one is doing science if

one is doing something very different from what scientists are
doing. Creation science was a good foil to use in teaching students
about the nature of science.

5   Philosophers of science can—and do—argue incessantly over
the definition of science. I don't know how many academic papers
have been written attempting to solve the "demarcation problem":
what qualifies as science and what does not. Some partisans even
go so far as to claim that science is impossible to define. I confess
to having little tolerance for such "how many angels can dance on
the head of a pin" type discussions. In my present job as director
of the National Center for Science Education, I regularly
encounter the public's misunderstanding of the most basic elements of science. I deal with people who nod in agreement with a
typical creationist statement that "neither evolution nor creationism is scientific because no one was there to observe it." I deal
with people who agree with creation scientists stating that "evolution isn't scientific because evolutionists are always changing
their minds." A very popular view is that we should "give the kids
all the options" in a science classroom, and teach them both data
demonstrating that evolution took place and "the evidence" for
the "alternate theory" that God created everything at one time in
its present form—two mutually exclusive views.

Against such a background, the philosopher's discussion of the
nuances of the demarcation problem becomes an intellectual luxury
far removed from what people need to hear. Doubtless to the frus-
tration of my colleagues in the philosophy of science, my job
requires me to simplify—probably beyond what they consider
acceptable. But in doing so, I can make a little progress in helping
the public to understand why science works, and also why creation
science isn't science. Maybe down the road the nonscientists I
encounter can tackle falsificationism and the demarcation problem;
right now, I'd be happy if they understood two basic rules of science
that I believe the majority of scientists would agree upon—however
much they might disagree on others. And—more importantly for
this discussion—creation science can be rejected as science based
even on this simplest of understandings of what science is.

THE NATURE OF SCIENCE

There are two basic principles of science that creationism violates. First, science is an attempt to explain the natural world in
terms of *natural* processes, not supernatural ones. This principle

is sometimes referred to as *methodological naturalism*. In time, a consensus of how some aspect of nature works or came about is arrived at through testing alternate explanations against the natural world. Through this process, the potential exists to arrive at a truly objective understanding of how the world works.

Please allow a digression here. I am not presenting a cut-and-dried formula—"the scientific method"—as if the process of science were a lockstep algorithm. It's much untidier than that. Of course science reflects the time and culture in which it is found. Of course scientists, being human, have biases and make mistakes. Yet the growth of knowledge in a field is not the result of individual achievement, but rather is a function of a number of minds working on the same and different problems over time. It's collective process, rather than being the result of actions of a solitary genius. Individual scientists may be biased, closed-minded, and wrong, but science as a whole lurches forward in spite of it all thanks to its built-in checks.

An important check is that explanations must be tested against the natural world. Thus there is an external standard against which a scientist's views are measured, regardless of his biases or the biases of his opponents. Unpopular ideas may take longer to be accepted, and popular ideas may take longer to be rejected, but the bottom line determining acceptance or rejection is whether the ideas work to describe, predict, or explain the natural world. The Soviet geneticist Lysenko foisted a Lamarckian (inheritance of acquired characteristics) theory of heredity upon the Soviet scientific establishment because Lamarckian genetics was more politically compatible with Marxism than was Mendelism. His politically biased science set Soviet genetics back a full generation, but today Russians employ Mendelian genetics, not Lysenkoism. Wheat raised in refrigerators doesn't grow any better in Siberia than regular wheat, and after a series of five-year plans gone bust, eventually the Soviet government figured out that Lysenko had to go. Mendelism works; Lysenkoism doesn't.

Science is nothing if not practical. The explanations that are retained are those that work best, and the explanations that work best are ones based on material causes. Nonmaterial causes are disallowed.   10

The second minimal principle of science is that explanations (which is what theories are) are tentative, and may change with new data or new theory. Now, don't misunderstand me: I am not claiming that all scientific explanations *always* change, because in fact some do not. Nonetheless, scientists must be willing to revise explanations in light of new data or new theory. The core ideas of science tend not to change very much—they might get tinkered with around the edges—whereas the frontier ideas of science may change a lot before we feel we understand them well.

Here then are two critical strictures on modern science: science must explain using *natural* causes, and scientists must be willing to change their explanations when they are refuted. Viewed in the light of these two basic tenets of science, creation science fails miserably.

EXPLAINING THROUGH NATURAL CAUSE

When a creationist says, "God did it," we can confidently say that he is not doing science. Scientists don't allow explanations that include supernatural or mystical powers for a very important reason. To explain something scientifically requires that we test explanations against the natural world. A common denominator for testing a scientific idea is to hold constant ("control") at least some of the variables influencing what you're trying to explain. Testing can take many forms, and although the most familiar test is the direct experiment, there exist many research designs involving indirect experimentation, or natural or statistical control of variables.

Science's concern for testing and control rules out supernatural causation. Supporters of the "God did it" argument hold that God is omnipotent. If there are omnipotent forces in the universe, by definition, it is impossible to hold their influences constant; one cannot "control" such powers. Lacking the possiblity of control of supernatural forces, scientists forgo them in explanation. Only natural explanations are used. No one yet has invented a *theometer*, so we'll just have to muddle along with material explanations.

15   Another reason for restricting ourselves to natural explanations is practical. It works. We've gone a long way toward building more complete, and we think better, explanations through methodological naturalism, and most of us feel that if it ain't broke, don't fix it. Also, being able to say, "God (directly) did it" is a "science stopper," in the words of philosopher Alvin Plantinga (1997). To say, "God did it" means one does not need to look further for a natural explanation. For example, creationist literature abounds with criticisms of origin of life research.

Because scientists have not yet reached a consensus on how the first replicating molecule came about, creationists argue, this is an intractable problem that should just be attributed to "God did it." Well, if we stop looking for a natural explanation for the origin of life, surely we will never find it. So even if we haven't found it yet, we must nonetheless slog on.

Creation science, for all its surface attempts (especially in its presentation to the general public) to claim to abide by a strictly scientific approach, relying solely on empirical data and theory, eventually falls back to violating this cardinal rule of methodological naturalism. Sometimes one has to go a bit deep in an argument, but eventually, as in the well-known Sidney Harris cartoon, "then a miracle occurs."

For example, to a creation scientist holding to Flood Geology, Noah's Flood was an actual historical event, and representatives of all land animals plus Noah, his wife, their sons, and their sons' wives were on a large boat. Q: *All* land animals? A: Sure. The Ark is the size of the *Queen Mary*. Q: But there are thousands of species of beetles, alone! How could *all* land animals be on the Ark? A: Oh, Noah didn't take two of every *species*. He took pairs of each *kind*, and kinds are higher taxonomic levels than species. Q: But how could only eight people take care of a *Queen Mary*-sized boat full of animals? How could they feed, water, and clean out the stalls? A: They didn't have that much work, because the rocking movement of the boat caused most of the animals to estivate, or go dormant, obviating the need for feeding, watering, and stall-cleaning. Q: But the Ark floated around for almost a year before landing! Small mammals such as mice and shrews have a high surface area:body mass ratio, and have to eat almost their weight in food each day just to keep their metabolism up. These animals couldn't have survived estivation. A: Well, then, a miracle occurred.

Push a creationist argument far enough, and sure enough, it will become necessary to resort to a miracle. But miracle-mongering cannot be part of science.

In addition to the familiar creation science that got me interested in this particular pseudoscience, in the last ten years or so a newer form of antievolutionism has made its appearance: "Intelligent Design" (ID) creationism. ID harkens back to the 1802 position of clergyman William Paley that structural complexity (such as the vertebrate eye for Paley or the structure of DNA for his latter-day bedfellows) is too complicated to have come about through a natural process. Therefore it must have been designed by an "intelligence." The "intelligence" of course is God, and attributing natural causality to a supernatural power of course violates methodological naturalism. Recognizing that methodological naturalism is the standard of modern science, ID proponents argue that it should be scuttled and replaced with what they call "theistic science," which possesses the enviable ability to invoke the occasional miracle when circumstances seem to require it (Scott 1998). ID proponents are content to allow methodological naturalism for the vast amount of science that is done; they wish to leave the possibility of supernatural intervention only for those scientific problems that have theological implications, such as the big bang, the origin of life, the appearance of "kinds" of animals (the Cambrian Explosion), and the origin of humans. The strength of methodological naturalism is perhaps best illustrated by its general acceptance by both the ID and creation science wings of the antievolution movement— except when it comes to religiously sensitive topics.

THE IMPORTANCE OF CHANGING YOUR MIND

20 So creationists violate the first cardinal rule of science, the rule of methodological naturalism, but they also violate the second cardinal rule, that of being willing to change or reject one's explanation based on good evidence to the contrary. This is most clearly revealed by creationist treatment of empirical data. Now, the problem is not that creationists sift through the scientifc literature to find data that support the creation "model," that in itself is not out of line. Scientists do seek confirming data (in the real world, as well as in the literature). But creationists *ignore evidence that disconfirms their view*, because they are not willing to change their explanations in the light of new data or theory.

Judges are not famous for their scientific acuity (witness Justice Scalia's dissent in the 1987 Supreme Court's *Edwards* v. *Aguillard* case), but one judge got it remarkably right. William Overton, in the decision in *McLean* v. *Arkansas* wrote,

> The creationists' methods do not take data, weigh it against the opposing scientific data, and thereafter reach the conclusions stated in section 4(a).
>
> Instead, they take the Book of Genesis and attempt to find scientific support for it.
>
> While anybody is free to approach a scientific inquiry in any fashion they choose, they cannot properly describe the

methodology used as scientific, if they start with a conclusion and refuse to change it regardless of the evidence developed during the course of the investigation.

A theory that is by its own terms dogmatic, absolutist and never subject to revision is not a scientific theory.

For decades now, creationists have claimed that the amount of meteoritic dust on the Moon disproves evolution. The argument goes like this: Based on scientific measurements, the amount of meteoritic dust falling on the Earth is X tons per year; a proportionate amount must also fall on the Moon. If the Earth and Moon were ancient as evolutionists claim, then the amount of dust on the Moon would be several hundreds of feet thick, since in the scant atmosphere of the Moon, the dust would not burn up as it does on Earth. When astronauts landed on the Moon, they found only a few inches of dust, proving that the Moon is young, so the Earth is young, so that there is not enough time for evolution, so that evolution didn't happen and God created the Earth, the Moon, and everything else in the universe ten thousand years ago.

Decades ago, creationists were told that the data they use for the amount of dust falling on the Earth was inaccurate. More accurate measurements of the amount of meteoritic dust influx to the Earth is degrees of magnitude smaller than the original estimates cited by creationists. Before astronauts landed on the Moon, satellites had accurately measured the amount of dust occurring in space, and NASA predicted the surface of the Moon would be covered by no more than a few inches of dust—exactly what astronauts found. Even though this information has been available for decades, and evolutionists time and again have pointed out flaws in the creationist argument, the dust on the Moon argument still is touted as "evidence against evolution." A normal scientific theory would have been abandoned and forgotten long ago, an empirical stake in its heart, but this creationist zombie keeps rising again and again.

It's hard to argue that one is doing science when one can never bring oneself to abandon a refuted argument, and creation science is littered with such rejects. More modern forms of creationism such as "intelligent design theory" have not been around as long, and have not built up quite as long a list of refuted claims, but things don't look very good for them at this point. Michael Behe (1996) has proposed the idea that certain biochemical functions or structures are "irreducibly complex": because all components must be present and functioning, such structures could not have come about through the incremental process of natural selection. The examples he uses in his book, *Darwin's Black Box*, such as the bacterial flagellum and the blood clotting cascade, appear not to be irreducibly complex after all. Worse, even granting the theoretical possibility that an irreducibly complex structure could exist, there is no reason it could not be produced by natural selection. A (theoretically) irreducibly complex structure would not have to have all of its components assembled in its present form all at one time. The way natural selection works, it is perfectly reasonable to envision that some parts of such a structure could be assembled for one purpose, other parts for another, and the final "assembly" results in a structure that performs a function different from any of the "ancestral" functions. As complex a biochemical sequence as the Krebs cycle has recently been given an evolutionary explanation of this sort (Melandez-Hevia, Waddell, and Cascante 1996).

25   I'm willing to give Intelligent Design (ID) a little more time to demonstrate that it is, as it aspires to be, a truly scientific movement. To be able legitimately to claim that ID is scientific, however, will require that its proponents be willing to abandon ideas in the light of refuting evidence—something that their ideological ancestors, the creation scientists, have been unable to demonstrate, and which we have seen precious little of from the leaders of the ID movement.

LOGICAL PROBLEMS

Needless to say, in addition to violating the two key principles of science, the science of creationsim demonstrates other weaknesses, its logic being one. Creation scientists posit a false dichotomy of only two logical possibilities: one being special creationism as seen in a literal interpretation of Genesis, and the other being evolution. Therefore, if evolution is disproved, then creationism is proved; arguments against evolution are arguments *for* creationism. Creation science literature is largely composed of a careful sifting of legitimate scientific articles and books for anomalies that appear to "disprove" evolution.

        But of course, to disprove one view is not to prove another; if I am not at home in Berkeley, that doesn't mean I am on the Moon. To accept the "if not A, then B" form of argument requires that there are only two possibilities. If the only two possibilities are that I am in Berkeley or on the Moon, then indeed, evidence that I am not in Berkeley is evidence that I am on the Moon, but clearly there are more than two alternatives as to my whereabouts. Similarly, there clearly are far more alternatives to scientific evolution than biblical creationism. There are several Hopi origin stories, several Navajo ones, scores of other Native American views, several dozen sub-Saharan African tribal explanations, and we haven't even looked at South Asia, Polynesia, Australia, or views no longer held such as those of the ancient Norse and ancient Greeks. Even if evolution were disproved, biblical literalists would have to find ways of disproving all of these other religious views, so the logic fails.

MORE THAN A PHILOSOPHICAL EXERCISE

For many years, then, my interest in creationism was largely academic. It was an interesting exercise in the philosophy of science. But a few years after I left Missouri, my professor Jim Gavan unwisely accepted an invitation to debate the ICR's Dr. Duane Gish. Gish had perfected a hugely effective technique for persuading the public that evolution was shaky science, and that folks should really consider his "scientific alternative." I and some of my Kentucky students drove from Lexington to Missouri to attend the debate, and it was an eye-opener. I counted thirteen buses from local church groups parked outside the big University of Missouri auditorium, and after seeing the enthusiasm with which the audience received Gish and his message, the cold water of the social and political reality of this movement hit me for the first time. It was no longer just an academic exercise. People were taking this pseudoscience very seriously.

The late Jim Gavan was an excellent scientist, a former president of the American Association of Physical Anthropology, a smart and articulate man well-grounded in philosophy of science. He had done his homework: he had studied creationist literature for several months, and came as prepared as anyone could be expected to be. Clearly, his scientific arguments were superior, but judged from the perspective of who won the hearts and minds of the people, Gish mopped him up.

So I realized that there was a heck of a lot more in this creationism and evolution business than just the academic issues. I went back to Lexington and my job of teaching evolution to college students with a new appreciation of a growing movement that had as its goal the undermining of my professional discipline, 30 to say nothing of the scientific point of view. But still—there were pressures to publish, and a high teaching load, and I was still learning my job, so I didn't take an active role in the controversy quite yet.

Then in 1976, I went to Kansas University in Lawrence, as a visiting professor. As I walked across campus one day, I saw a poster advertising a debate between two KU professors, Edward Wiley and Pat Bickford, and Duane Gish and Henry Morris from the ICR. My first thought was, Do these guys know what they are getting in for? I jotted down the names of the professors and called up Ed Wiley. I told him that I had a collection of creationist materials that I was happy to make available to him, and offered to discuss the upcoming debate with him some time. We met and shared resources, and because of Ed's strategy I began to think that maybe this debate would be different.

Gish's usual stock in trade was to attack Darwinian gradualism because virtually all of his evolutionist opponents defended it. Ed Wiley had recently arrived from the American Museum of Natural History, where he had been converted to some new approaches to evolutionary biology that Gish had not heard of yet. Whereas Gish anticipated that his opponent would defend Darwinian gradualism, Ed merely sniffed that Dr. Gish had not kept up on the latest scholarship and went on to explain punctuated equilibrium and cladism. Worse for Duane, not only did Wiley ignore Darwinian gradualism, he almost ignored evolution completely, concentrating instead on attacking creation science as being a nonscience, and as being empirically false.

This debate was a disaster for the creationism side. Gish didn't know what to say: his target had disappeared, and he was faced with new information with which he was totally unfamiliar (needless to say, by his next debate, he had figured out a "refutation" of punctuated equilibrium, and no other evolutionist opponent would ever catch him unprepared on *this* topic). It was pleasant to behold, especially after having seen my mentor and friend Jim Gavan skunked by Gish a couple of years before.

But the most memorable moment in the debate didn't have anything to do with science. Geologist Pat Bickford was paired with the avuncular founder of creation science, Henry M. Morris, and did a good job showing the scientific flaws of Morris's "flood geology model" (according to which all the world's important geological features were formed by Noah's Flood), although I don't know how many in the audience understood much of his technical presentation. As with the Gavan/Gish debate, the audience was dominated by people who had arrived on buses from regional churches, and they were there to cheer their champions Gish and Morris. I was sitting behind a young girl of eleven or so and her mother.

Bickford began his presentation by pointing out that he was   35 an active churchgoer, had been one for many years, and found this not at all incompatible with his acceptance of evolution. The girl in front of me whirled to face her mother and said, "But you told me———" and her mother, equally shocked and intent on hearing more, said, "Shhhhhhhh!" They had come to the debate convinced that one had to choose between evolution and religion. Bickford's testimonial exposed them to empirical evidence that this was not true. I suspect that they wondered what else they had been told that was not true. I noticed that they listened to Bickford far more intently than they had listened to Wiley, and left with a thoughtful look in their eyes.

But my true baptism into realizing the depth and extent of the social and political importance of the creation science movement came in 1980 in Lexington, Kentucky, when the "Citizens for Balanced Teaching of Origins" approached the Lexington school board to request that "creation science" be introduced into the curriculum. Because I had a collection of creationist literature collected over the years, I became a focal point for the opposition to this effort. After over a year of controversy, our coalition of scientists and liberal and moderate clergy (who objected to biblical literalism being presented in the public schools) managed to persuade the Lexington Board of Education to reject the proposal—by a scant 3–2 margin.

CREATIONISM AND PSEUDOSCIENCE

What happened in Lexington has happened in community after community across the United States, although the evolution side has not always prevailed. I learned from the Lexington controversy (and from observing creation/evolution debates) that creation science is not a problem that will be solved merely by throwing science at it. And I suspect that this is generally also the case with other pseudosciences. Like other pseudosciences, creation science seeks support and adherents by claiming the mantle of science. Proponents argue that creation science should be taught in science class because it supposedly is a legitimate science. This point must be refuted, and scientists are the best ones to make the point. But showing that creationism is unscientific (and just plain factually wrong) is insufficient, however necessary. People who support creation science do so for emotional reasons, and are reluctant or unwilling to relinquish their belief unless those needs or concerns are otherwise assuaged. I suspect the same thing can be said for believers in UFOs, or out-of-body experiences, or paranormal phenomena in general: these beliefs are meeting some emotional needs, and consequently will be very difficult to abandon.

In the case of creation science, the needs being met are among those associated with religion, which makes the adherence to creationism particularly difficult to give up. Creationism is most closely associated with a particular theology of special creationism; not all religion is inimical to evolution, as demonstrated both by scientists who are religious and religious non-scientists who accept evolution. But if your theology requires you to interpret your sacred documents in a literal fashion (whether the Bible, the Torah, the Koran, or the Vedas), in most cases, evolution will be difficult to accommodate with faith.

Some antievolutionists—most of the ID supporters, for example—think that evolution is incompatible with faith not because their theology is biblically literalist, but because they believe that a God who works through evolution is too remote; their theology requires a very personal God who is actively involved with individual human lives and who therefore gives purpose and meaning to life. The God of the theistic evolutionist, the one who uses evolution to construct living things much as Newton's God used gravitation to construct the Solar System, is too remote; evolution to them is a step down the slippery slope toward deism.

40   But whether in the form of biblical literalism or not, religious sensibilities are the engine driving antievolutionism. Religion is a powerful force in human lives. If religion didn't meet many human needs, it wouldn't be a cultural universal; obviously we are dealing with many complex psychological issues. No matter how sound Jim Gavan's science was during his debate with Gish, he failed to move most of his listeners because they came to the debate convinced that evolution was fundamentally incompatible with their religion. Pat Bickford's casual mention that he was a churchgoer was critical to the success of the Kansas debate, because it forced audience members to grapple with a new idea: that one could be an evolutionist and also a Christian. In Lexington, scientists could point out that creation science wasn't

science, but the clergy could assuage the public's emotional concerns that by "believing" in evolution, they were giving up something important to them. Scientists alone could not have won the day. If ninety-five clergymen hadn't signed a petition stating that evolution was fine with them, and that they felt that the schools should not be presenting a religious doctrine as science, community sentiment would not have allowed the board of education to make the decision it did.

Those of us concerned about pseudoscience and its attraction to the public would be well advised to consider the emotional needs that are met by beliefs in ESP, alien abduction, astrology, psychic powers, and the like, and address them as well as criticizing the poor science invoked to support the pseudoscience. We skeptics sometimes feel that the people we are trying to reach are impenetrable—and some of them are! The public is divided into three parts: confirmed believers, confirmed skeptics, and a much larger middle group that doesn't know much science, but doesn't have the emotional commitments that might lead it to embrace a pseudoscientific view. In the case of creation science, the emotional commitment (among many) is to the particular theology of biblical literalism; in the case of UFO abductees, it may be a need for a quasi-religious benevolent protector (or conversely, the fear of an omnipresent threat against which one is powerless). I have found that I am most effective with that large middle group, and hardly ever effective with the true believers; I suspect most skeptics have had similar experiences.

But after all, reaching that large middle group is also the goal of the proponents of pseudoscience. If, like most skeptics, you feel that we'd all be better off with more science and less pseudoscience, then that is where we should be focusing our energies, rather than fruitlessly arguing with people who will never agree with us. But to reach that group that is potentially reachable, we must also be aware that a scientific explanation is necessary but not sufficient to change someone's mind; if I have learned anything from over twenty-five years in the skeptic business, it is that it is necessary to deal with the emotional reasons that make our species susceptible to these beliefs, as well as the scientific.

References

Behe, M. 1996. *Darwin's Black Box*. New York: Free Press.
Plantinga, A. 1997. "Methodological Naturalism Is True by Definition." *Origins and Design* 18, no. 2: 22–34.

Scott, E. C. 1998. "'Science and Religion,' 'Christian Scholarship,' and 'Theistic Science': Some Comparisons." *Reports of the NCSE* 18, no. 2: 30–32.

Melandez-Hevia, Enrique, Thomas G. Waddell, and Marta Cascante. 1996. "The Puzzle of the Krebs Citric Acid Cycle: Assembling the Pieces of Chemically Feasible Reactions, and Opportunism in the Design of Metabolic Pathways During Evolution." *Journal of Molecular Evolution* 43: 293–303.

For Discussion and Writing

1. Scott says that "creation science was a good foil to use in teaching students about the nature of science." What does she mean by "foil"? In what ways might thinking about a non-science teach you about science?

2. "When a creationist says, 'God did it,' we can confidently say that he is not doing science," writes Scott. Explain her argument here. What is the difference between "God did it" and "it all began with a big bang"?

3. Why does Scott refer to creationist claims about dust on the moon? What did creationists think about the depth of dust on the moon? How does their clinging to this argument violate the "second cardinal rule" of science?

4. What does the author mean when she says that creationism posits a false dichotomy in its view of creation? Let's suppose that both evolution and creation are rejected. What other account could one come up with for the origins of life on this planet? Would these explanations be "scientific"?

5. Scott allows that religion and science are compatible. Explain her thinking here. Is a literal reading of the creation account in Genesis compatible with science? Explain your thinking.

6. What is "methodological naturalism"?

Dr. Down's Syndrome
STEPHEN JAY GOULD

The late Stephen Jay Gould got his Ph.D. from Columbia University and was, for many years, professor of geology and zoology at Harvard University. Among his many publications are the books Ever Since Darwin, Ontogeny and Phylogeny, *and* The Mismeasure of Man. *A regular contributor to* Nature Magazine, *Gould published many collections of his nature essays, among them* Hen's Teeth and Horses Toes *and* The Panda's Thumb, *from which the following essay is taken. In this wonderfully concise piece, Gould manages to review reproductive biology, nineteenth-century racialized science, and modern genetics, all in a tour of science gone wrong.*

———————————— ✦ ————————————

Meiosis, the splitting of chromosome pairs in the formation of sex cells, represents one of the great triumphs of good engineering in biology. Sexual reproduction cannot work unless eggs and sperm each contain precisely half the genetic information of normal body cells. The union of two halves by fertilization restores the full amount of genetic information, while the mixing of genes from two parents in each offspring also supplies the variability that Darwinian processes require. This halving, or "reduction division," occurs during meiosis when the chromosomes line up in pairs and pull apart, one member of each pair moving to each of the sex cells. Our admiration for the precision of meiosis can only increase when we learn that cells of some ferns contain more than 600 pairs of chromosomes and that, in most cases, meiosis splits each pair without error.

Yet organic machines are no more infallible than their industrial counterparts. Errors in splitting often occur. On rare occasions, such errors are harbingers of new evolutionary directions. In most cases, they simply lead to misfortune for any offspring generated from the defective egg or sperm. In the most common of meiotic errors, called non-disjunction, the chromosomes fail to split. Both members of the pair go to one sex cell, while the other comes up one chromosome short. A child formed from the union of a normal sex cell with one containing an extra chromosome by nondisjunction will carry three copies of that chromosome in each cell, instead of the normal two. This anomaly is called a trisomy.

In humans, the twenty-first chromosome suffers nondisjunction at a remarkably high frequency, unfortunately rather tragic in effect. About 1 in 600 to 1 in 1,000 newborn babies carry an extra twenty-first chromosome, a condition technically known as "trisomy-21." These unfortunate children suffer mild to severe mental retardation and have a reduced life expectancy. They exhibit, in addition, a suite of distinctive features, including short and broad hands, a narrow high palate, rounded face and broad head, a small nose with a flattened root, and a thick and furrowed tongue. The frequency of trisomy-21 rises sharply with increasing maternal age. We know very little about the causes of trisomy-21; indeed, its chromosomal basis was not discovered until 1959. We have no idea why it occurs so often, and why other chromosomes are not nearly so subject to nondisjunction. We have no clue as to why an extra twenty-first chromosome should yield the highly specific set of abnormalities associated with trisomy-21. But at least it can be identified *in utero* by counting the chromosomes of fetal cells, thus providing an option for early abortion.

If this discussion strikes you as familiar, but missing in one respect, I have indeed left something out. The common designation for trisomy-21 is Mongolian idiocy, mongolism, or Down's syndrome. We have all seen children with Down's syndrome and I feel certain that I have not been alone in wondering why the condition was ever designated *Mongolian* idiocy. Most children with Down's syndrome can be recognized immediately, but (as my previous list demonstrates) their defining traits do not suggest anything oriental. Some, to be sure, have a small but perceptible epicanthic fold, the characteristic feature of an oriental eye, and some have slightly yellowish skin. These minor and inconstant features led Dr. John Langdon Haydon Down to compare them with orientals when he described the syndrome in 1866. But there is far more to the story of Down's designation than a few occasional, misleading, and superficial similarities; for it embodies an interesting tale in the history of scientific racism.

5   Few people who use the term are aware that both words, Mongolian and idiot, had technical meanings for Dr. Down that were rooted in the prevailing cultural prejudice, not yet extinct, for ranking people on unilinear scales with the ranker's group on top. Idiot once referred to the lowest grade in a threefold classification of mental deficiency. Idiots could never master spoken language; imbeciles, a grade above, could learn to speak but not to write. The third level, the slightly "feeble-minded," engendered considerable terminological controversy. In America, most clinicians adopted H. H. Goddard's term, "moron," from a Greek word meaning foolish. Moron is a technical term of this century, not an ancient designation, despite the length of metaphorical whiskers on those terrible, old moron jokes. Goddard, one of three major architects for the rigidly hereditarian interpretation of IQ tests, believed that his unilinear classification of mental worth could be simply extended above the level of morons to a natural ranking of human races and nationalities, with southern and eastern European immigrants on the bottom (still, on average, at moron grade), and old American WASP's on top. (After Goddard instituted IQ tests for immigrants upon their arrival at Ellis Island, he proclaimed more than 80 percent of them feeble-minded and urged their return to Europe.)

Dr. Down was medical superintendant of the Earlswood Asylum for Idiots in Surrey when he published his "Observations on an ethnic classification of idiots" in the London Hospital Reports for 1866. In a mere three pages, he managed to describe Caucasian "idiots" that reminded him of African, Malay, American Indian, and Oriental peoples. Of these fanciful comparisons, only the "idiots who arrange themselves around the Mongolian type" survived in the literature as a technical designation.

Anyone who reads Down's paper without a knowledge of its theoretical context will greatly underestimate its pervasive and serious purpose. In our perspective, it represents a set of flaky and superficial, almost whimsical, analogies presented by a prejudiced man. In his time, it embodied a deadly earnest attempt to construct a general, causal classification of mental deficiency based upon the best biological theory (and the pervasive racism) of the age. Dr. Down played for stakes higher than the identification of some curious noncausal analogies. Of previous attempts to classify mental defect, Down complained:

> Those who have given any attention to congenital mental lesions must have been frequently puzzled how to arrange, in any satisfactory way, the different classes of this defect which have come under their observation. Nor will the difficulty be lessened by an appeal to what has been written on the subject. The systems of classification are generally so vague and artificial, that, not only do they assist but feebly, in any mental arrangement of the phenomena which are presented, but they fail completely in exerting any practical influence on the subject.

In Down's day, the theory of recapitulation embodied a biologist's best guide for the organization of life into sequences of higher and lower forms. (Both the theory and "ladder approach" to classification that it encouraged are, or should be, defunct today. See my book *Ontogeny and Phylogeny*, Harvard University Press, 1977.) This theory, often expressed by the mouthful "ontogeny recapitulates phylogeny," held that higher animals, in their embryonic development, pass through a series of stages representing, in proper sequence, the adult forms of ancestral, lower creatures. Thus, the human embryo first develops gill slits, like a fish, later a three chambered heart, like a reptile, still later a mammalian tail. Recapitulation provided a convenient focus for the pervasive racism of white scientists: they looked to the activities of their own children for comparison with normal, adult behavior in lower races.

As a working procedure, recapitulationists attempted to identify what Louis Agassiz had called the "threefold parallelism" of paleontology, comparative anatomy, and embryology—that is, actual ancestors in the fossil record, living representatives of primitive forms, and embryonic or youthful stages in the growth of higher animals. In the racist tradition for studying humans, the threefold parallel meant fossil ancestors (not yet discovered), "savages" or adult members of lower races, and white children.

10   But many recapitulationists advocated the addition of a fourth parallel—certain kinds of abnormal adults within superior races. They attributed many anomalies of form or behavior either to "throwbacks" or "arrests of development." Throwbacks, or atavisms, represent the spontaneous reappearance in adults of ancestral features that had disappeared in advanced lineages. Cesare Lombroso, for example, the founder of "criminal anthropology," believed that many lawbreakers acted by biological compulsion because a brutish past lived again in them. He sought to identify "born criminals" by "stigmata" of apish morphology— receding forehead, prominent chin, long arms.

Arrests of development represent the anomalous translation into adulthood of features that arise normally in fetal life but should be modified or replaced by something more advanced or complicated. Under the theory of recapitulation, these normal traits of fetal life are the adult stages of more primitive forms. If a Caucasian suffers developmental arrest, he may be born at a lower stage of human life—that is, he may revert to the characteristic forms of lower races. We now have a fourfold parallel of human fossil, normal adult of lower races, white children, and unfortunate white adults afflicted with atavisms or arrests of development. It is in this context that Dr. Down had his flash of fallacious insight: some Caucasian idiots must represent arrests of development and owe their mental deficiency to a retention of traits and abilities that would be judged normal in adults of lower races.

Therefore, Dr. Down scrutinized his charges for features of lower races, just as, twenty years later, Lombroso would measure the bodies of criminals for signs of apish morphology. Seek, with enough conviction aforethought, and ye shall find. Down described his search with obvious excitement: he had, or so he thought, established a natural and causal classification of mental deficiency. "I have," he wrote, "for some time had my attention directed to the possibility of making a classification of the feeble-minded, by arranging them around various ethnic standards—in other words, framing a natural system." The more serious the deficiency, the more profound the arrest of development and the lower the race represented.

He found "several well-marked examples of the Ethiopian variety," and described their "prominent eyes," "puffy lips," and "woolly hair . . . although not always black." They are, he wrote, "specimens of white negroes, although of European descent." Next he described other idiots "that arrange themselves around the Malay variety," and still others "who with shortened fore-heads, prominent cheeks, deep-set eyes, and slightly apish nose" represent those people who "originally inhabited the American continent."

Finally, mounting the scale of races, he came to the rung below Caucasian, "the great Mongolian family." "A very large number of congenital idiots," he continued, "are typical Mongols. So marked is this, that when placed side by side, it is difficult to believe that the specimens compared are not children of the same parents." Down then proceeded to describe, with fair accuracy and little indication of oriental features (beyond a "slight dirty yellowish tinge" to the skin), a boy afflicted with what we now recognize as trisomy-21, or Down's syndrome.

Down did not confine his description to supposed anatomical   15 resemblances between oriental people and "Mongolian idiots." He also pointed to the behavior of his afflicted children: "They have considerable power of imitation, even bordering on being mimics." It requires some familiarity with the literature of nineteenth-century racism to read between these lines. The sophis-tication and complexity of oriental culture proved embarrassing to Caucasian racists, especially since the highest refinements of Chinese society had arisen when European culture still wallowed in barbarism. (As Benjamin Disraeli said, responding to an anti-Semitic taunt: "Yes, I am a Jew, and when the ancestors of the right honorable gentleman were brutal savages . . . mine were priests in the temple of Solomon.") Caucasians solved this dilemma by admitting the intellectual power of orientals, but attributing it to a facility for imitative copying, rather than to innovative genius.

Down concluded his description of a child with trisomy-21 by attributing the condition to developmental arrest (due, Down thought, to the tubercular condition of his parents): "The boy's aspect is such that it is difficult to realize that he is the child of Europeans, but so frequently are these characters presented, that there can be no doubt that these ethnic features are the result of degeneration."

220 Stephen Jay Gould

By the standards of his time, Down was something of a racial "liberal." He argued that all people had descended from the same stock and could be united into a single family, with gradation by status to be sure. He used his ethnic classification of idiots to combat the claim of some scientists that lower races represented separate acts of creation and could not "improve" towards whiteness. He wrote:

> If these great racial divisions are fixed and definite, how comes it that disease is able to break down the barrier, and to simulate so closely the features of the members of another division. I cannot but think that the observations which I have recorded, are indications that the differences in the races are not specific but variable. These examples of the result of degeneracy among mankind, appear to me to furnish some arguments in favor of the unity of the human species.

Down's general theory of mental deficiency enjoyed some popularity, but never swept the field. Yet his name for one specific anomaly, Mongolian idiocy (sometimes softened to mongolism), stuck long after most physicians forgot why Down had coined the term. Down's own son rejected his father's comparison of orientals and children with trisomy-21, though he defended both the low status of orientals and the general theory linking mental deficiency with evolutionary reversion:

> It would appear that the characteristics which at first sight strikingly suggest Mongolian features and build are accidental and superficial, being constantly associated, as they are, with other features which are in no way characteristic of that race, and if this is a case of reversion it must be reversion to a type even further back than the Mongol stock, from which some ethnologists believe all the various races of men have sprung.

Down's theory for trisomy-21 lost its rationale—even within Down's invalid racist system—when physicians detected it both in orientals themselves, and in races lower than oriental by Down's classification. (One physician referred to "Mongol Mongolians" but that clumsy perseverance never took hold.) The condition could scarcely be due to degeneration if it represented the normal state of a higher race. We now know that a similar set of features occurs in some chimpanzees who carry an extra chromosome probably homologous with the twenty-first of humans.

With Down's theory disproved, what should become of his 20
term? A few years ago, Sir Peter Medawar and a group of oriental
scientists persuaded several British publications to substitute
Down's syndrome for Mongolian idiocy and mongolism. I detect
a similar trend in this country, although mongolism is still
commonly used. Some people may complain that efforts to
change the name represent yet another misguided attempt by
fuzzy-minded liberals to muck around with accepted usage by
introducing social concerns into realms where they don't belong.
Indeed, I do not believe in capricious alteration of established
names. I suffer extreme discomfort every time I sing in Bach's
St. Matthew Passion and must, as an angry member of the Jewish
crowd, shout out the passage that served for centuries as an "official" justification for anti-Semitism: Sein Blut komme über uns
und unsre Kinder—"His blood be upon us and upon our
children." Yet, as he to whom the passage refers said in another
context, I would not change "one jot or one title" of Bach's text.

But scientific names are not literary monuments. Mongolian
idiocy is not only defamatory. It is wrong on all counts. We no
longer classify mental deficiency as a unilinear sequence.
Children with Down's syndrome do not resemble orientals to any
great extent, if at all. And, most importantly, the name only has
meaning in the context of Down's discredited theory of racial
reversion as the cause of mental deficiency. If we must honor the
good doctor, then let his name stand as a designation for trisomy-
21—Down's syndrome.

For Discussion and Writing

1. Dr. Down was accurate in his description of children born with the set of
   defects constituting the syndrome that now bears his name. Briefly restate
   the thinking behind "Mongolian idiocy" and "trisomy-21." In what sense can
   the earlier theory be seen as scientific in its day?
2. How does Cesare Lombroso fit into Gould's essay? What dangers do you see
   in trying to link criminal behavior to body type? In your view, what makes
   such analysis attractive to researchers?
3. What does Gould mean when he says that Down was something of a racial
   liberal ("by the standards of his time")? Which aspects of his thinking might
   be construed as less racist than the simplistic hierarchy that fixed white
   people at the crown of creation?
4. Gould's essay offers a fine opportunity to consider the relation of theory to
   fact. Write a short paper that separates the facts Down worked with and the
   theory he spun to account for those facts.

5. Suppose that next week a group of researchers announced that they had isolated the gene that causes boys to become rapists. Imagine a group of concerned citizens who, hearing this, advocate aborting any fetus bearing the gene. What are some of the ideas that you could use from this essay in responding to such advocacy?

Remembering Dangerously
ELIZABETH LOFTUS

In the 1980s a story that had spectacular features exploded into public view: abused children, satanic ritual, and the recovery in therapeutic settings of terrible memories long repressed. Rumors combining Satanism and child abuse ran across the country. Years after trials and convictions, investigators revealed that the "recovered" memories were simply not reliable. As recently as October of 2005 one of the witnesses in the McMartin Pre-School case recanted his testimony. Psychologist Elizabeth Loftus has investigated the phenomenon of recovered memory and performed experiments to show how false memories can be manufactured. The following essay appeared in the March/April 1995 issue of Skeptical Inquirer.

◆

We live in a strange and precarious time that resembles at its heart the hysteria and superstitious fervor of the witch trials of the sixteenth and seventeenth centuries. Men and women are being accused, tried, and convicted with no proof or evidence of guilt other than the word of the accuser. Even when the accusations involve numerous perpetrators, inflicting grievous wounds over many years, even decades, the accuser's pointing finger of blame is enough to make believers of judges and juries. Individuals are being imprisoned on the "evidence" provided by memories that come back in dreams and flashbacks—memories that did not exist until a person wandered into therapy and was asked point-blank, "Were you ever sexually abused as a child?" And then begins the process of excavating the "repressed" memories through invasive therapeutic techniques, such as age regression, guided visualization, trance writing, dream work, body work, and hypnosis.

One case that seems to fit the mold led to highly bizarre satanic-abuse memories. An account of the case is described in detail by one of the expert witnesses (Rogers 1992) and is briefly reviewed by Loftus and Ketcham (1994).

A woman in her mid-seventies and her recently deceased husband were accused by their two adult daughters of rape, sodomy, forced oral sex, torture by electric shock, and the ritualistic murder of babies. The older daughter, 48 years old at the time of the lawsuit, testified that she was abused from infancy until age 25. The younger daughter alleged abuse from infancy to age 15. A granddaughter also claimed that she was abused by her grandmother from infancy to age 8.

The memories were recovered when the adult daughters went into therapy in 1987 and 1988. After the breakup of her third marriage, the older daughter started psychotherapy, eventually diagnosing herself as a victim of multiple-personality disorder and satanic ritual abuse. She convinced her sister and her niece to begin therapy and joined in their therapy sessions for the first year. The two sisters also attended group therapy with other multiple-personality-disorder patients who claimed to be victims of satanic ritual abuse.

In therapy the older sister recalled a horrifying incident that   5
occurred when she was four or five years old. Her mother caught a rabbit, chopped off one of its ears, smeared the blood over her body, and then handed the knife to her, expecting her to kill the animal. When she refused, her mother poured scalding water over her arms. When she was 13 and her sister was still in diapers, a group of Satanists demanded that the sisters disembowel a dog with a knife. She remembered being forced to watch as a man who threatened to divulge the secrets of the cult was burned with a torch. Other members of the cult were subjected to electric shocks in rituals that took place in a cave. The cult even made her murder her own newborn baby. When asked for more details about these horrific events, she testified in court that her memory was impaired because she was frequently drugged by the cult members.

The younger sister remembered being molested on a piano bench by her father while his friends watched. She recalled being impregnated by members of the cult at ages 14 and 16, and both pregnancies were ritually aborted. She remembered one incident in the library where she had to eat a jar of pus and another jar of scabs. Her daughter remembered seeing her grandmother in a black robe carrying a candle and being drugged on two occasions and forced to ride in a limousine with several prostitutes.

The jury found the accused woman guilty of neglect. It did not find any intent to harm and thus refused to award monetary damages. Attempts to appeal the decision have failed.

Are the women's memories authentic? The "infancy" memories are almost certainly false memories given the scientific literature on childhood amnesia. Moreover, no evidence in the form of bones or dead bodies was ever produced that might have corroborated the human-sacrifice memories. If these memories are indeed false, as they appear to be, where would they come from? George Ganaway, a clinical assistant professor of psychiatry at the Emory University School of Medicine, has proposed that unwitting suggestions from therapy play an important role in the development of false satanic memories.

WHAT GOES ON IN THERAPY?

Since therapy is done in private, it is not particularly easy to find out what really goes on behind that closed door. But there are clues that can be derived from various sources. Therapists' accounts, patients' accounts, and sworn statements from litigation have revealed that highly suggestive techniques go on in some therapists' offices (Lindsay and Read 1994; Loftus 1993; Yapko 1994).

10   Other evidence of misguided if not reckless beliefs and practices comes from several cases in which private investigators, posing as patients, have gone undercover into therapists' offices. In one case, the pseudopatient visited the therapist complaining about nightmares and trouble sleeping. On the third visit to the therapist, the investigator was told that she was an incest survivor (Loftus 1993). In another case, Cable News Network (CNN 1993) sent an employee undercover to the offices of an Ohio psychotherapist (who was supervised by a psychologist) wired with a hidden video camera. The pseudopatient complained of feeling depressed and having recent relationship problems with her husband. In the first session, the therapist diagnosed "incest survivor," telling the pseudopatient she was a "classic case." When the pseudopatient returned for her second session, puzzled about her lack of memory, the therapist told her that her reaction was typical and that she had repressed the memory because the trauma was so awful. A third case, based on surreptitious recordings of a therapist from the Southwestern region of the United States, was inspired by the previous efforts.

INSIDE A SOUTHWESTERN THERAPIST'S OFFICE

In the summer of 1993, a woman (call her "Willa") had a serious problem. Her older sister, a struggling artist, had a dream that she reported to her therapist. The dream got interpreted as evidence of a history of sexual abuse. Ultimately the sister confronted the parents in a videotaped session at the therapist's office. The parents were mortified; the family was wrenched irreparably apart.

Willa tried desperately to find out more about the sister's therapy. On her own initiative, Willa hired a private investigator to pose as a patient and seek therapy from the sister's therapist. The private investigator called herself Ruth. She twice visited the therapist, an M.A. in counseling and guidance who was supervised by a Ph.D., and secretly tape-recorded both of the sessions.

In the first session, Ruth told the therapist that she had been rear-ended in an auto accident a few months earlier and was having trouble getting over it. Ruth said that she would just sit for weeks and cry for no apparent reason. The therapist seemed totally disinterested in getting any history regarding the accident, but instead wanted to talk about Ruth's childhood. While discussing her early life, Ruth volunteered a recurring dream that she had in childhood and said the dream had now returned. In the dream she is 4 or 5 years old and there is a massive white bull after her that catches her and gores her somewhere in the upper thigh area, leaving her covered with blood.

The therapist decided that the stress and sadness that Ruth was currently experiencing was tied to her childhood, since she'd had the same dream as a child. She decided the "night terrors" (as she called them) were evidence that Ruth was suffering from post-traumatic-stress disorder (PTSD). They would use guided imagery to find the source of the childhood trauma. Before actually launching this approach, the therapist informed her patient that she, the therapist, was an incest survivor: "I was incested by my grandfather."

During the guided imagery, Ruth was asked to imagine   15
herself as a little child. She then talked about the trauma of her parents' divorce and of her father's remarriage to a younger woman who resembled Ruth herself. The therapist wanted to know if Ruth's father had affairs, and she told Ruth that hers had, and that this was a "generational" thing that came from the grandfathers. The therapist led Ruth through confusing/sugges-tive/manipulative imagery involving a man holding down a little girl somewhere in a bedroom. The therapist decided that Ruth

was suffering from a "major grief issue" and told her it was sexual: "I don't think, with the imagery and his marrying someone who looks like you, that it could be anything else."

The second session, two days later, began:

> Pseudopatient: You think I am quite possibly a victim of sexual abuse?
>
> Therapist: Um-huh. Quite possibly. It's how I would put it. You know, you don't have the real definitive data that says that, but, um, the first thing that made me think about that was the blood on your thighs. You know, I just wonder, like where would that come from in a child's reality. And, um, the fact that in the imagery the child took you or the child showed you the bedroom and your father holding you down in the bedroom . . . it would be really hard for me to think otherwise. . . . Something would have to come up in your work to really prove that it really wasn't about sexual abuse.

Ruth said she had no memory of such abuse but that didn't dissuade the therapist for a minute.

> Pseudopatient: . . . I can remember a lot of anger and fear associated with him, but I can't recall physical, sexual abuse. Do people always remember?
>
> Therapist: No. . . . Hardly ever. . . . It happened to you a long time ago and your body holds on to the memory and that's why being in something like a car accident might trigger memories. . . .

The therapist shared her own experiences of abuse, now by her father, which supposedly led to anorexia, bulimia, over-spending, excessive drinking, and other destructive behaviors from which the therapist had presumably now recovered. For long sections of the tape it was hard to tell who was the patient and who was the therapist.

Later the therapist offered these bits of wisdom:

> I don't know how many people I think are really in psychiatric hospitals who are really just incest survivors or, um, have repressed memories.
>
> It will be a grief issue that your father was—sexualized you— and was not an appropriate father.
>
> You need to take that image of yourself as an infant, with the hand over, somebody's trying to stifle your crying, and feeling pain somewhere as a memory.

The therapist encouraged Ruth to read two books: *The Courage To Heal*, which she called the "bible of healing from childhood sexual abuse," and the workbook that goes with it. She made a special point of talking about the section on confrontation with the perpetrator. Confrontation, she said, wasn't necessarily for everyone. Some don't want to do it if it will jeopardize their inheritance, in which case, the therapist said, you can do it after the person is dead—you can do eulogies. But confrontation is empowering, she told Ruth.

Then to Ruth's surprise, the therapist described the recent confrontation she had done with Willa's sister (providing sufficient detail about the unnamed patient that there could be little doubt about who it was).

> Therapist: I just worked with someone who did do it with her parents. Called both of her parents in and we did it in here. . . . Its empowering because you're stepping out on your own. She said she felt like she was 21, and going out on her own for the first time, you know, that's what she felt like. . . .
>
> Pseudopatient: And, did her parents deny or—
>
> Therapist: Oh, they certainly did—
>
> Pseudopatient: Did she remember, that she—she wasn't groping like me?
>
> Therapist: She groped a lot in the beginning. But it sort of, you know, just like pieces of a puzzle, you know, you start to get them and then eventually you can make a picture with it. And she was able to do that. And memory is a funny thing. It's not always really accurate in terms of ages, and times and places and that kind of thing. Like you may have any variable superimposed on another. Like I have a friend who had an ongoing sexual abuse and she would have a memory of, say, being on this couch when she was seven and being abused there, but they didn't have that couch when she was seven, they had it when she was five. . . . It doesn't discount the memory, it just means that it probably went on more than once and so those memories overlap. . . .
>
> Pseudopatient: This woman who did the confrontation, is she free now? Does she feel freed over it?
>
> Therapist: Well, she doesn't feel free from her history . . . but she does feel like she owns it now and it doesn't own her . . . and she has gotten another memory since the confrontation. . . .

The therapist told Ruth all about the "new memory" of her other patient, Willa's sister:

> Therapist: [It was in] the early-morning hours and she was just lying awake, and she started just having this feeling of, it was like her hands became uncontrollable and it was like she was masturbating someone. She was like going faster than she could have, even in real life, so that she knew, it was familiar enough to her as it will be to you, that she knew what it was, and it really did not freak her out at all. . . . She knew there was a memory there she was sitting on.

20   Before Ruth's second therapy session had ended, Ruth's mother was brought into the picture—guilty, at least, of betrayal by neglect:

> Therapist: Well, you don't have to have rational reasons, either, to feel betrayed. The only thing that a child needs to feel is that there was probably a part of you that was just yearning for your mother and that she wasn't there.
>
> And whether she wasn't there because she didn't know and was off doing something else, or whether she was there and she knew and she didn't do anything about it. It doesn't matter. All the child knew was that Mom wasn't there. And, in that way she was betrayed, you know, whether it was through imperfection on your mother's part or not, and you have to give yourself permission to feel that way without justification, or without rationalization because you were.

Ruth tried again to broach the subject of imagination versus memory:

> Pseudopatient: How do we know, when the memories come, what are symbols, that it's not our imagination or something?
>
> Therapist: Why would you image this, of all things. If it were your imagination, you'd be imaging how warm and loving he was. . . . I have a therapist friend who says that the only proof she needs to know that something happened is if you think it might have.

At the doorway as Ruth was leaving, her therapist asked if she could hug her, then did so while telling Ruth how brave she was. A few weeks later, Ruth got a bill. She was charged $65 for each session.

Rabinowitz (1993) put it well: "The beauty of the repressed incest explanation is that, to enjoy its victim benefits, and the distinction of being associated with a survivor group, it isn't even necessary to have any recollection that such abuse took place." Actually, being a victim of abuse without any memories does not sit well, especially when group therapy comes into play and women without memories interact with those who do have memories. The pressure to find memories can be very great.

Chu (1992:7) pointed out one of the dangers of pursuing a fruitless search (for memories): it masks the real issues from therapeutic exploration. Sometimes patients produce "ever more grotesque and increasingly unbelievable stories in an effort to discredit the material and break the cycle. Unfortunately, some therapists can't take the hint!"

The Southwestern therapist who treated Ruth diagnosed   25
sexual trauma in the first session. She pursued her sex-abuse agenda in the questions she asked, in the answers she interpreted, in the way she discussed dreams, in the books she recommended. An important question remains as to how common these activities might be. Some clinicians would like to believe that the problem of overzealous psychotherapists is on a "very small" scale (Cronin 1994: 31). A recent survey of doctoral-level psychologists indicates that as many as a quarter may harbor beliefs and engage in practices that are questionable (Poole and Lindsay 1994). That these kinds of activities can and do sometimes lead to false memories seems now to be beyond dispute (Goldstein and Farmer 1993). That these kinds of activities can create false victims, as well as hurt true ones, also seems now to be beyond dispute.

THE PLACE OF REPRESSED MEMORIES IN MODERN SOCIETY

Why at this time in our society is there such an interest in "repression" and the uncovering of repressed memories? Why is it that almost everyone you talk to either knows someone with a "repressed memory" or knows someone who's being accused, or is just plain interested in the issue? Why do so many individuals believe these stories, even the more bizarre, outlandish, and outrageous ones? Why is the cry of "witch hunt" now so loud (Baker 1992: 48; Gardner 1991)? *Witch hunt* is, of course, a term that gets used by lots of people who have been faced by a pack of accusers (Watson 1992).

"Witch hunt" stems from an analogy between the current allegations and the witch-craze of the sixteenth and seventeenth centuries, an analogy that several analysts have drawn (McHugh 1992; Trott 1991; Victor 1991). As the preeminent British historian Hugh Trevor-Roper (1967) has noted, the European witch-craze was a perplexing phenomenon. By some estimates, a half-million people were convicted of witchcraft and burned to death in Europe alone between the fifteenth and seventeenth centuries (Harris 1974: 207–258). How did this happen?

It is a dazzling experience to step back in time, as Trevor-Roper guides his readers, first to the eighth century, when the belief in witches was thought to be "unchristian" and in some places the death penalty was decreed for anyone who burnt supposed witches. In the ninth century, almost no one believed that witches could make bad weather, and almost everyone believed that night-flying was a hallucination. But by the beginning of the sixteenth century, there was a complete reversal of these views. "The monks of the late Middle Ages sowed: the lawyers of the sixteenth century reaped; and what a harvest of witches they gathered in!" (Trever-Roper 1967: 93). Countries that had never known witches were now found to be swarming with them. Thousands of old women (and some young ones) began confessing to being witches who had made secret pacts with the Devil. At night, they said, they anointed themselves with "devil's grease" (made from the fat of murdered infants), and thus lubricated they slipped up chimneys, mounted broomsticks, and flew off on long journeys to a rendezvous called the witches' sabbat. Once they reached the sabbat, they saw their friends and neighbors all worshipping the Devil himself. The Devil sometimes appeared as a big, black, bearded man, sometimes as a stinking goat, and sometimes as a great toad. However he looked, the witches threw themselves into promiscuous sexual orgies with him. While the story might vary from witch to witch, at the core was the Devil, and the witches were thought to be his earth agents in the struggle for control of the spiritual world.

Throughout the sixteenth century, people believed in the general theory, even if they did not accept all of the esoteric details. For two centuries, the clergy preached against the witches. Lawyers sentenced them. Books and sermons warned of their danger. Torture was used to extract confessions. The agents of Satan were soon found to be everywhere. Skeptics, whether in universities, in judges' seats, or on the royal throne, were denounced as witches themselves, and joined the old women at the burning stake. In the absence of physical evidence (such as a pot full of human limbs, or a written pact with the Devil), circumstantial evidence was sufficient. Such evidence did not need to be very cogent (a wart, an insensitive spot that did not bleed when pricked, a capacity to float when thrown in water, an incapacity to shed tears, a tendency to look down when accused). Any of these "indicia" might justify the use of torture to produce a confession (which was proof) or the refusal to confess (which was also proof) and justified even more ferocious tortures and ultimately death.

When did it end? In the middle of the seventeenth century the basis of the craze began to dissolve. As Trevor-Roper (1967: 97) put it, "The rubbish of the human mind, which for two centuries, by some process of intellectual alchemy and social pressure, had become fused together in a coherent, explosive system, has disintegrated. It is rubbish again."

Various interpretations of this period in social history can be found. Trevor-Roper argued that during periods of intolerance any society looks for scapegoats. For the Catholic church of that period, and in particular their most active members, the Dominicans, the witches were perfect as scapegoats; and so, with relentless propaganda, they created a hatred of witches. The first individuals to be so labeled were the innocently nonconforming social groups. Sometimes they were induced to confess by torture too terrible to bear (e.g., the "leg screw" squeezed the calf and broke the shinbone in pieces; the "lift" hoisted the arms fiercely behind and back; the "ram" or "witch-chair" provided a heated seat of spikes for the witch to sit on). But sometimes confessions came about spontaneously, making their truth even more convincing to others. Gradually laws changed to meet the growth of witches—including laws permitting judicial torture.

There were skeptics, but many of them did not survive. Generally they tried to question the plausibility of the confessions, or the efficacy of torture, or the identification of particular witches. They had little impact, Trevor-Roper claims, because they danced around the edges rather than tackling the core: the concept of Satan. With the mythology intact, it creates its own evidence that is very difficult to disprove. So how did the mythology that had lasted for two centuries lose its force? Finally, challenges against the whole idea of Satan's kingdom were launched. The stereotype of the witch would soon be gone, but not before tens of thousands of witches had been burned or hanged, or both (Watson 1992).

Trevor-Roper saw the witch-craze as a social movement, but with individual extensions. Witch accusations could be used to destroy powerful enemies or dangerous persons. When a "great fear" grips a society, that society looks to the stereotype of the enemy in its midst and points the finger of accusation. In times of panic, he argued, the persecution extends from the weak (the old women who were ordinarily the victims of village hatred) to the strong (the educated judges and clergy who resisted the craze). One indicia of "great fear" is when the elite of society are accused of being in league with the enemies.

Is it fair to compare the modern cases of "de-repressed memory" of child sexual trauma to the witch-crazes of several centuries ago? There are some parallels, but the differences are just as striking. In terms of similarities, some of the modern stories actually resemble the stories of earlier times (e.g., witches flying into bedrooms). Sometimes the stories encompass past-life memories (Stevenson 1994) or take on an even more bizarre, alien twist (Mack 1994).[1] In terms of differences, take a look at the accused and the accusers. In the most infamous witch hunt in North America, 300 years ago in Salem, Massachusetts, three-fourths of the accused were women (Watson 1992). Today, they are predominantly (but not all) men. Witches in New England were mostly poor women over 40 who were misfits, although later the set of witches included men (often the witches' husbands or sons), and still later the set expanded to include clergy, prominent merchants, or anyone who had dared to make an enemy. Today, the accused are often men of power and success. The witch accusations of past times were more often leveled by men, but today the accusations are predominantly leveled by women. Today's phenomenon is more than anything a movement of the weak against the strong. There is today a "great fear" that grips our society, and that is fear of child abuse. Rightfully we wish to ferret out these genuine "enemies" and point every finger of accusation at them. But this does not mean, of course, that every perceived enemy, every person with whom we may have feuded, should be labeled in this same way.

35   Trevor-Roper persuasively argued that the skeptics during the witch-craze did not make much of a dent in the frequency of bonfires and burnings until they challenged the core belief in Satan. What is the analogy to that core today? It may be some of the widely cherished beliefs of psychotherapists, such as the belief in the repressed-memory folklore. The repression theory is well articulated by Steele (1994: 41). It is the theory "that we forget

events because they are too horrible to contemplate; that we cannot remember these forgotten events by any normal process of casting our minds back but can reliably retrieve them by special techniques; that these forgotten events, banished from consciousness, strive to enter it in disguised forms; that forgotten events have the power to cause apparently unrelated problems in our lives, which can be cured by excavating and reliving the forgotten event."

Is it time to admit that the repression folklore is simply a fairy tale? The tale may be appealing, but what of its relationship to science? Unfortunately, it is partly refuted, partly untested, and partly untestable. This is not to say that all recovered memories are thus false. Responsible skepticism is skepticism about some claims of recovered memory. It is not blanket rejection of all claims. People sometimes remember what was once forgotten; such forgetting and remembering does not mean repression and de-repression, but it does mean that some recently remembered events might reflect authentic memories. Each case must be examined on its merits to explore the credibility, the timing, the motives, the potential for suggestion, the corroboration, and other features to make an intelligent assessment of what any mental product means.

THE CASE OF JENNIFER H.

Some writers have offered individual cases as proof that a stream of traumas can be massively repressed. Readers can be massively repressed. Readers must beware that these case "proofs" may leave out critical information. Consider the supposedly ironclad case of Jennifer H. offered by Kandel and Kandel (1994) to readers of *Discover* magazine as an example of a corroborated de-repressed memory. According to the *Discover* account, Jennifer was a 23-year-old musician who recovered memories in therapy of her father raping her from the time she was 4 until she was 17. As her memories resurfaced, her panic attacks and other symptoms receded. Her father, a mechanical-engineering professor, denied any abuse. According to the *Discover* account, Jennifer sued her father, and at trial "corroboration" was produced: Jennifer's mother testified that she had seen the father lying on top of Jennifer's 14-year-old sister and that he had once fondled a baby-sitter in her early teens. The defendant's sister recalled his making passes at young girls. Before this case becomes urban legend and is used as proof of something that it might not be proof of, readers are entitled to know more.

Jennifer's case against her father went to trial in June 1993 in the U.S. District Court for the District of Massachusetts (*Hoult* v. *Hoult*, 1993). The case received considerable media attention (e.g., Kessler 1993). From the trial transcript, we learn that Jennifer, the oldest of four children, began therapy in the fall of 1984 with an unlicensed New York psychotherapist for problems with her boyfriend and divided loyalties surrounding her parents' divorce. Over the next year or so she experienced recurring nightmares with violent themes, and waking terrors. Her therapist practiced a "Gestalt" method of therapy; Jennifer describes one session: "I started the same thing of shutting my eyes and just trying to feel the feelings and not let them go away really fast. And [my therapist] just said 'Can you see anything?' . . . I couldn't see anything . . . and then all of a sudden I saw this carved bedpost from my room when I was a child. . . . And then I saw my father, and I could feel him sitting on the bed next to me, and he was pushing me down, and I was saying, 'No.' And he started pushing up my nightgown and . . . was touching me with his hands on my breast, and then between my legs, and then he was touching me with his mouth . . . and then it just all like went away. It was like . . . on TV if there is all static. . . . It was, all of a sudden it was plusssssh, all stopped. And then I slowly opened my eyes in the session and I said, 'I never knew that happened to me'" (pp. 58–59).

Later Jennifer would have flashbacks that were so vivid that she could feel the lumpy blankets in her childhood bed. She remembered her father choking her and raping her in her parents' bedroom when she was about 12 or 13 (p. 91). She remembered her father threatening to rape her with a fishing pole in the den when she was about 6 or 7. She remembers her father raping her in the basement when she was in high school. The rape stopped just as her mother called down for them to come to dinner. She remembered her father raping her at her grandparents' home when she was in high school, while the large family were cooking and kids were playing. She remembered her father threatening to cut her with a letter opener, holding a kitchen knife to her throat (p. 113). She remembered him chasing her through the house with knives, trying to kill her, when she was about 13 years old (p. 283).

40   Jennifer also remembered a couple of incidents involving her mother. She remembered one time when she was raped in the bathroom and went to her mother wrapped in a towel with blood dripping. She remembered another incident, in which her father was raping her in her parents' bedroom and her mother came to the door and said, "David." The father then stopped raping her

and went out to talk to the mother. Jennifer's mother said she had no recollection of these events, or of any sexual abuse. An expert witness testifying for Jennifer said it is common in cases of incest that mothers ignore the signs of abuse.

During the course of her memory development, Jennifer joined numerous sexual-abuse survivor groups. She read books about sexual abuse. She wrote columns. She contacted legislators. Jennifer was involved in years of therapy. She wrote letters about her abuse. In one letter, written to the President of Barnard College on February 7, 1987, she said "I am a victim of incestuous abuse by my father and physical abuse by my mother" (p. 175). In another letter to her friend Jane, written in January 1988, she talked about her therapy: "Well, my memories came out . . . when I would sit and focus on my feelings which I believe I call visualization exercises because I would try to visualize what I was feeling or be able to bring into my eyes what I could see" (pp. 247–248). She told Jane about her Gestalt therapy: "In Gestalt therapy, the sub-personalities are allowed to take over and converse with one another and hopefully resolve their conflicts. Each personality gets a different chair, and when one new one starts to speak, the individual changes into that personality's seat. It sounds weird, and it is. But it is also an amazing journey into one's self. I've come to recognize untold universes within myself. It feels often very much like a cosmic battle when they are all warring with one another" (pp. 287–288; see also page 249).

In one letter, written on January 11, 1989, to another rape survivor, she said that her father had raped her approximately 3,000 times. In another letter, dated January 30, 1989, she wrote: "Underneath all the tinsel and glitter was my father raping me every two days. My mother smiling and pretending not to know what the hell was going on, and probably Dad abusing my siblings as well" (pp. 244–245). In a letter written on April 24, 1989, to *Mother Jones* magazine she said that she had survived hundreds of rapes by her father (p. 231).

Before October 1985, Jennifer testified, she didn't "know" that her father had ever put his penis in her vagina, or that he had put his penis in her mouth, or that he had put his mouth on her vagina (p. 290). She paid her terapist $19,329.59 (p. 155) to acquire that knowledge.

In sum, Jennifer reported that she had been molested by her father from the ages of 4 to 17 (p. 239); that she was molested hundreds if not thousands of times, even if she could not remember all of the incidents; that this sometimes happened with many family members nearby, and with her mother's "involvement" in some instances; and that she buried these memories until she was 24, at which time they purportedly began to return to her. No one saw.

45   These are a few of the facts that the Kandels left out of their article. Jennifer was on the stand for nearly three days. She had "experts" to say they believed her memories were real. These experts were apparently unaware of, or unwilling to heed, Yapko's (1994) warnings about the impossibility, without independent corroboration, of distinguishing reality from invention and his urgings that symptoms by themselves cannot establish the existence of past abuse. At trial, Jennifer's father testified for about a half-hour (Kessler 1993b). How long does it take to say, "I didn't do it"? Oddly, his attorneys put on no character witnesses or expert testimony of their own, apparently believing—wrongly—that the implausibility of the "memories" would be enough. A Massachusetts jury awarded Jennifer $500,000.

GOOD AND BAD ADVICE

Many of us would have serious reservations about the kinds of therapy activities engaged in by Jennifer H. and the kind of therapy practiced by the Southwestern therapist who treated pseudopatient Ruth. Even recovered-memory supporters like Briere (1992) might agree. He did, after all, say quite clearly: "Unfortunately, a number of clients and therapists appear driven to expose and confront every possible traumatic memory" (p. 136). Briere notes that extended and intense effort to make a client uncover all traumatic material is not a good idea since this is often to the detriment of other therapeutic tasks, such as support, consolidation, desensitization, and emotional insight.

Some will argue that the vigorous exploration of buried sex-abuse memories is acceptable because it has been going on for a long time. In fact, to think it is fine to do things the way they've always been done is to have a mind that is as closed and dangerous as a malfunctioning parachute. It is time to recognize that the dangers of false-memory creation are endemic to psychotherapy (Lynn and Nash 1994). Campbell (1994) makes reference to Thomas Kuhn as he argues that the existing paradigm (the theories, methods, procedures) of psychotherapy may no longer be viable. When this happens in other professions, a crisis prevails and the profession must undertake a paradigm shift.

It may be time for that paradigm shift and for an exploration of new techniques. At the very least, therapists should not let sexual trauma overshadow all other important events in a patient's life (Campbell 1994). Perhaps there are other explanations for the patient's current symptoms and problems. Good therapists remain open to alternative hypotheses. Andreasen (1988), for example, urges practitioners to be open to the hypothesis of metabolic or neurochemical abnormalities as cause of a wide range of mental disorders. Even pharmacologically sophisticated psychiatrists sometimes refer their patients to neurologists, endocrinologists, and urologists. For less serious mental problems we many find, as physicians did before the advent of powerful antibiotics, that they are like many infections—self-limiting, running their course and then ending on their own (Adler 1994).

When it comes to serious diseases, a question that many people ask of their physicians is "How long have I got?" As Buckman and Sabbagh (1993) have aptly pointed out, this is a difficult question to answer. Patients who get a "statistical" answer often feel angry and frustrated. Yet an uncertain answer is often the truthful answer. When a psychotherapy patient asks, "Why am I depressed?" the therapist who refrains from giving an erroneous answer, however frustrating silence might be, is probably operating closer to the patient's best interests. Likewise, nonconventional "healers" who, relative to conventional physicians, give their patients unwarranted certainty and excess attention, may make the patients temporarily feel better, but in the end may not be helping them at all.

Bad therapy based on bad theory is like a too-heavy oil that,   50
instead of lubricating, can gum up the works—slowing everything down and heating everything up. When the mental works are slowed down and heated up, stray particles of false memory can, unfortunately, get stuck in it.

To avoid mucking up the works, constructive advice has been offered by Byrd (1994) and by Gold, Hughes, and Hohnecker (1994): Focus on enhancement of functioning rather than uncovering buried memories. If it is necessary to recover memories, do not contaminate the process with suggestions. Guard against personal biases. Be cautious about the use of hypnosis in the recovery of memories. Bibliotherapeutic and group therapy should not be encouraged until the patient has reasonable certainty that the sex abuse really happened. Development and evaluation of other behavioral and pharmacological therapies that minimize the possibility of false memories and false diagnoses should be encouraged.

Instead of dwelling on the misery of childhood and digging for childhood sexual trauma as its cause, why not spend some time doing something completely different? Borrowing from John Gottman's (1994) excellent advice on how to make your marriage succeed, patients might be reminded that negative events in their lives do not completely cancel out all the positives (p. 182). Encourage the patient to think about the positive aspects of life— even to look through picture albums from vacations and birthdays. Think of patients as the architects of their thoughts, and guide them to build a few happy rooms. The glass that's half empty is also half full. Gottman recognized the need for some real basis for positive thoughts, but in many families, as in many marriages, the basis does exist. Campbell (1994) offers similar advice. Therapists, he believes, should encourage their clients to recall some positive things about their families. A competent therapist will help others support and assist the client, and help the client direct feelings of gratitude toward those significant others.

FINAL REMARKS

We live in a culture of accusation. When it comes to molestation, the accused is almost always considered guilty as charged. Some claims of sexual abuse are as believable as any other reports based on memory, but others may not be. However, not all claims are true. As Reich (1994) has argued: "When we uncritically embrace reports of recovered memories of sexual abuse, and when we nonchalantly assume that they must be as good as our ordinary memories, we debase the coinage of memory altogether" (p. 38). Uncritical acceptance of every single claim of a recovered memory of sexual abuse, no matter how bizarre, is not good for anyone—not the client, not the family, not the mental-health profession, not the precious human faculty of memory. And let us not forget one final tragic consequence of overenthusiastic embracing of every supposedly depressed memory; these activities are sure to trivialize the genuine memories of abuse and increase the suffering of real victims who wish and deserve, more than anything else, just to be believed.

We need to find ways of educating people who presume to know the truth. We particularly need to reach those individuals who, for some reason, feel better after they have led their clients—probably unwittingly—to falsely believe that family members have committed some terrible evil. If "truth" is our goal, then the search for evil must go beyond "feeling good" to include standards of fairness, burdens of proof, and presump-. tions of innocence. When we loosen our hold on these ideals, we risk a return to those times when good and moral human beings convinced themselves that a belief in the Devil meant proof of his existence. Instead, we should be marshaling all the science we can find to stop the modern-day Reverend Hale (from *The Crucible*), who, if he lived today would still be telling anyone who would listen that he had seen "frightful proofs" that the Devil was alive. He would still be urging that we follow wherever "the accusing finger points"!

Note

1. John Mack details the kidnappings of 13 individuals by aliens, some of whom were experimented upon sexually. Mack believes their stories, and has impressed some journalists with his sincerity and depth of concern for the abductors (Neimark 1994). Carl Sagan's (1993:7) comment on UFO memories: "There is genuine scientific paydirt in UFO's and alien abductions—but it is, I think, of distinctly terrestrial origin."

References

Adler, J. 1994. The age before miracles. *Newsweek*, March 28, p. 44.
Andreasen, N. C. 1988. Brain imaging: Applications in psychiatry. *Science*, 239: 1381–1388.
Baker, R. A. 1992. *Hidden Memories*. Buffalo, N.Y.: Prometheus Books.
Briere, John N. 1992. *Child Abuse Trauma*. Newbury Park, Calif.: Sage Publications.
Buckman, R., and K. Sabbagh, 1993. *Magic or Medicine? An Investigation into Healing*. London: Macmillan.
Byrd, K. R. 1994. The narrative reconstructions of incest survivors. *American Psychologist*, 49:439–440.
Campbell, T. W. 1994. *Beware the Talking Cure*. Boca Raton, Fla: Social Issues Resources Service (SirS).
Chu, J. A. 1992. The critical issues task force report: The role of hypnosis and Amytal interviews in the recovery of traumatic memories. *International Society for the Study of Multiple Personality and Dissociation News*, June, pp. 6–9.
CNN. 1993. "Guilt by Memory." Broadcast on May 3.
Cronin, J. 1994. False memory. *Z Magazine*. April, pp. 31–37.
Gardner, R. A. 1991. *Sex Abuse Hysteria*. Creskill, N.J.: Creative Therapeutics.

Gold, Hughes, and Hohnecker. 1994. Degrees of repression of sexual-abuse memories. *American Psychologist*, 49:441–442.

Goldstein, E., and K. Farmer, eds. 1994. *True Stories of False Memories*. Boca Raton, Fla.: Social Issues Resources Service (SirS).

Gottman, J. 1994. *Why Marriages Succeed or Fail*. New York: Simon & Schuster.

Harris, M. 1974. *Cows, Pigs, Wars, and Witches: The Riddles of Culture*. New York: Vintage Books.

Hoult v. Hoult. 1993. Trial testimony. U.S. District Court for District of Massachusetts. Civil Action No. 88–1738.

Kandel, M., and E. Kandel. 1994. Flights of Memory. *Discover*, 15 (May): 32–37.

Kessler, G. 1993a. Memories of abuse. *Newsday*, November 28, pp. 1, 5, 54–55.

———. 1993b. Personal communication, *Newsday*, letter to EL dated December 13, 1993.

Lindsay, D. S., and J. D. Read. 1994. Psychotherapy and memories of childhood sexual abuse: A cognitive perspective. *Applied Cognitive Psychology*, 8:281–338.

Loftus, E. F. 1993. The reality of repressed memories. *American Psychologist*, 48: 518–537.

Loftus, E. F., and K. Ketcham. 1994. *The Myth of Repressed Memory*. New York: St. Martin's Press.

Lynn, S. J., and M. R. Nash. 1994. Truth in memory. *American Journal of Clinical Hypnosis*, 36: 194–208.

Mack, J. 1994. *Abduction*. New York: Scribner's.

McHugh, P. R. 1992. Psychiatric misadventures. *American Scholar*, 61: 497–510.

Neimark, J. 1994. The Harvard professor and the UFO's. *Psychology Today*, March–April, pp. 44–48, 74–90.

Poole, D., and D. S. Lindsay. 1994. "Psychotherapy and the Recovery of Memories of Childhood Sexual Abuse." Unpublished manuscript, Central Michigan University.

Rabinowitz, Dorothy. 1993. Deception: In the movies, on the news. *Wall Street Journal*, February 22. Review of television show "Not in My Family."

Reich, W. 1994. The monster in the mists. *New York Times Book Review*, May 15, pp. 1, 33–38.

Rogers, M. L. 1992. "A Case of Alleged Satanic Ritualistic Abuse." Paper presented at the American Psychology-Law Society meeting, San Diego, March.

Sagan, C. 1993. What's really going on? *Parade Magazine*, March 7, pp. 4–7.

Stevenson, I. 1994. A case of the psychotherapist's fallacy: Hypnotic regression to "previous lives." *American Journal of Clinical Hypnosis*, 36: 188–193.

Steele, D. R. 1994. Partial recall. *Liberty*, March, pp. 37–47.

Trevor-Roper, H. R. 1967. *Religion, the Reformation, and Social Change*. London: Macmillan.

Trott, J. 1991. Satanic panic. *Cornerstone*, 20: 9–12.

Victor, J. S. 1991. Satanic cult "survivor" stories. *Skeptical Inquirer*, 15: 274–280.

Watson, B. 1992. Salem's dark hour: Did the devil make them do it? *Smithsonian*, 23: 117–131.

Yapko, M. 1994. *Suggestions of Abuse*. New York: Simon & Schuster.

For Discussion and Writing

1. Describe the process by which a therapist might bring repressed memories to the surface. In what ways does the therapist interpret for the patient? How could an observer distinguish between interpreting and implanting a memory?
2. One pseudo patient tells the therapist that she can't recall sexual abuse. How does the therapist respond?
3. What parallels does Loftus make between recovered memory/ritual abuse and sixteenth-century accounts of witches? Look closely at therapists' "proofs" and at proofs of one's being a witch. What similarities can you see? How is attacking the concept of repressed memories similar to attacking the concept of Satan in these two topics?
4. How does Jennifer H.'s public life change after she remembers early childhood abuse? Who are some of the people she contacts about her alleged abuse? Why is she telling them about this?
5. Loftus claims we live in a culture of accusation. What do you think this means? Why is an accuser likely to be believed? Do some preliminary research on tales of satanic ritual abuse (you may come across a fine article entitled "Remembering Satan" from the late 1980s). Discuss your findings. What do they add to your understanding of Loftus' piece?

Science and Pseudoscience: Research and Writing Possibilities

1. Junk science has begun to occupy the attention of many in our culture these days. For example, Jerrold P. Anders and Edward M. Kock note in their article on junk science that "in Grady v. Frito-Lay, Inc., 839 A.2d 1038, the Supreme Court held that a scientific expert's methodology must enjoy general

acceptance among the scientific community" (http://www.whitewms.com/CM/Publications/Publications327.asp). In *Sleeping with Extra-terrestrials*, a book about the rise of the irrational in American life, Wendy Kaminer devotes a chapter to junk science, targeting the pseudoscientific language and methods of Deepak Chopra, Napoleon Hill, Sophy Burnham, and others. Write a paper that defines junk science, distinguishing it in several crucial aspects from legitimate science. You might begin by reading Kaminer's chapter and then looking into Robert Park's *Voodoo Science*, which details some well-known instances of this phenomenon.

2. The Y2K crisis was just one of many dire scenarios that fizzled at or near the turn of the millennium. Look into it and other forms of cosmic doom such as the one detailed by Philip Plait in this chapter. Analyze the language and logic of several such predictions, trying not only to see how they are shaped but what makes them so fascinating to audiences. You could include disaster movies, too, like the classic *Dr. Strangelove* or more recent depictions of cataclysmic natural events.

3. Compare a creationist account of the origins of life on earth with a concise science-based account. Is there any middle ground? Does either side allow for alternative accounts? Decide whether a faith-based account can be taught in the way that a science-based account can be: alongside proofs and open to inquiry. You might start by looking into historical roots of the current debates, say the Scopes trial of the early twentieth century.

4. In the 1980s in America there quite suddenly appeared a national interest, even panic, in cases of the "satanic ritual abuse" of children. One engine driving the panic was the therapeutic recovery of suppressed memories. These memories played a role in court cases that led to convictions, some later overturned. Investigate this phenomenon, and decide what role skepticism might have played in preventing unjust convictions. You could start by looking into Lawrence Wright's book, *Remembering Satan: A Tragic Case of Recovered Memory*. It might also be useful to read an account of New England witch trials and executions. Indeed, such reading could lead to an interesting comparison of the two historical moments.

5. Cold fusion, if possible, would be an extraordinary boon to mankind. Researchers see it as a solution to major problems plaguing humanity today, but it has so far eluded scientists, reminiscent of alchemists' attempts to turn lead into gold. In 1989, two electrochemists in Salt Lake City, Utah, announced that they had witnessed controlled nuclear fusion in a laboratory setting. Further inquiry and experiment failed to reproduce the effects reported in Utah, but the quest goes on. Research the 1989 "findings," and argue for or against further efforts—and expense—devoted to cold fusion. Read widely on all sides of the controversy before you commit to a position. What does this controversy tell you about "pure" science, about financial pressures, and about human frailty in the business of research? If you can,

reproduce cold fusion in your own lab. Then plan a long, extravagant retirement.

6. Gould's essay ("Dr. Down's Syndrome") raises the specter of science led astray by a priori notions based on mythologies of race. Human measuring and ranking has always been a risky business, with the self-interest of those who measure influencing their findings. Read the four essays in Chapter 4 of Gould's *The Panda's Thumb*. Consider the implications and consequences of scientific work carried on under the influence of bias. You might find it helpful to look at parts of longer works like Gould's *Mismeasure of Man* or William H. Tucker's *The Science and Politics of Racial Research*. Write an essay that explores some implications and dangers of such tainted research.